To Edith,
  a belated birthday
gift from Eleanor

11-3-06

So They Will Not Forget

An Autobiography by
ELEANOR ERICKSON

authorHOUSE™

1663 LIBERTY DRIVE, SUITE 200
BLOOMINGTON, INDIANA 47403
(800) 839-8640
WWW.AUTHORHOUSE.COM

AuthorHouse™
1663 Liberty Drive, Suite 200
Bloomington, IN 47403
www.authorhouse.com
Phone: 1-800-839-8640

AuthorHouse™ UK Ltd.
500 Avebury Boulevard
Central Milton Keynes, MK9 2BE
www.authorhouse.co.uk
Phone: 08001974150

First published by AuthorHouse 8/21/2006

ISBN: 1-4259-0162-X (sc)

Printed in the United States of America
Bloomington, Indiana

This book is printed on acid-free paper.

THIS AUTOBIOGRAPHY IS
IN MEMORY OF MY MOTHER
who was dignified in every way and under every
circumstance. She set an example of strength and
courage and she loved me as only a mother can love.

———————

My children often recounted stories of their mother's
life and her family. The stories have changed many
times over the years. I promised to tell my story in my
own words, so I wrote this book
FOR MY CHILDREN,
CATHERINE & STEVEN
and for their children —

So They Will Not Forget . . .

I Dedicate This Book
To My Husband

who kept his promises, encouraged me
and stood by me when I despaired

Acknowledgments

I wish to express my gratitude and appreciation
to the following people:

Beatrice Holmes, my editor, for her
perceptive comments and suggestions,
as well as for her sensitivity and
understanding of my feelings as
portrayed in this book.

Jay Holmes, who took the time to give
me his view as a journalist as well as a
lot of constructive advice.

My husband, who provided constant
help and extensive computer
knowledge.

Irma Wachtel, for proofreading.

Many of my friends, for their
encouragement to write this book.

A special thank-you to Publisher
Willmuth Arenhövel for permission to
use selected photos from the book,
Berlin 1945 Eine Dokumentation.

For all that is our life we sing our thanks and praise;

for all life is a gift which we are called to use

to build the common good

and make our own days glad.

For sorrow we must bear, for failures, pain, and loss

for each new thing we learn, for fearful hours that pass:
we come with praise and thanks

for all that is our life.

by Bruce Findlow

Two verses from *For All That Is Our Life*

from the Unitarian Universalist Hymnal

Singing the Living Tradition.

TABLE OF CONTENTS

A P P E N D I X

Introduction

It was February 1944. I was ten. I stepped through the front door of my parents' country home, called *Der Heidehof* that means Heather Farm. I could smell the fresh air, filled with the fragrance of pine trees all around me. The sky was a brilliant blue without a cloud. In this part of the world – then my world – cloudless skies were uncommon in the month of February. By now I knew that when the skies were cloudless, bomber squadrons would soon be overhead to carry their deadly load toward Berlin. They flew much too high to be seen, but the penetrating roar of their engines could not be mistaken. Usually they came over Hannover-Braunschweig and then, invariably over us. That thought gave me chills.

So far, no bombs had been dropped anywhere near this quiet farmland. All the tall straight pine trees, at the edge of the Spree Forest, seemed to shield us from the air raids on Berlin.

I was born in Berlin, located only 35 miles northwest of the Heidehof, but in those days, it took us the better part of a day to get there.

Mutti, my mother, had to stay in Berlin during the week. Ever since I could remember, I had nightmares about losing her, and being left alone in this world to fend for myself. Vati, my father, was also loving and protective, but he lived in his own world, worrying about his business and fighting his private war against Hitler. His disdain for the Nazi Regime made him a time bomb waiting to self-destruct. At this time, Frau Typke was looking after me. She had been my first-through-third grade school teacher in Berlin. She was well-educated, self-reliant, and had never married. I admired her from the first day I met her, and she never lost my admiration and respect. My father managed to get her a teaching job in our little town of Märkisch-Buchholz. The town was located one-and-a-half miles from our farm and had a population of about a thousand. Märkisch-Buchholz prided itself on having the only school in a five-mile radius. I walked 25 minutes to get there, straddling the wagon furrows, deeply embossed in the sandy road.

I shall always remember the stillness in the air, the dew on the trees and grass and the smell of pine on my way to school. To my left stretched a forest of tall pines with no underbrush, and to my right were cultivated fields, small and defined. Beyond them, I could see the river Dahme, a tributary to the river Spree that flows through the heart of Berlin.

I could not remember a time without war. Telling me of peacetime was like telling me a fairy tale. I loved to listen to my father, when he talked about the way Berlin used to be before the war, 'at night it was as bright as the day!' He would tell me that when he was young, he used to buy one bowl of soup at *Aschinger's* and with it he got all the rolls he wanted at no extra charge. That was his daily fare during university days. – No ration cards! As far as I knew, only one thing could be bought without ration cards and that was soup made from hot water and a bouillon cube. We used to order it at the railroad restaurant in Königs-Wusterhausen where we had to change trains, halfway between Berlin and Halbe. It took the waiter at least twenty minutes to bring this so-called 'soup' and when we asked, "What took so long?" he answered, "The bones were not tender yet!" That was considered *Berliner Humor.* No matter how bad conditions were, and how impertinent the remarks, everybody laughed. Laughing relieved the tension we all felt. I learned early how important it is to have a sense of humor, in spite of frustration.

I was born the very year Hitler came to power, and I started school when the Nazis declared the Second World War. A world of ration cards, blackouts and bombs was all I knew.

I cannot remember being afraid, although many a night I sat in an air-raid cellar during bombing attacks. My Catholic faith made me confident that there was a personal God who was looking out for me. Proof to me was that He had blessed me with such loving parents.

I was not quite so sure though that God could keep my father out of jail. Vati voiced his angry opinion constantly. Whenever he was late, Mutti and I worried that we would never see him again. For some unknown reason, I was also afraid of losing my mother. I must have felt instinctively that she was in danger, but I did not know why. I certainly could not have known in how 'much' danger she really was.

My mother made most decisions regarding me. Only when I was summoned to join the Hitler-youth, my father's 'No!' was not to be contradicted. Mutti then came up with the idea of telling the authorities that I had joined a group in Berlin, and because of our out-of-town location I could not attend meetings. I certainly did not enjoy always being different, but I had to get used to it.

I realized early that there was a threatening world out there, and that it was special to be so protected and feel so loved. I never took my relationship with my parents for granted. I knew from early on that, somehow, I had these parents not by accident of birth, but by some other circumstance about which I was to wonder until I was thirteen.

PART ONE

CHILDHOOD

Early Childhood Memories

On this beautiful February morning of 1944, I was reflecting on the past ten years of my life.

I was born in Berlin in the Kaiserallee, now renamed Bundesallee. From there my parents moved to Prager Platz 4. The new apartment was extraordinarily large with an endless corridor, long enough to practice riding my first bicycle. At that time my governess was Erna. She was quite important in my life because I spent most of my day with her, and since she lived with us, I had to put up with her more than I liked. In fact, I did not like her at all. Even at the tender age of three, I realized that she was more interested in men than in children. She stopped to talk to every man who showed her the least bit of interest.

Once she talked to a policeman who was directing traffic. At that time, traffic lights were not fully automatic. I remember policemen turning a lever on a dial. That process fascinated me. When one of such policemen became engrossed in a conversation with Erna, I decided to turn the lights for him. I changed them from one color to another at frightening speed. It was great fun to watch the cars, coming from all directions, screeching to a halt. And there were lots of cars, because it happened at one of the busiest intersections of the Kurfürsten Damm. I was very proud of the excitement I caused and could not wait to tell my father about it. It amused him greatly, to my governess' dismay. My mother was not amused either but that did not keep my father from retelling the story over and over again.

My father and I were buddies in our dislike for Erna. Since parodies were Vati's forté, he did not miss the opportunity to insert Erna's name into some unflattering songs. I remember one of them, *"In Rixdorf is' Musike, da tanzt die dicke Ricke, DIE ERNA!"* which said something like, 'in Rixdorf there is music, there dances the big goat, ERNA!' Mutti was not amused with that either, and Erna was offended and angry to have her authority undermined!

Every day, Erna took me on a walk to the *Stadtpark*. There I found my first special friend, Tommi. His governess had chosen the same playground for their daily outing. Tommi was wonderful. We had such good times playing together that I could hardly wait for the next day, when we would meet again. His parents were well-to-do. His father was a pharmacist and owner of a very prestigious pharmacy on the Kaiser Allee.

My mother met the Happs, Tommi's parents, when she brought me to his birthday party. From then on, we never missed Tommi's birthday celebration. At his 9th birthday party, I saw him for the last time. It was an exciting, happy day. I remember how much Mutti and I laughed on our way home. We did not take a bus, we walked home to avoid my problem with motion sickness. It was spring and April showers made the long walk challenging. Mutti had a brand-new *Knirps,* a collapsible umbrella that remained a puzzle to her. Each time when she had managed to open it, it had stopped raining. When she finally got it closed, it poured again. By the time we arrived home, we were cold and soaked. Still, Mutti was always able to laugh at herself, even in the face of adversity.

One evening, I overheard my mother talking to my father. She spoke of the Happs' 'lovely and cultured home.' "It distinguishes the Jews from their Christian counterparts!" I heard her say. From then on I knew that Tommi was Jewish. Thank goodness, I was too young to realize what danger that distinction meant for Tommi and his family!

Erna watching Tommi and me at the Stadtpark

Tom Axel Happ and I – best of friends

Absender: Tom Issel Happ
Bln – Schöneberg
Innsbruckerstr 54 II

Postkarte

Viele Grüße
auch an Deine
Eltern Dein

Tommi

Schisi Uhlenbrook

Berlin – W

Rosenheimerstr 5 IV

Liebe Shisi!

Du wirst mich sicher nicht mehr
kennen, aber ich kenne Dich, denn
ich weiß wo Du wohnst. Du wirst
Diech sicher über meinen Absender
wundern weil ich doch in der
Kaiserallee 156 gewohnt habe. Ich
schreibe Dir ...
weil ich Dich mal ... Besuchen will,
und Du auch mich.

Tommi's post card telling me that he has a new address
that I need to know so we can visit each other again

I received a postcard from him in July of 1942 that I have kept for more than fifty years. I only had the chance to speak to Tommi one more time and only by coincidence. Whenever I think about Tom Axel Happ, it revives in me all the anger and frustration that I feel about the cruelty of the human race. I still hope against hope that the Happ family survived the Nazi horror.

I was always lonely for playmates. There were no relatives, nor did my parents have friends with children. Two girls were living in our building at Prager Platz. Their father was a pediatrician. Part of their apartment was used for his practice, the way ours was used for my father's offices. The girls were twins. We discovered each other through our kitchen windows facing the back courtyard. It was so exciting when I was first invited to visit the twins. The greatest fun was their swing that was fastened to the doorframe between two rooms. Since the rooms had twelve-foot ceilings and high doorframes, their openings were perfect for the installation of a swing. I loved being active, and a swing was a dream come true. I don't remember that they ever visited me, but then, of course, I had no swing! Eventually I did get one, but that was later in our Rosenheimer-Strasse apartment.

I was sad that my mother was so reserved and had so little interest in making friends or meeting new people. Only her family seemed important to her. I felt very close to my mother, and I knew how much she loved me. She never said that she loved me, but she often told me that 'I was her sunshine and her reason for living.'

I had no idea then, what a burden I must have been for her! She did not let on how much she worried about her ability to raise me, especially in the situation in which she found herself. She saved me from knowing that her marriage to my father was all that was protecting her. She never shared any of this with me until she was out of danger, many years later . . .

7

My First Trip to Italy
and the Loss of Our Apartment

When I was four, Mutti and I took an exciting trip to Italy. We went by train and stayed overnight in Basel, Switzerland. It was fun to ride in the plush train, but once the newness wore off, the hours became endless. I was bored easily, and sitting still was not my strong suit. To keep me occupied, Mutti allowed me to unpack and re-pack her large alligator handbag. There were all kinds of compartments for travel items: one for the comb, one for the mirror, the soap container, perfume bottles and for a small brush. I took everything out and stuck it back at least a hundred times. I am sure Mutti wondered what would be missing when we arrived. Once it got dark, I occupied myself by looking out of the window of the rolling train. I was astonished that the moon was able to keep up with us, no matter how fast we went, even when we rode around corners and were hidden behind trees. Playing hide and seek with the moon entertained me until we finally arrived in Basel. There we stayed in a hotel close to the station. I was happy I could sleep in the same room with my mother. I had a vivid imagination and was afraid to sleep alone. (In our bedroom at home, I saw spindly creatures jump out of our wardrobe, no matter which way I turned. Even when I covered my head, I could not escape them.)

The next day we continued our train ride to Rome where we met my sister Ruth, Mutti's eldest daughter. I had heard my parents talk about her, but we had never met. Ruth had left Germany in 1934 to move to Italy. I seem to remember hearing that she was twenty-one. In my imagination, Ruth remained twenty-one forever, because I saw her only that one time during my childhood.

My mother never mentioned age. In fact, she tried to keep everybody's age, but mine, a secret. That was not easy, because my father was very proud of his years and even added a few to impress others. I remember him always being in his sixties.

When we arrived in Rome, we also met *Tante Clara* (Aunt Clara). I can still see her coming down the wide marble steps of one of those huge public buildings in Rome. Mutti said to me, "Give your *Tante Clara* a kiss." I resisted by saying, *"Ich mag die Italiener nicht!"* which meant, "I do not like the Italians."

This meeting with 'Aunt' Clara and my rejection of the Italians was often retold laughingly. I wondered for a long time why it was so important to like the Italians, when they don't even speak our language. I saw no humor in not wanting to kiss a stranger! Only two years later I could have understood, but by then, I had forgotten about the incident with 'Aunt Clara' and never saw the connection.

Ruth and I in Rapallo – 1937

After visiting Rome, we went with Ruth to Alassio where I had a wonderful time. I loved Ruth at first sight. She was young and full of fun. She pushed me ahead of her on a raft as she swam way out into the Ligurian Sea. While it worried Mutti, it made Ruth and me friends for life. During our time together, Ruth bought a little toy for me every day. Gifts were only given for birthdays and Christmas, but my generous sister ignored those rules! Before returning home, we traveled to Rapallo. There,

I remember meeting my grandparents. My grandmother promised to buy me a doll, but then forgot all about it. So did I. I only know this story from Ruth who had no problem remembering it. In fact, she never forgave my grandmother for her thoughtlessness.

Soon after we returned home to Berlin, we were informed that our apartment building at Prager Platz was to become offices for the *Luftfahrtministerium* (Air Defense Ministry). Therefore, in 1938, we were forced to vacate our twelve-room apartment, the one with the long central hallway; where my bedroom was at one end and Vati's two-room office suite at the other. Our move ended the little ritual of my father and me: every morning when I woke up, I called at the top of my voice, *"Vati, wo bist Du? "* (where are you?) and then I waited for his voice to come back, *"Im Bureau! "* And I would rhyme *"Ach sooo! "* (Really!)

By then, Vati and I had become united in rebellion against Hitler – very much against my mother's will. I often overheard her warn my father, "A child should not be burdened with the political opinions of a family that opposes everything she hears in the world around her." Mutti told him many times, "It will confuse the child, and it is also very dangerous. How can she know not to repeat what you say?" (I remember feeling sneaky. I understood much more than my parents suspected.) But it was impossible to reason with my father, especially when he had an outlet for his frustrations concerning the 'Hitler hoodlums.' He would not miss a chance to rhyme a parody for every Nazi song or poem he heard, and he was good at it! It was the only time I saw him laugh and have fun!

I was only five then, but to this day I recall the very first anti-Hitler jingle I heard. It went something like this, 'Do you have a Hitler picture? No, no, I don't have one yet. I am waiting for Stalin to get one first!' Of course, in German it rhymed and had a tune.

It was Bimmi who sang the jingle first. He was the son of close family friends. He was much older than I, but he was like a brother to me. He also came to all my early birthday parties and I loved him. His real name was Jobst Haedenkamp. The last time I saw him was in 1942 at the Heidehof, before he was shipped out to Stalingrad. He told us that he had taken the offer of receiving his 'emergency' *Abitur* (Examination of Maturity and prerequisite for entering university) in exchange for joining the army. My mother was horrified! When she asked him, whether he had considered his mother's feelings, propaganda had already done its job. He shrugged and said, "What other German Mothers can endure, my mother can handle as well!" After that, none of us ever heard from him again. His mother never gave up hope that he was still alive. She waited for him to her dying day, forty-two years later.

Every conversation one had with my father was turned into a lecture on history. It always included his opinions about the state of the war and, last but not least, the 'Hitler hoodlums.' He incessantly predicted doom, pointing downward to tell us where we were heading. He lectured about Germany invading the USSR, ignoring the treaty of 1922 at Rapallo that made the two countries trading partners. He also talked about the non-aggression pacts of 1926 and 1939. "In 1942, when Germany's soldiers trampled their bloody path through the Ukraine, the Ukrainians welcomed them as 'liberators'," my father said. "They did not realize that Hitler had learned most of his methods from Stalin!" he added. As far as the offensive against Stalingrad was concerned, "Only the Russian climate was more murderous than the Nazis!" He referred to the fact that the German troops first got stuck in mud, caused by torrential rains. Then in September of 1942, when temperatures suddenly plunged to 55° F below zero, there were no winter clothes available. Those who did not freeze to death, starved to death! Bimmi was probably one of them.

From then on, whenever Hitler shouted over the airwaves, "I have calculated everything!" Vati shouted even louder, "But you forgot the winter clothing!"

I remember the quote, "In war there are no winners and no losers, only survivors." It soon looked as if there were not going to be any survivors either – at least no Germans.

Rosenheimer Strasse

I was told that we were very lucky to find an apartment in Rosenheimer Strasse 5, in Berlin-Schöneberg. Nobody wanted to rent to my parents, for reasons I did not understand.

Our new apartment was much smaller than the one before. Mutti was thrilled because it was very bright. Through very large windows (no screens) the southern sun flooded the dining room, study and sitting room with its warm light. The windows had white curtains that made the rooms even brighter. Whenever possible, the windows and balcony doors were wide open. I loved the fresh cool incoming air. It smelled so clean, and everything looked so polished when I came home from school, especially after our cleaning woman had just finished.

Our apartment was on the top floor at the southeast corner of the building. The bedrooms faced East, where the sun greeted us in the morning. The dining room was a big corner room with large windows on two sides, in addition to a glass door leading to the east balcony. Under the windows on the south side was a wide, covered radiator. I love to sit there. It was warm and I could look far down the street. I particularly remember one twenty-fourth of December, the afternoon of Christmas Eve. All stores had closed at noon, and the streets were almost deserted. A light, powdery snow fell. I looked out, preoccupied in anticipation of what Christmas might bring, when Mutti joined me. We could see a woman holding the hand of a girl, about my age, walking swiftly. Mutti pointed her out and told me, how sad she had been when she was young, after her mother had died. She had often sat in front of their living room window, with tears running down her face, envying other girls who still had a mother. – It was not often that Mutti talked about herself; so when she did, I listened very carefully. This time, I could feel her pain as if it were my own. I even felt guilty that I was so fortunate to have a mother!

My desk was placed in the dining room, in the corner between the windows. It was a reminder that homework was to be done right after the midday meal. There were two wide French pocket-doors that opened into my father's large study-library we called the *Herrenzimmer*. It had a wide window next to double glass doors leading to a large balcony. The room also had a second set of pocket doors, opening into the living room. It was so designed that when both sets of sliding doors were opened, the three rooms became one expansive suite. In summer we ate outside on the balcony. Its southern exposure was a luxury in the middle of the city.

Vati and I

The *Herrenzimmer* was furnished with two big leather armchairs and a couch covered with a beautiful Persian rug. Three square matching pillows stood stiffly against the back wall, making the couch a sofa. A heavy, black oak wall-unit surrounded it. On each side were tall cabinets with beveled glass doors. The inside of the cabinets were light cherry wood.

During advent – before Christmas – dried, sugared orange peels and home-baked ginger snaps were stored in there. Their fragrance penetrated the wood. To this day, that smell, as well as tangerines and candle wax, recreates for me the Christmas seasons of long ago.

In front of the sofa and between the armchairs was a square oak table, especially designed for playing cards and other games. On the opposite side of the room, in front of the windows, was a massive desk and chair. Next to it were the balcony doors. There was only enough space between those doors and the adjoining wall to accommodate the depth of our bookcase, also with beveled-edge glass doors to keep the dust away from the many books. There were about eight important inches between the wall on the balcony side and the bookcase. This space was significant because, as fate had it, it was to become the final resting place for the smallest Nazi flag of its time.

Every so often my father held a business meeting in this *Herrenzimmer.* I remember those meetings only too well, even though I was only five years old. I often was called in to be introduced. I could see the pride in my father's face as I entered to shake hands and curtsy. I could also feel the men's stares like daggers. It never took long until one of them wondered aloud, (I suppose, considering my father's age) whether I was his grandchild? In reply, my father would say, "No," with more than necessary emphasis. Then, invariably, he proceeded to whisper something into the stranger's ears. It was not hard for me to guess that he was explaining something about my relationship to him. It embarrassed me so much that I just wished I could make myself invisible. I felt responsible for whatever was said about me and ashamed because I knew it made me different from all the other kids. I dreaded those business meetings. I was more afraid of them than our nightly visits to the air-raid cellar. I did not dare to ask my father what he was whispering about. I was afraid that the answer might even be more hurtful. Maybe I would never be the same, or maybe, it would jeopardize the relationship with my parents! In addition, I worried that my questions might embarrass him. That thought was very uncomfortable for me. By then I knew how painful embarrassment was! From early on, I tried not to put anybody else into an embarrassing situation. I knew that my father had no idea what he did to me. He would never have consciously hurt me because he loved me too much.

Every Sunday, Vati and I went to church together. I was not yet six years old and therefore not required to attend Sunday mass in our church. But it was fun joining my father, while Mutti cooked our Sunday dinner. It was served at 1:00 pm sharp. After mass, Vati and I used to go by taxi to *Café Kranzler.* He would order a cup of coffee and listen to the soft, live music, while I was doing my best to get him to order some ice cream for me. Ice cream was a treat we did not have at home, because we did not have freezers. Often we were home late for our meal and I had no appetite. I was never hungry as a child, but after ice cream, I could not to be talked into eating at all. Mutti would lament about the dinner she could not keep warm and, in addition, was upset about my eating before dinner.

This every-Sunday ritual changed abruptly, when the discrimination against the Jews became more pronounced. Now, after church, we went to visit Vati's Jewish clients, and we went by streetcar.

One such Sunday morning, we were on our way to the Wagner family. Vati and I sat a few rows apart because the streetcar was rather empty and I could seek out a seat next to an open window that prevented my motion sickness. Two young, uniformed men entered the compartment where Vati and I were sitting. One of them shouted, "All Jews stand up!" Immediately, I could feel my heart thumping, anticipating what was about to happen. Vati stood up and commanded, "All Jews remain seated!" Trying to ignore my father, the young man repeated his original order. Vati, not to be ignored, raised his voice even more. This scene was repeated a third time, and this time my father shouted like he was commanding a battalion. By now I cried hysterically, so afraid of what was to come next. One of the uniformed men walked over to me, bent over and said right into my face in a very harsh voice "Why is that brat crying?" Not waiting for an answer, he turned on his heel and said to my father, "You are arrested!" The streetcar driver, positioned on the left of the steps, could not have missed that scene! My father proceeded to the front platform, where the driver was sitting, while being ordered to exit at the next stop. Amazingly, in all the commotion, the young Nazis still remembered their manners. They got off first to assist my much older and distinguished-looking father, with his cane, down the steep streetcar steps. Just at the very moment when the two had stepped off the streetcar, and before Vati could step down, the driver drove off, leaving the uniformed men standing in the street. A hero! He probably saved my father's life.

That Sunday morning was an unforgettable nightmare for me. I was so unnerved by the dread of what could have happened, that I kept crying for hours afterwards. I could not wait to tell Mutti every detail of the ordeal as soon as we returned home. She comforted me and promised that I did not ever have to do those Sunday runs with Vati again. Mutti only showed concern and compassion for me. Much later did I realize, how afraid and distraught she must have been when she heard about the incident.

Often on Sundays, *Tante* Hempel came to dinner. I called her Tante, the German word for aunt. She loved me and acted as if she were my closest relative. I never questioned this relationship either. I was very fond of her and looked forward to the little gifts, she never forgot to bring for me.

Mutti said that our Rosenheimer-Strasse apartment was more pleasant than any of the other places we had lived before. Vati was not pleased, because the house had no elevators.

That meant walking up eight flights of stairs, eleven or twelve steps each. It was quite an exercise to go up and down those stairs several times a day, especially when one was used to elevators. Soon my father invested in some black stools. He placed them strategically on every second landing, to pause there and catch his breath. He had to replace them several times, because they were always stolen. It made Mutti snicker when my more-than-frugal father had to replace his chairs repeatedly. No matter how hard it was for him to part with his money, his legs needed the rest.

Besides the absence of elevators, the apartment had only one bathroom. That represented a real problem. In fact, it was close to a tragedy! Vati could not adhere to any reasonable schedule. He was not willing to yield us privacy in the bathroom, even for the shortest time. He considered an apartment with only one bathroom unacceptable, and we were punished for it daily. The minute either of us used that room, he banged on the door unless, of course, he was not home.

He had rented the corner store of our building, which was converted into offices. The two tall store windows were covered with drapes. A bronze plate outside proclaimed, *Friedrich August Uhlenbrock, Wasserversorgung und Baugesellschaft, GmbH, seit 1909* (Friedrich August Uhlenbrock, Water Supply Design and Installation, Ltd., since 1909).

Whenever possible, I postponed doing homework by climbing on my radiator in front of the big window. I was given a little square of chocolate after the meal, as long as the supply lasted. I knew the chocolate had been sent by my Italian grandmother, the one I had met only once in Rapallo. I never thought about whose mother she could be and I never asked. I do not remember ever writing a thank-you letter to her. I knew that Mutti's mother had died when she was a young girl, and Vati's mother was dead, as well.

When we moved to Rosenheimer Strasse, Erika who was young, creative and fun replaced Erna. Erika had been a kindergarten teacher and knew how to keep me interested in whatever we were doing. She taught me how to make little gifts out of leather kits. We made eyeglass cases and key holders for my parents. I loved giving gifts from very early on, so Erika had no problem motivating me. Unfortunately, she did not stay with us very long. I can still see her with her suitcases, walking through the swinging doors that divided the central hall from the entrance hall. It was the first time in my life that I experienced the sadness of having to say good-bye to someone I loved and not knowing whether I would ever see her again. But sometimes strange things happen in life. Mutti and I happened to meet Erika again in Jelleff's, a clothing store in Arlington, Virginia, 20 years later.

When my mother enrolled me in Catholic kindergarten, she let Erika go. I hated that place! I had to sit still a lot and, among other things, I had to sing. Sitting still and singing were the two things I was least able to do! The consolation was that I always managed to find a special friend. In kindergarten I met my very first 'best' girlfriend, Klärchen.

Klärchen and I with Mutti & Vati – 1938

This was the time I started to feel that I was different from others. I had a nickname, nobody else had – a constant reason for embarrassment! I also disliked my bangs. Maybe it added to being different from the other girls! After a lot of begging, the haircut was changed, but there was no way of getting rid of my nickname *Cisi*. My father would call my name so loud that everyone turned around to look at me. I soon realized I had no choice but to get used to being different!

I remember making a lot of fuss about not wanting to go to kindergarten. I believed I could not do anything as well as the other kids and it made me feel miserable. I begged Mutti to keep me home. She did not give in until I told her that Sister Marianne had spanked a child for vomiting. My mother checked the story out, found it to be true and was upset enough that my kindergarten-days were over. Klärchen had no problems. She could do everything well, even sing! Although, our kindergarten togetherness was shortened by a few months, Klärchen and I remained friends for life.

First School Years
and First Communion

Klärchen and I lived just a block apart, and therefore were assigned to the same public school. It just so happened that our mothers, who knew each other from accompanying us to kindergarten, were in school to enroll us on the same day, at the same time. It was as if it were meant to be – and it changed my childhood years forever!

In April 1939 I started school. When my first school year was entering its second half, the Second World War was entering its first round. My little world – the home front – was affected immediately. The fathers of two school friends, who lived in my street, had been drafted. Annemarie Schwarz's father was killed in action as early as the end of 1939, *"für Führer, Volk und Vaterland,"* (for our Leader, the people and the Fatherland) as the notification read. Annemarie had almost taken Klärchen's place as my 'best' friend, when her mother, after the loss of her husband,

My first school day with Mutti

took her daughter and moved to Stendahl. Again I had that empty and sad feeling of losing somebody very special to me. The other

23

friend was Ingrid Feuerherm. Her father was sent to Africa to fight under Rommel's command. I remember it well, because Ingrid's father was able to buy and mail home a wristwatch for me 'from the front', that none of my friends was privileged to have. It became my most cherished Christmas gift. To buy a watch, then a luxury item, one had to have connections. I felt like a millionaire! Later it occurred to me that maybe the watch was meant to teach me punctuality, a 'must' for my mother. When I was as much as five minutes late, Mutti became very worried, as well as very angry.

My first school building was located three blocks from where we lived. It became a war hospital almost immediately, so we were moved. The new school was 'bombed out' at a time when only a few bombs were dropped, and our nightly air raids were mostly designed to destroy our nerves and deprive us of sleep. Again, we were moved to another building. Temporarily, we were in an Intermediate School around the corner from us, on Barbarossa Square. Eventually we ended up at the Kyffhäuser Strasse in a dark, old school building that also had a 'Help-School' section for learning-disabled children.

Frau Typke was my first grade teacher. She stayed with our class for the first three years. She was very strict and did not allow any noise in her classroom. She had to be able to hear a pin drop, which was next to impossible in a room with 50 little girls. She had little use for children who could not sit still. Therefore, she could hardly tolerate me. But that did not discourage me from admiring her. I even daydreamed that I would be allowed to sit on her lap one day. But there was little chance of that! On the contrary, notes were sent to my mother, summoning her to school. Frau Typke had justifiable complaints. Too often, my head was turned to face the children behind me, rather than paying attention to her. I was constantly dropping things from my slanted desktop. While I retrieved one thing, another one fell. It got really bad, when the little slate blackboard, on which I practiced writing, came crashing to the floor!

My mother pleaded with Frau Typke to be patient, because I was so much younger than most girls in my class. She also suggested seating me in the last row, where I had no reason to turn my head. "If she is 'so' young, she does not belong in school!" Frau Typke responded. My mother explained that because of her age, she wanted me to complete school as early as possible. Frau Typke was angry that she had to sacrifice her sacred recess to listen to useless excuses, and none of Mutti's suggestions seemed to interest her. Mutti grew more and more frustrated with her, as well as with me.

My second grade class picture with Frau Typke in the middle. I am standing right behind her. To the right of me is Klärchen, and on the very far right in the same row is my friend Ulla Neumann

After one of those encounters with Frau Typke, I heard Mutti tell my father that she usually had 'some' rapport with people, but this teacher was 'unapproachable!' Still, my adoration for Frau Typke never wavered, and I was only too happy when I could proclaim, "Frau Typke is not a Nazi!"

We were sitting at our dining table, which seated twelve – twenty-four when extended. The table was so large that a large-size Persian prayer rug was used under the tablecloth to protect its surface. Mutti always sat at one end, my father at the other, and I was placed around the corner next to my mother. By saying that Frau Typke was not a Nazi, I had my parents' undivided attention from both ends of the table. When questioned further, I explained that every day, before the school bell rang, we were allowed to congregate around Frau Typke's desk. There we could tell her about all the exciting things on our minds. One girl, with the name of Ruth Richter, said that an old, blind woman had asked her for help across the street. She was about to do so when she saw the yellow Star of David with *Jude* on her coat – which all Jews were required to wear – so she refused. I don't remember Frau Typke's exact words, but I remember her outrage. She was red in her face and her message was unmistakable, "How dare you refuse your help! She is a human being just like you! How would YOU feel, if YOU were blind and helpless?"

I knew how that story would be received. By now, I had no doubt about my parents' hatred for Hitler and their sympathy for the Jews. My father was not only vocal about it, he was perpetually engaged in his private war. I devilishly enjoyed reciting every newly memorized poem that had to do with the praise of Hitler. It provoked him so much that we would hear his version no later than the next morning. His parodies were so good that I had a hard time remembering the original. The following poem I never forgot, because it put us into a terribly dangerous situation. It went like this:

> *Einer ist da, der alle führt,*
> One is there who leads us all,
> *Einer, dem aller Dank gebührt,*
> one who deserves all gratitude
> *Einer, den, wenn wir ihn täglich schauen,*
> one when we see him daily

Voller Liebe und voll Vertrauen

full of love and full of trust

Betet zu Gott, dass Er ihn uns bewahre

pray to God that He'll keep him for us

Unseren Führer für viele Jahre

Our Leader for many years to come

The parody went like this:

Einer ist da, der alle verführt

One is there who misleads us all

Einer, dem die schlimmste Strafe gebührt

 one, who deserves the worst punishment

Einer, den, wenn wir ihn täglich schauen,

one, when we see him daily

Am liebsten in die Fresse hauen

desire to punch into his big mouth

Bete zu Gott, dass der Bursche verrecke

pray to God that the villain perishes

Und wie ein Hund krepiert in der Ecke.

 and, like a dog, expires in the corner

I loved my father's 'artistic' changes, and I memorized them immediately.

The following year, we had to recite a poem we remembered. I chose this one. I was called to stand in front of the class. Very self-conscious and nervous, suddenly I could only remember the parody. I choked on the words, turned beet red and started crying and could not stop. I was horrified that I had said too much already. – Nobody suspected what was troubling me. I was led out of the classroom to be calmed down and comforted. Thank goodness, I realized in time that it was better to be thought strange than to end up in a concentration camp!

In those years I really enjoyed going to our church, because the sermons subtly reinforced my parents' political orientation. I was convinced that all Catholics were against Hitler. It felt good to be part of a group of people who seemed to have the same convictions as my family.

In 1941, when I was eight years old, I was preparing for my First Communion ceremony. We needed to wear all white: dress, stockings and shoes and we had to carry a long candle. None of this was easy to find. Coupons were required for everything, and only practical things were on the shelves, if there was anything at all. But sooner or later, my mother managed to get it all together. She bartered and ran all over Berlin to dress me as beautifully as possible. I remember how she beamed, when I tried on the white stockings and the smocked white dress. She was so proud of her accomplishment and pleased with the way I looked. I was probably the best-dressed girl in the Communion procession and I was so excited.

Erna, Uncle Alfred's wife

On the Sunday of my First Communion, our dining room had a festive table waiting, and my uncle Alfred and his wife came to join us to celebrate the occasion. My parents gave me a golden necklace with a cross, and I received from the church a small, framed picture of Jesus holding a lamb. On the back of the picture were the signatures of the three parish priests.

Uncle Alfred was Mutti's older brother; her younger

brother had died in a French prisoner-of-war camp, at the end of the First World War. Uncle Alfred was blind and had to be lead by his wife, Aunt Erna. I remember how dear and kind Uncle Alfred was and how he congratulated me with a warm hug. Suddenly I saw something yellow under his lapel. It frightened me, because only Jews wore a yellow star! I thought about it for a moment, and then suspected that it was probably something to indicate that he was blind, like the band that blind people wear around their sleeves in Germany.

I loved Uncle Alfred, even though I was always a bit in awe of him. I thought he must be a saint to be so kind and cheerful, even though he was not able to see. He never complained about his disability and certainly was much more cheerful than my father. Somehow he even managed to operate his own cigar store.

Not long after my First Communion, Uncle Alfred's wife died of a sudden heart attack. I did not know then that it meant I would never see my Uncle Alfred again.

The Revelation

Klärchen and I were best friends. We often visited each other after school and played together for many hours.

Erika's room had become my playroom. But whenever we could get away with it, we played in Inge's Room. Inge was my other sister, two years younger than Ruth, but also much older than I. Inge had left for the United States in 1939. As a child, I never had much of a relationship with Inge. She did not like me much and I remember a time when I made her particularly nervous. She had sprained her ankle skiing. Whenever I came close to her bed, she screamed in anticipation of what I might do to her painful leg. But I don't remember her having much patience with me even when she was well. She avoided me and I don't recall spending any time with her. It did not surprise me, because I was often described as a 'very active' child. Many people, in our apartment house, complained when I slid down the banisters of the eight flights of stairs. They were annoyed by the loud thumps when I reached the landings. One of our neighbors told my mother that she did not believe "Anything worthwhile will ever become of that child!" Mutti's love for me weathered all predictions and she repeated them to my father with a warm, little smile.

Why Inge had left, I did not know. I cannot recall a good-bye, nor that I missed her, but I do remember that her room was a fun playroom. It was even more attractive because it was not to be used for playing. Inge's room was furnished with our winter-garden furniture, made from rattan. The chair cushions were covered with shrimp-colored raw silk. A matching bedspread covered her metal bed. (Many years later, we salvaged the spread from under the debris, and made my first long gown out of it.) There was a matching three-mirrored vanity, just perfect for playing 'fine ladies'. In front of the window was a Pfaff sewing machine. The sewing machine had a wide foot pedal to move up and down that made the needle work. That sewing machine was a 'no-no' to play with and therefore the main attraction.

On this particular day in 1939, Klärchen and I were sitting in Inge's room, in front of the sewing machine, pretending to sew. Suddenly, Klärchen looked troubled. I asked her what was the matter? She told me – now looking torn – that she knew something about me, but had promised her mother not to tell. Even though Klärchen was just seven years old, she did not take a promise lightly. She had strong ideas about friendship, as well. She was convinced that friends should not keep secrets from each other. She had a great conflict; to break a promise to her mother or to keep a secret from her best friend. After an endless time discussing the situation, I finally convinced her that being true friends carried more weight than honoring a promise. When that left doubt, I threatened her with the end of our friendship. That finally tipped the scales! And then she said it: "You are not German, you are Italian!" She continued explaining, "My mother was there when you were registered for school, and she saw it with her own eyes!"

I felt like the floor had opened up under me. I suddenly was a stranger to myself. I could only think, 'Who am I?' and 'It is the worst fate not to be German like everybody else!' Klärchen must have read my mind. She tried to comfort me, as she explained, "It would be a lot worse if you were English. England is our enemy, you know, but Italy is fighting on our side!" I did not care who was fighting with or against whom. I only wanted to be German like everybody else! I remembered Klärchen's consolation throughout the years, but it did not help.

I never once questioned the validity of what had been said to me, nor did I ask my parents about it. I was much too scared of what else might be different about me – but most of all, afraid of what I could lose! My father's business meetings came to my mind, and I felt embarrassed and worthless, because I was not German! The question never left me, 'Why am I different?' I went as far as finding a duplicate key to my mother's personal wardrobe in my parents' bedroom. Whenever I sneaked in, I was so nervous that I could not read fast enough, or understand well enough, to find any information that would give me a clue.

WAR DAYS

The war was becoming more apparent and the struggle for survival had become the number one pre-occupation for everyone.

We had to have black shades in front of all windows, so no inside light could be seen from the outside. If light peeked through, it cost a hefty fine and worse than that, one was treated like a traitor. The streets were pitch black at night. People wore reflective buttons on their coats so they would not run into each other. Even the flashlights, they carried to avoid stumbling over the curbs, had to have dark shades. Sirens had been installed on the rooftop of every second or third house. When they sounded their alarm, the whole city screamed as though to awaken the dead. Bathtubs had to be filled with water at all times, and buckets full of sand had to be placed in front of every entrance door. Runners and carpets were removed from the halls and stairways. The underground cellars were sectioned off to become air-raid shelters. It was important that neither gas nor water lines were located in the shelter section. A safe-like door became the entrance to our nightly hideout. Each of us had to provide our own chair that was placed in the cellar waiting for us.

It was not long into the war that the sirens sounded first once then twice a night. We soon counted on it. We jumped out of bed, got dressed, grabbed our individual small suitcases packed with essentials, and descended the eight flights of steps to the ground floor. We proceeded to the outside of the house and made a U-turn to go further down the cellar steps. A strip of grass with a lilac bush separated the front door from the entrance to the cellar.

Rosenheimer Strasse 5 Air Raid Shelter Door

I am trying to open the same Air Raid Shelter door 50 years later

The all-clear sirens were usually heard in about forty-five minutes to an hour, after which we climbed back up into our beds. I always shivered and never quite knew whether it was out of fear or a reaction to getting pulled out of a deep sleep in the middle of the night. For a long time, we did not see much damage after these nightly trips. The only evidence of bombing was small crater-like holes in the streets. Collecting bomb splinters became the popular thing to do and a favorite pastime for us kids.

Then one day, the meaning of war became more real to me. Once a week, a group of kids and I went to Catholic religious instruction in a private home. One week, when I went there, twin girls were missing from the group. We were told that they had been buried under the rubble of their apartment building, when it collapsed in a bombing raid. That was so horrible that I remember consciously blocking it out of my thoughts. But, whenever I was in our shelter, hearing bombs whistling on their way down, I wondered about the building above us. Would we get out from under, or would we be buried alive like the twins?

We had been instructed what to do during an air raid. We had to stick our fingers into our ears and open our mouths, so the noise and pressure would not break our eardrums. I can still see the meager source of light; a dangling light bulb, flickering ominously, while I had my fingers poked into my ears and my mouth opened wide.

As conditions worsened, my father became more and more stubborn and rebellious. The only time we could listen to the radio was for news. Then he was constantly interrupting by shouting at the commentators and announcers. He corrected the news as it was read, to the point where he even changed the name of the commentator. His name was 'Dr. Ley.' Whenever his name was mentioned, my father shouted from the top of his lungs, "Levy is the name!" This must have been the ONLY Jew he hated. I was confused about why he insisted on that name! Neither Mutti nor I believed he was correct, but after the end of the war, we heard it confirmed by others. I still wonder why Dr. Ley, alias Levy, had been allowed to join the Nazis, even if he so desired? And then there was the commentator, Hans Fritsche. *"Das Schwein schon wieder."* (the equivalent would be "that jackass again") my father screamed every evening on cue, as if he did not know that Fritsche spouted Goebbels' propaganda on a daily basis! Thank goodness for thick walls between the apartments! Still, we lived in constant fear that somebody could hear him, if not through the walls, then through the entrance door. But there was absolutely no stopping my father.

Things only got worse. One day, Vati decided that he had enough of going night after night into the air raid cellar. At that point, my shivering was joined by tears. There was nothing more dangerous than being on the top floor during an air attack. Nobody stayed there, unless one was Jewish, hidden away and afraid to be seen. Then, of course, there were the poor soldiers manning the anti-aircraft cannons on the rooftops. My father weakened when he saw me crying so bitterly and heard my begging. But it did not keep him from instigating the same scene every night, before being dragged to the cellar.

I never doubted that my father's hatred and anger was justified. But I wanted so much to be like everyone else. I wanted to believe that there was justification for this war, and that we could win it. But more than that, I wanted to be proud to be German! We were taught that a German child was, 'As hard as Krupp-steel, as tough as leather and as fast as the greyhounds!' I was not any of this, not even German! I heard my mother beg my father over and over again, "Please, do not burden our child with the hopelessness of the situation!" To no avail. As I grew older, I became more aware of what was happening in the war and at the home front. I remember the day my father announced, "It is just a matter of time, until the United States will join the war!" and "We will all march into hell together!" The line came from 'his' version of the *Horst Wessel* song. It was his favorite line and he recited it constantly while pointing his right index finger toward the floor. He drew circles in the air and then his finger went straight down. I hated that motion and dreaded it, because he did it in public whenever somebody talked about winning the war. It did not seem to bother him that people wondered what he was doing. I am sure, while I held my breath, he was hoping they would ask him, so he could add the words to the motion. All my friends seemed happy in their belief that we were winning, and that there was a future besides hell. I envied them!

The second time I became aware of the deadly seriousness of our existence, was when I walked down our street to see why people were lining the entrance to a neighboring building. An ambulance was waiting at the curb. I was scared but curious, so I joined the crowd to see what was happening. After a long wait, I saw them carry out four stretchers, each with a body covered by a sheet. I overheard people saying that it was a young family; father, mother and two children, a boy and a girl. They had taken their own lives – they had committed suicide.

I don't remember whether it was mentioned that they were Jewish, but somehow I knew! I was horrified and kept wondering how they all died? Why did these parents not protect their children and prevent them from dying? I was only seven or eight then and I wonder today, why I was too uncomfortable to ask my parents about the incident. Somehow, I must have sensed that the subject would cause even more upheaval in my family. Maybe they knew and tried to keep it from me? We had a large Jewish population in our neighborhood, called the Bavarian quarter, because we lived close to the Bavarian Square. Not long after that horrible incident, I became aware that the Jews were 'picked up!' On the second floor of our building lived a middle-aged Jewish lady with a hunchback. We called her *Sternchen,* little Star, because *Stern* was her name and she was so short. We kids loved her. She owned a small candy store in our building, next to my father's office. She was always friendly and kind when we bought our measly one-penny piece of black licorice that we could tear into five separate strings. Often she gave us an extra long piece or another piece of candy with it. She was a part of our young lives just like a member of the family.

One day, she was not there anymore. There was talk that she had been 'picked up.' Nobody knew exactly what happened to people who were 'picked up', but we knew that they were taken from their homes and not heard from again. Mutti said they were put into concentration camps. She predicted that no one would survive there. (I believe to this day that most people, who were not involved with the operation, thought them to be detention or labor camps. Who could have fathomed that they were extermination camps?)

Vati became more brooding and angry depending on the time of day. Mutti seemed more and more serious. She did not say much, but I knew she worried a lot as she became more and more protective of me. She was trying as hard as she could to keep things calm – a full time job considering my father's behavior. He kept on fighting his private war. The victims were my mother and me.

The next crisis came soon. Vati was very proud of the honor of having been awarded the 'Iron Cross' during World War I. Unfortunately, this award for distinguished service was also given out by Hitler. The difference was a swastika in the center. Every veteran with the original version was graciously sent the new edition. At the time of receipt of the new medal, the original one had to be returned. Needless to say, Vati sent the 'new' one back! The authorities must have thought it was an involuntary error and sent it back to us. My father was now more outraged than before. He had a run-in with the mailman, who luckily returned it without reporting the incident to the police. From then on, Mutti and I monitored the mail so we would catch and hide the medal, should it come back again. Vati was waiting for it as well, because now he wanted to return it in person. Thank goodness, Mutti caught it, we hid it and a disaster was prevented.

Just when we were relieved to have solved the Iron Cross incident, we were officially notified that we were remiss in not flying the Nazi-flag on holidays. That meant Vati had to buy and fly a flag. This gave Vati another occasion to voice his opinion in the stationery store that handled the sale of flags. Mutti knew what lay ahead, so she stayed home. I loved to go to this type of store, hoping to get some new school supplies. I always thought that new copybooks and pencils would make it more exciting to study. I eagerly took advantage of any opportunity to get some money out of my father. That was a chore even for the price of a pencil! This time, I could forget about his buying anything for me, because my father could not be interrupted while purchasing a flag – and not just any old flag. With great effort and unnecessary explanations, he selected the smallest flag that was manufactured at the time. It had a three-foot pole and sold for two *Reichsmark*. The rule was that the flag had to be mounted 'in plain sight.' That was an impossibility with this flag, considering the height of our balcony. Our flag could only be seen from the balcony itself. You had to have very keen eyesight to detect it from the street. My father was pleased; after all, that was the idea. Not too long after that, he had an even better idea. It had to do with a very peculiar incident, which made me remember the flag story, in the first place.

In November 1941, we had the first serious bombing attack. All men still around, most of them too old or too feeble to be on the front lines, were ordered to patrol inside the houses, looking for firebombs. Small fires caused by these bombs could be extinguished with sand, stored in containers at the doors, or with the water in the tubs. The only time my father obeyed the order to patrol the apartments, was the one time that I could not get him to go downstairs to the shelter. He just stayed upstairs, and then it happened. Our little flag, stored standing up in the narrow space between the bookcase and the wall next to the balcony door, was bombed. A small firebomb had come through the ceiling, right above the narrow space where the flag was standing. The thick wall of the bookcase was charred, and so was the parquet floor underneath. And there was a hole in the ceiling above. Mutti and I looked at that site a lot and checked it very carefully! Lo and behold, our newly acquired flag was burned without a trace. Vati loved to tell about having thrown the bomb from the balcony, which would have been plausible, if the bomb had never ignited. It was amazing how he enjoyed telling everybody that he lost his flag in this peculiar way! I wonder to this day, how the bomb could have been handled, after it had burned the flag. My mother and I suspected that my father helped that miracle along! "The fact that we lost the flag, and *only* the flag, must have been God's will!" so my father said. The story of the flag and the heroic bomb disposal was added to my father's repertoire of obnoxious stories he told, whenever he was talking to somebody suspected of being a Nazi. He always added to his story that he had wasted two *Reichsmark* on a flag that he did not want, and obviously was not meant to have – at least not for long!

EVACUATION

After the flag incident, our nightly travels to the air-raid cellar continued without major attacks on our particular part of the city. Deafening sirens, at all hours of the night, had become a part of our lives. I got used to my shivering attacks whenever the sirens blasted to wake up the city. It sounded as if the whole world could hear them! But I could not get used to worrying about whether my father would go with us to the cellar, at least one more time, because he never failed to threaten, "This is the last time!" His toll on our nerves exceeded that of the British bombers. More and more, we appreciated the high-pitched 'all-clear' sirens. When we emerged from the cellar into the street, there was a sigh of relief that we had been spared another night.

In March of 1943 all of that changed. We headed for the cellar for a routine visit to our reserved chairs. I remember stepping outside the front door. We were greeted by a full moon that shone brightly from a clear sky. It was a cold night, but peaceful and quiet after the sirens had stopped and the bomber squadrons were still too far away to be detected with the naked ear. We had just sat down on our chairs, when the earth began to shake from the impact of the bombardment. The one bulb, dangling from the ceiling, went out. It was dark for what seemed a long time. The light eventually came back on. I held my breath thinking that this was what Vati had predicted: 'We are on our way to hell!' The whistling of falling bombs was incessant, only interspersed with the noise of our anti-aircraft cannons (FLAK). Did we still have a house above us? If not, would we be able to dig ourselves out? All,

43

but the children younger than I, pondered those questions. I knew it, although nobody spoke. Forty-five minutes later, we heard the all-clear sirens. We carefully opened the heavy door, wondering – It opened! Up the worn brick cellar steps we climbed to reach the outside. Dense smoke choked us. After our eyes got used to the burning darkness, we could see some flames in the middle of enormous black smoke clouds. The fire seemed some distance away. We looked up at our own house. We were unable to tell whether the top floors were still there. The clear night-sky had been replaced by one huge cloud of smoke that seemed to have swallowed our entire city. We climbed the stairs with the eerie feeling that we may fall off the end. We expected that there was nothing, where we had climbed out of bed just an hour ago. We never went up those many steps so easily because, with each flight of stairs, we became more hopeful and got closer to our beds.

We had been luckier than most people on our street. When we saw it all in daylight, we could not believe our eyes. The fire-safe walls were all that was left of most of the buildings. They stood stark and lonely like memorials to the war. Some of those walls had a sink or a toilet bowl still attached by its plumbing pipes. Countless families were homeless and had lost everything. Anyone who had an undamaged apartment, with more than one bedroom, had to take in families who were bombed out. 'Bombed out' became the new household word. We were assigned a couple named Guhr, who moved in with us. All I remember about them was that they were both very tall and had no children.

Bunkers had been built in many places. They were rumored to be bomb-proof. Only women with children were allowed inside. Those who lived close enough scurried to try to get in. Others ran to hide in deep, underground subwaystations. Some true believers thought God would protect the churches. But they soon noticed that the churches were the first to be damaged, if only because their steeples were blown off. It became increasingly harder to believe in a benevolent God. Where was justice? More Nazis than objectors seemed to survive. I hoped that *Die Vorsehung,* (predestination), as Hitler called God, would not just save him, while we all perished.

We did not have to wait long for the next *Großalarm,* the second major air attack on Berlin. It was the time when Hitler declared *'den totalen Krieg'* (the total war). That meant fighting until no one was left alive. Hitler called it 'a fight until *Selbstvernichtung,'* namely, self-destruction. But before that, mothers and children were to leave the *Reichshauptstadt,* the capital of Germany, and relocate immediately.

I was in the third grade. In our schools, the regular air raid drills had become so sophisticated that they included learning how, and when, to use gas masks. The drills became the real thing, when air attacks became part of our days, as well as our nights.

One morning, while I was in school, the sirens started blasting. Our class was about to be ushered into the shelter, located under our school building, when my mother appeared out of nowhere, grabbed me, and pulled me into the cellar of a house nearby. After the all-clear sirens sounded, we went straight to the *Görlitzer* train station, to leave for the Heidehof. I never found out why we fled in such a hurry.

I only came back to Berlin a couple of times before the end of the war. I came back to be released from the Berlin-school, to transfer to the school in Märkisch-Buchholz. That last school day in Berlin was very exciting, because I was allowed to take Mutti's purple vase with big, white hydrangeas to school, as a good-bye gift for Frau Typke. Letting go of the vase was no sacrifice for Mutti, because she never liked it and it also had a chip missing on the rim. I had seen my classmates bring flowers before, but I never had the courage myself. I feared Frau Typke might refuse them, since I thought she still barely tolerated me! However, on this special occasion, it seemed reasonable for me to take the chance. To my surprise, Frau

Typke was delighted with the flowers, and very interested in where I was moving. That gave me the chance to invite her to visit us at the Heidehof. Since I was not going to be in her class any longer, Mutti had given me permission to invite her, should the opportunity arise. (According to law, parents could not have social contact with their children's teachers, to prevent favoritism.)

I could not have guessed then that Frau Typke kept that purple vase with her, wherever she went, in an effort to return it. Therefore it was not lost, as all her other belongings were. It is hard to believe that she brought it with her in 1964 – twenty-one years later – on her first visit to Virginia. We have it to this day, still missing the chip. Now it is a precious memory of a friend, with whom we stayed in close contact until her death in 1980.

Soon after we left, all of Berlin's schools were evacuated. They were relocated to smaller, safer towns. The local people had to make room for teachers and pupils alike. Our school was sent to Vetschau, further away from Berlin than the Heidehof, but in the same general direction.

The second time I came back to Berlin was to take my entrance examinations for a college preparatory high school.

THE HEIDEHOF AND MÄRKISCH-BUCHHOLZ

The Heidehof was idyllic. The previous owner was Victor Bake, in his eighties, when my father met him. Victor Bake was an artist who had painted a picture of a beautiful farmhouse, and then had one built to match. He placed it in a countryside of purple heather, surrounded by some birches and many pine trees, far away from urban noise.

The train usually was my father's favorite place to get into political discussions, even though warning signs were posted on every window, **"Careful With Conversations, Enemy Listens!"** Of course, the Nazis and my father had different enemies in mind.

My father happened to meet Mr. Bake on a train. The two men found each other to be of the same political persuasion. This put Bake into the 'friend' category which, in turn, gave him the opportunity to show Vati his painting of the Heidehof. When Vati heard that Mr. Bake had decided to sell his picturesque farm and was looking for a buyer, my father was immediately interested. He had just been forced to sell his park property in Saarow-Pieskow, for use as an air-supply field. He was looking to acquire some land in its stead, preferably where riding-horses could be kept. Ever since the First World War, where he had been issued his own horse, riding had become his passion. To own a horse was his dream for a tomorrow that never came.

The Heidehof was exactly what Vati had wanted. He shared the purchase with his brother, Fritz. Each of them paid one hundred thousand *Reichsmark*. I often heard it mentioned that it was a 'bargain', because it came complete with 'living

Die Dahme bei Märkisch-Buchholz

Aerial photo of the Heidehof right of lower center, also showing the Dahme River, the northern border of our property

48

and dead inventory.' I still remember that peculiar terminology. It meant that it came completely furnished and the stables were filled with animals. All but horses! There was an ox, two cows, two pigs, a family of ducks and some chickens. When I first saw the Heidehof, the ducks were swimming merrily in the oval duckpond in front of the stables, just like the picture that Mr. Bake had painted.

The stables, as well as the barn, were attached to the main house – the barn on one end, the stables on the other. The outside of the house was off-white, rough stucco, interrupted by dark brown exposed beams that protruded just enough to show the wood's natural beauty. In front of the house was a big veranda under an equally large covered balcony. The entrance was through the open veranda into a spacious reception room.

Inside, all walls were paneled with cherry wood, which was patterned near the top with a row of inlaid ebony diamonds. The furniture and the built-in cupboards were made of the same wood. The wooden benches and chairs were made out of thin strips, which were bent into continuous curved backs and seats.

One side of the room was furnished with a large rectangular dining table in front of a built-in bench. On the other side of the entrance was a small round smoking table with two impressive wooden wingback chairs, covered with square leather cushions. Facing the entrance door, across the room, were two swinging doors, symmetrically placed between cupboards. One of the cupboard doors hid a dumbwaiter to the kitchen below. The swinging door on the left, led to a stairway going to the upstairs bedrooms. If you went through the right swinging door, you had a choice of going straight ahead to the farm manager's quarters, or taking the stairway on the left, down to the kitchen.

The house was a split-level with two stories in front and three in the back. The kitchen was built on a concrete slab, with a door leading out to the back of the house. The two cellars – both accessible from inside the kitchen and on the same level – were under the front half of the house. They only had dirt floors and no windows. One was the potato cellar; the other one became our shelter in the final battle of the war.

The left extension of the kitchen was a so-called 'milk-kitchen', a separate room equipped with a 'government-disabled' centrifuge. Since all milk had to be turned in daily, the authorities confiscated the parts of the centrifuge that were necessary to separate the cream from the milk. This way, the milk could not be skimmed. This milk-kitchen became the future site of my father's famous water holding-tank.

We had barely moved to the Heidehof, when Vati had lavatories built into all upstairs bedrooms. In order to have running water upstairs, water had to be pumped into the holding tank and put under pressure. Since there was no electricity at the Heidehof, it required industrial-strength muscles and even greater determination to get sufficient pressure. Unfortunately, not long after all the new equipment was installed, no one was willing to do the pumping job.

Next to the milk and pump room there was another large room, soon to be occupied by the farmer's daughter and her child. In fact, it wasn't long before all the rooms in the Heidehof were in use by non-paying guests.

Next to the quarters of the caretaker, on the right, was an especially big, heavy door. It opened into a space wide enough to accommodate a window, and doors to two indoor 'outdoor-type' toilet stalls. Each toilet consisted of a wooden bench with a round hole. Ten feet below was a covered trench to the vegetable garden. Later, when the whole area became Germany's final battlefield, I threw a leather-bound edition of Hitler's book, *Mein Kampf,* into one of those holes. I had found it lying on the ground. I was very interested in it until I heard that the Russians shot everybody, who owned Hitler paraphernalia. I disposed of the book fast!

The barn was on the left side of the house. Over it were two guest rooms with a common, covered balcony in front. They became the home of our Russian laborers, a woman and her adult son. They had been deported from Russia, and forced upon us to help with farming. They were supposed to replace the manpower sent away to fight the war. These Russians had no intention to do work, and my father had none to make them. We could not communicate, but they seemed content and happy. Unfortunately, they disappeared during the final battle. It would have been nice, had they stayed to put in a good word for us, when their victorious and vengeful countrymen arrived!

Upstairs, over the large entrance room was our combination bed-and-sitting room. It was the most prominent room, facing the front of the house and opened onto the covered balcony above the entrance-veranda. We also had a real bathroom with bathtub. It was useless, because there was not enough pressure pumped for running cold water, and there was certainly no hot water available. So, the beautiful new bathtub became the storage bin for our Persian rugs brought from Berlin, as well as the home for some mice that nibbled holes into them.

The Heidehof consisted of thirty-five acres of land. Of those acres there was only enough cultivated to feed one family. The remaining land consisted of spruce and pine forests and sandy ground covered with heather, and a few birches around the house.

Whoever came to visit, was doomed to take the one and one-half hour walk around the boundary of our property. It was my father's favorite sport. It was not my idea of a good time, but every one of our guests took the long walk in stride and even seemed to enjoy it.

Märkisch Buholz Market Place - 1943

Soon after we had moved to the Heidehof, Frau Typke took us up on our invitation to visit. When she took the path through the pines off the main road, she suddenly stood at a bright opening. About one hundred seventy-five feet ahead of her, she saw the Heidehof. It was love at first sight. She stopped in surprise, and immediately named the Heidehof, *Heideschloß* 'Heather Castle' instead of 'Heather Farm'. It was not long until Frau Typke asked my father to talk to the school principal about a teaching job in the one and only school in the area, the elementary school of Märkisch-Buchholz.

A mile and a half of a quiet country road led from the Heidehof to Märkisch-Buchholz. The sandy road had deep ruts from oxen-drawn wagons that townspeople used to reach their fields. The surrounding scenery was beautiful. There was the tall pine forest on one side of the road, and the meadows that stretched to the Dahme river on

Road through the pine forest

the other side. The meadows were only interrupted by some gardens, symmetrically squared. I don't remember ever meeting anyone on my way to school. There was not a house to be seen until one entered the 'city.' At that time, Märkisch-Buchholz had a population of about a thousand, qualifying it to be called a 'city.' That new law, decreed by Hitler, gave the people great pride; so much so, that Vati believed it made the majority of them instant Nazis. Since everybody knew everybody else in town, those of opposing views were very careful – everyone but my father!

I was with Vati, when he first walked into the mayor's office. One look at the two overpowering pictures, one of Hitler and the other of von Hindenburg, hanging side by side, staring at him from the wall, made him crazy. My father exclaimed, pointing at Hitler, "He has got to go!" Then he pointed at Hindenburg, "Too bad that he was senile in his later years!" When the mayor showed some interest in what my father was saying, he felt encouraged enough to continue: "Hitler sure is getting a lot of mileage out of the old aristocrat, who was too feeble to know what he was doing when he betrayed the German people. After all, von Hindenburg was elected, not Hitler! How could he have handed his power over to his opponent, this 'hoodlum' (my father's favorite word for Hitler) who lost the election!" I had never been taught anything like this in school and I did not understand what Vati was talking about. But I cringed under that black cloud of fear – so familiar to me – while I wondered whether the mayor was going to have my father arrested.

Again my father was lucky! The mayor and his wife were among the few in town who agreed with what he had said. Even though the mayor and his wife were much younger than my parents, it was the beginning of a friendship. (In the mayor's house, I made my first potato pancakes. They tasted the best I had ever eaten, and I was proud of my cooking ability.)

It was no secret in Märkisch-Buchholz that Frau Hauck, the veterinarian's wife, had lost her teaching -job for refusing to join the Nazi party. Frau Hauck lived in a large, beautiful villa on the other side of the Dahme. (The Dahme formed the natural border on one side of our property, flowed through Märkisch-Buchholz and eventually into the Spree.) Frau Hauck was a lovely lady and a wonderful teacher. To this day,

I cannot imagine how she emotionally survived the loss of her husband and both her sons – in a war she hated. By 1945, she was the only survivor of her family. The communists who labeled her a capitalist took her home from her. Being 'privileged', was synonymous with 'capitalist.' Her house was filled with refugees from the areas east of the Oder/Neisse rivers. All that territory became Polish after the war. She had been 'graciously' given permission to live in one room in the basement of the house she had once owned. I saw her once more, five years after the war. She never allowed herself to complain, but her pain was written all over her face. Loneliness and hopelessness had become her existence.

In the Märkisch-Buchholz school, Berliners enjoyed the reputation of being smarter than the natives. This forced me to study hard, not to tarnish my status. It was reflected in my grades. I had never studied with so little distraction and so much motivation. The school was demanding and we learned a lot. Märkisch-Buchholz took Hitler's priority seriously: 'to prepare the guarantors of the future with a good education.'

Vati managed to get Frau Typke a job. Frau Hauck's loss became Frau Typke's gain, when she unknowingly stepped into the position left vacant by the dismissal of Frau Hauck. Since a teacher is a government employee, to be a party member was obligatory, especially in a small town. Frau Hauck had refused. The irony was that Frau Typke had never joined the Party either. Coming from Berlin, she was presumed a Nazi and never questioned. She moved in with us at the Heidehof, and she did not leave until my uncle Fritz and his wife arrived to claim their room. At that time, Frau Typke moved to the opposite end of town, into a room in the principal's house that he was willing to let her have. It was just beyond the Dahme's picturesque and quite noisy waterfall.

To travel to Berlin, we had to walk or bicycle to the nearest train station, which was Halbe. The bus transportation from Märkisch-Buchholz to Halbe had ceased, for lack of fuel. Now it took almost two hours from our house to the train station. Mutti and I walked it many times. Vati did it weekly when he commuted to Berlin. How exciting it was, when he managed to get permission to acquire a bicycle 'for business purposes.' It was a precious possession in wartime.

In 1943, I was in fourth grade. We took the train back to Berlin, so I could take the entrance examination for college preparatory school. This 'higher' school – as it was called – was strictly for the serious university candidates whose parents could afford to support their children through twelve years of school, as well as the university years. The children who had to support themselves as early as possible, stayed on in elementary school through the eighth grade. Others chose an intermediate school, qualifying them, at age sixteen, for a professional school. There they learned occupations like nursing, laboratory technician or home economics. Those who continued the elementary education, graduated from eighth grade, when they were fourteen. Then they entered into an apprenticeship agreement with an employer, their parents and the State, to learn a trade or secretarial work. They had to continue furthering themselves by evening classes, as part of the contract. Since it was impossible for any child or teenager to earn any money, their level of education depended on the affluence of their parents, as well as their ability to pass the required tests.

In Märkisch-Buchholz everybody continued elementary school, simply because there was no higher school available. In my case, there was never a question as to what education my parents wanted for me. Therefore, they made sure that I did not forfeit my eligibility.

While I was in Berlin to take my exams, the phone rang and I picked it up. It was my friend Tommi. He told me, "I am hiding out from the Gestapo and can not tell you where."

It was a moment in my life, I shall never forget. It must have been meant for me to be in Berlin, alone for that moment, the only one available to pick up the phone. (Ordinarily, children were not called, and therefore did not answer the telephone, when an adult was available.) When I heard Tommi on the other end, I knew something was not right and that it was serious. I am so glad that I did not fully understand what 'hiding from the Gestapo' meant and, I hope, neither did he! Mutti looked very worried when I told her about the call. Only much, much later did she tell me, that Tommi's mother had left to find refuge in England, to pave the way for her husband and son to follow. As far as Mutti knew, Tommi's mother had not been able to get her family out of Germany in time.

In those few days in Berlin, something else happened which was very upsetting to me. For the first time in my life, I saw my mother cry. Mutti was standing between the kitchen cupboard, filled with the well known onion-patterned Meissen porcelain, and the big butcher-block kitchen table. She opened a telegram from Auschwitz. It was a message that her brother – my uncle Alfred – had 'succumbed to pneumonia'. She read it while tears were running down her cheeks. When she looked at me, she said with a bitterness I had never heard before nor since, *"Der Dank des Vaterlands sei Dir gewiss! "* which means, 'You can be assured of the gratitude of the fatherland!' It was the sentence used during the First World War, when Mutti's family was officially notified that her younger brother, Erich, had died in a French prisoner-of-war camp, after having been on the front lines during the entire four years of that other senseless war.

The Years on the Farm

The closest neighbor to the Heidehof was a couple in their forties. How the husband had avoided the army remained an unanswered question. They had no children. I often went over to visit them at their house. It resembled a small summer cottage and was located near the river. I liked them very much. Sometimes they took me along in their kayak that we paddled down the river. Often I visited just to spend time with them, or watch her cook. I was quite isolated, because my school friends all lived in town, too far to visit.

Mutti felt sorry for me, and therefore allowed my 'best and number-one' friend, Klärchen, to come live with us. It was as if I had a sister. It was so wonderful, but only lasted for a short time. Klärchen and I had a lot of fun together. We seldom quarreled, except for one occasion. I don't know what possessed me! I started a rumor in school that Klärchen wet her pants. I think I got bored, and did it to add some excitement to my life. Well, boredom ceased immediately. Klärchen was rightfully furious and did not let a lie like this go unpunished. When she found out that I – of all people – was responsible, she was so angry that she jumped into my bed to beat me up. During the struggle, she bit my hand. She also made me admit my lie, and I had to apologize to her in front of the whole class. The embarrassment and the little scar on my hand did not let me forget my hurtful behavior for many years.

The other uncomfortable memory of that time happened in our music class in school. I was called upon to sing in front of three combined grades of boys and girls. Our very strict principal, Mr. Puls, taught music among other subjects. He could not believe that there were people who were not able to carry a tune. I was mortified when I had to demonstrate my inability to sing. It so happened that I had the misfortune of singing a simple little song correctly. That proved to Mr. Puls that everyone could sing. They only had to try hard enough.

Mutti and I on the veranda of the Heidehof

Since Klärchen was good at everything, she also sang well. One time, while I was holding my breath not to be called upon again, she finished singing in front of the class and came back to sit down next to me. Mr. Puls came over to shake Klärchen's hand very demonstratively. As he reached across me, I could not suppress a smile. Mr. Puls noticed it, and promptly slapped me in the face. My shock wore off, when it occurred to me that now I had something to report to my mother. I knew that under no circumstance would she allow a teacher to hit her child. I was right. She promptly went to see Mr. Puls. She must have stated her position so well that a fair arrangement was negotiated. I had to learn all the notes and the words of the songs. In return, I did not have to sing solo in front of the class! Again, I felt so thankful and lucky to have such a loving mother to defend me if she deemed it necessary.

Good old Mr. Puls was not easy. He put the fear of God into all of us, not just me. In his class we studied hard and learned a lot. He was a good teacher and a tough principal.

Only too soon, there was a disastrous Mothers' Day caper. It turned out to be the end of my having 'a sister.' The night before Mothers' Day, before Klärchen's family came to visit, we sneaked out of the house to steal flowers from the neighbors' garden-plots. We wanted them for Mothers' Day gifts. Since we were sleeping in the first floor guest room with the balcony, we climbed over the railing and jumped down. Mutti must have looked in on us and found our bedroom empty. She decided right then and there to send Klärchen home with her parents. She said that she could not take the responsibility for another child, 'since neither of us obeyed the rules.' We were devastated.

Mutti and I in front of the Heidehof stables

My first kitten and I showing the end part of the stables

As I think about it now, it probably gave Mutti a welcome excuse to relieve herself of an additional burden. How could she take care of another child, when she didn't know how much longer she could take care of me? – But how could Klärchen or I understand that? Mutti covered up her feelings so carefully that we had no idea how much she suffered and how scared she was.

Alone again, I had little distraction from my duties. In those years I remember being industrious and helpful. My parents were very pleased and praised me often. I worked hard in school and brought home good grades. Although time passed slowly and I was sometimes bored, I felt proud of myself. That is until one terrible day when I went to town to buy bread.

I rode my father's precious bike to town, which I loved to do. I had money and the family's ration cards in a basket. We all used them to carry groceries, because paper bags were not available.

Each monthly ration card was divided in stamps for different food groups. They were all on one sheet to save paper. (Formerly each food group had separate sheets in different colors.) While I was standing in line in the bakery waiting to be served, somebody stole the ration cards out of my basket. Ration cards were our livelihood, more valuable than money and irreplaceable. I felt as if I had lost our means of survival! Thank goodness, it happened toward the end of the month. Mutti seemed calm and collected. What was the use of making me feel even worse? None of us knew then that the loss of the ration cards was only a precursor of much worse things to come.

The Lübecks, the caretakers of the Heidehof at that time, were *Selbstversorger*. This meant that they were allowed to slaughter a pig or a cow per year for their own consumption and even keep a certain amount of the milk. Vegetables could be grown by anyone who had the land. Therefore *Selbstversorger* had much more food, but they were not eligible for food stamps. With the Lübecks' help and no one in our little family eating very much, we survived quite well without ration cards until the end of the month. At that time, the ration for the three of us was one pound of meat per week, which included lunchmeat. That was lost, but the Lübecks gave bread, lard and even some bacon to us. Mutti had her source of milk – she called it, 'stealing milk from our own cows.' Vegetables could be taken from the garden. We also had some sheep at the time. Their milk tasted so awful that it was not subject to collection by the city. Vati claimed that he had no tastebuds, so he did not mind eating sheep-butter and drinking some of that milk. He ate everything except cheese. He must have had a few taste buds, because he noticed the slightest bit of cheese mistakenly put on his sandwich – even in starvation times! Our dinners consisted mostly of boiled potatoes, with 'stolen milk' turned into something like cottage cheese. We did not know much about processing milk, but after we let it sit for a while, the milk thickened and cream formed on the top. We took that layer off to make butter and what was left we called 'cottage cheese'.(To this day, I think it was sour cream rather than cottage cheese, because of its smooth texture.) We mixed that cottage cheese with freshly cut chives and ate it cold over hot potatoes. That meal I really liked. I was seldom hungry before I was twelve. I could easily go without food, especially when we had boiled potatoes and vegetables seasoned only with a little salt or a bouillon cube. Once a year, if we were lucky, we could buy a roasting chicken. Usually the chicken was so old that we had to boil it for hours and then roast it. It made the best soup, and it also made the tough old bird edible.

One day, my father came home with a whole basket full of little chicks. All of them were brownish red, only one of them was grey. I don't know how Vati was able to obtain them and why one of them looked so different. We called the grey one *Prätorius* because it had a goat-beard just like a man in town with the name Prätorius. That chicken became our pet. The special attention made him (or her) behave like a dog. When we called him by his name, he came immediately. One day, when he had become a grown-up chicken, Prätorius ventured into the stables and got kicked by the ox. I heard him scream in pain. I screamed even louder and ran for help. The Lübecks came running, but Prätorius could not be saved. I cried until late into the night and, needless to say, none of us ate Prätorius – we buried him.

Soon after Klärchen left, I moved in with my parents to make room for our 'hard working' deported Russians. I am sure my father enjoyed spoiling them; that was part of his anti-Hitler stand!

Throughout my childhood, I had a recurring nightmare in which my mother was dying or had died. For a long time, I did not tell Mutti why I woke up crying so often. I was afraid it would frighten her. On one occasion, when I was sobbing, Mutti kept urging me to tell her what was wrong. She said that she could make it all go away if only she knew what it was. I finally broke down and told her. She comforted me by saying, "Don't worry, my sweetheart, that ALWAYS means a long life for the person who dies in a dream!" Hesitantly, I chose to believe her; and I made a point of believing it throughout my years – clinging to a welcome superstition.

THE WAR INTENSIFIES

In Berlin, my friend Ulla lived across the street from us, just about a block away. She had been enrolled in Frau Typke's first grade class, as I was, but she had the measles when school started. That made her miss the first three weeks. Our mothers walked us to school and picked us up afterwards. On one of those occasions, Ulla's mother asked me to give Ulla some help, so she could catch up. I was flattered. I not only helped her with homework, but I took her under my wing, taught her bicycle riding, roller skating, and later even swimming. Her mother was over-protective. Ulla was an only child, small for her age and she appeared fragile. Although I was a half-year younger, she clung to me as to an older sister. In fact, she became so attached to me, that eventually she started and ended every sentence with my name. This sounded especially funny, because of Ulla's fast manner of speaking. It drove my father crazy!

Ulla's mother – Frau Neumann – repeated every bit of Nazi propaganda as if it were gospel. It took only one casual meeting of my father and Frau Neuman, for her to become his number one target of ridicule. When the rumor of 'The Crates' started to make its rounds, Frau Neumann used every opportunity to spread the news. "The crates contain Hitler's secret weapon," she told my father. "All Hitler has to do is to order them opened, and we shall win

Ulla Newmann

the war," Frau Neumann said, while my father stared at her in disbelief. From that time on, whenever he saw Ulla's mother, he did not wait for her to get close enough to have a conversation. He shouted across the street, "Frau Neumann, have the crates been opened yet?" or, "I hope Hitler does not forget about his crates!" or, "The crates should be opened soon. Do you notice that time is running out?" – Mutti was appalled. "Aren't you embarrassed to behave like this?" she scolded him. It was useless to say anything, because my father enjoyed his own sarcasm much too much, and – unfortunately – he was never embarrassed!

Ulla had not been evacuated with our school. Her parents worried about her living with strangers, so she was sent to her well-to-do cousin, to get away from the bombing. The cousin was much older than Ulla and already had three girls of her own. They had escaped to a large rented property, not far from Berlin. Only too soon, Ulla's cousin grew tired of taking care of a fourth child. She sent Ulla back to Berlin, where she was stranded without schooling. Over and over, her mother repeated to my mother, how terribly worried she was to have her child in Berlin. (Berlin, by now, had severe bombing attacks at night as well as during the day.) Eventually, my mother felt sorry enough that she gave in to Frau Neumann's begging and brought Ulla to stay with us.

Ulla was very happy to join me at the Heidehof. She slept on the sofa in our one and only bed-and-sitting room. At night she would call my name several times. "Even in her sleep!" my father complained. Once, she accidentally spilled the ink out of the inkpot onto my father's precious desk. The top of the desk had a wood-framed cover of green billiard-cloth instead of the usual ink-blotter. Vati loved the unusual handmade furniture he had bought with the Heidehof, and the ink-spill created uproar. But it didn't faze Ulla. She explained, "He is only grouchy. It doesn't mean that he dislikes me!" I don't ever remember that my father was really angry at us children, so maybe Ulla was right.

I was happy that it was like having a sister again, with whom I could go to school. Twice a week we went for private English instruction to Frau Hauck's house. We were at that giggle-age where everything seemed funny, and once we started laughing, we couldn't stop. Sometimes it made Mutti very nervous, and it also got us into a lot of trouble with Frau Hauck. Some English words just sounded so funny to us that they triggered a laughing attack. On one occasion, our laughing was so obnoxious that Frau Hauck lost patience and threw us out. Mutti just happened to be in town and saw us moping around at the Marketplace. Mutti immediately made us go back to apologize. It wasn't easy, but we did it, and it worked!

Ulla had no problem singing in Mr. Puls' class, but she was so afraid of him that she could not remember the words to the songs. No matter how hard she memorized the lyrics, once she stood in front of the class, she got mixed up. So the nightingale in a song was *'hochbetagt'* that meant 'high in age', instead of *'hochbegabt'* that meant 'highly talented'. That caused Mr. Puls much grief and gave me a chance to practice self-control. It was not easy to keep from laughing. But the fear of being slapped a second time, made me strong!

Ulla also managed to lose the folders containing our report cards in the deep snow. Gone were the records for previous years as well! Fortunately, it happened on the way home, after having had them signed by my parents and approved by the school. We worried about them until spring came. When the snow melted, there they lay somewhat smeared and unattractive, but we had them back.

After returning home with her parents, Klärchen had been 'evacuated' with her Berlin class to Vetschau. Teachers and pupils were housed in local homes in that small town. Klärchen became very jealous, when she learned that my mother had allowed Ulla to live with us now. In fact, it made her so angry that she wrote nasty letters with made-up stories, which threatened to end our friendship.

Mutti looked pale and sick. She had constant problems with her digestion and often fainted for no apparent reason. She collapsed in the milk-store and soon thereafter at home, where she fell onto the concrete floor of our kitchen and was severely bruised. After that she burned herself. She was carrying a pot of boiling hot coffee when the swinging door to the big entrance hall hit her arm. Her deep burns required daily visits by a doctor. The odor from the burned flesh, combined with the cod-liver-oil ointment, penetrated the whole room with a terrible odor, whenever the doctor changed the dressing. Mutti appeared more and more frail every day, and I became obsessed with worrying about her.

Soon, after her arms had somewhat healed, Mutti lost her ration card eligibility. It was like condemning her to starvation. I could not understand why, and my parents did not discuss it. I was only told that Mutti had to move back to Berlin and could possibly visit us on occasional weekends.

Frau Typke was put in charge of us. Together, Ulla and I worried as we watched the bombing attacks on Berlin. It looked like fireworks along the horizon, where the pine trees seemed to touch the sky. As far as we could tell, Frau Typke did not share our fear and seemed to have little sympathy for us. I guessed that she had become somewhat numb. After all, she had already lost everything in Berlin, the night her apartment house was leveled by bombs.

Because we had been denied a ration-card for Mutti, the Lübecks agreed to share one meal a day with us. Unfortunately, this arrangement was short-lived. Fritz and his wife, as part-owners, learned about the Lübecks' help for us. They insisted on the same privilege, even though they were aware that the Lübecks went into the arrangement because of the denial of my mother's ration-card. My uncle's greed resulted in the Lübecks not feeding any of us.

Those were scary days and nights. It seemed as if I could hear the rumble of bomber-squadrons from the time they took off from England to start their bloody missions. While on their approach to Berlin, they dropped masses of flares that brightened up the sky as if it were daylight. No bombs had been dropped yet anywhere between the Heidehof and Berlin, but still we would get dressed and stand outside. We thought it safer than taking the chance of having the house collapse over us. Standing there in the bright light made us feel like a perfect target. I kept reminding myself that the planes were too high to zero in on three people standing below. Still, it was creepy! Ulla whimpered constantly. She insisted that the flares were going to 'explode'. But it was only Frau Typke who exploded! She showed little fear, only annoyance that her sleep was disturbed. I don't remember being very afraid for myself either, only so scared for my parents in Berlin. And when I did not worry about bombs killing them, I had my father's private war against Hitler on my mind. What was he saying now? What was he planning to do next? How much longer until they arrested him? Mutti always said, "Nobody comes back – once in their hands."

Frau Typke had little compassion for either of us, because 'we had no self-discipline.' (For self-discipline, she sure was the best example.) According to her, we were only making a bad situation worse. All of us had to go to school in the morning, but she had to teach! More than once she said, "Grit your teeth and take charge of your emotions!"

Ulla also had a problem with thunderstorms. That tried Frau Typke's patience even more. One stormy night, one of us was supposed to run downstairs to fetch the dinner plates. I usually answered the command, but this time Frau Typke insisted that Ulla get the plates. Ulla, scared to death of thunder and lightning, only descended reluctantly. Just when she grabbed the plates, there was a loud bang of thunder. Ulla was so startled that she accidentally hit a vase standing behind her. We could hear the glass shatter. Ulla came running upstairs, covering her ears with her hands, convinced that a lightning bolt had broken the window. Frau Typke, red-faced and exasperated, decided to assess the damage herself. It was a funny scene. I could not help laughing, when I saw what had happened. Frau Typke's anger made it even funnier. My laughing further enraged her so that she slapped me across the face. She must have thought I was laughing at her, rather than at the situation. She proceeded to sweep up the broken glass, and instructed Ulla to take it and throw it down the hole of the toilet.

We saw Ulla shakily walking to open the door to get to the toilets. Then we heard a high-pitched scream again. Ulla pointed at the window and exclaimed, "I cannot go there, there is where the lightning hit!" Looking out of the window, we saw a beautiful large red ball at the horizon, the setting sun after the storm. Frau Typke now looked as if she were going to have a stroke! I enjoyed the scene. Even though I revered Frau Typke, she was not at all motherly, and when we needed emotional support, Ulla and I felt like orphans.

When we entered the final months of the war, the frequency and severity of the attacks on Berlin were steadily increasing. Ulla became almost hysterical from fright. She had to be taken back to her parents.

I was approaching twelve years of age. Now, in spite of the long distance between the Heidehof and Märkisch-Buchholz, my classmates and I were often allowed to visit each other. Vati had brought my swing from Berlin, and had fastened it between two pine trees. I loved swinging, and practiced all kinds of acrobatic tricks on the rings, as well as the cross bar. My swing was also one of the reasons my friends liked to visit me.

We had wonderful apple trees in our garden, but they only bore fruit every second or third year. One of the trees had the most delicious apples I ever tasted. The apple harvest was divided very carefully between all parties. I remember stealing a few of those special apples before they were counted. Even though I knew it was wrong, and I had to keep track of my sins – for the purpose of confession – I thought those apples were worth it. I hoped that nobody would notice, and that God would understand and forgive me.

One day, I was hanging upside down from my swing, sharing a stolen apple with one of my school friends, when she told me something frightening – but interesting. She said, "a girl in our class, just a little older, suddenly saw blood when she went to the bathroom." I did not understand. My friend explained, "I know that this is going to happen to us, too" and she continued, "This is normal for all girls." It sounded to me like death, so I chose not to think about it any further, because – just maybe – I would be lucky enough to be spared!

At other times, I went to town to visit my friends. One of them lived in a house with a hayloft, from which we could jump into mountains of hay below. I remember that day for having had the most fun of all my two and a half years in the country. I wished that day had never ended.

In early 1945, Frau Typke and I started walking home from school together. Now, even she was afraid to walk alone. We took the back way to the Heidehof, though longer, because it had 'cover'. Ditches and bushes became valuable hiding places to prevent being seen by the small Russian fighter planes that suddenly dove down out of a clear blue sky. They shot at pedestrians, as well as passengers who got off trains. (In many small towns, the stations had only a partial roof.) We learned to duck under bushes or dive into ditches, whenever we heard propeller noise. I despised planes. I hated the sound of their engines, whether close or high above. There was no outrunning them! One could only hope not to be seen, or lucky enough to be missed by their bullets.

Frau Typke took a nap every afternoon. I wandered aimlessly around the grounds when I had finished my homework. One day, Lübeck, the caretaker, was sitting at the far side beyond the stables. Mr. Lübeck had a very nice and voluptuous wife, two adult daughters and one grandchild. They all lived on our farm now. It was rumored that Lübeck had murdered his first wife and that he had been in a penitentiary before he came to replace our first caretakers, the Webers. Others claimed to know that he was a Communist, and that this was the reason for his prior imprisonment. We only knew for sure that he was not in the Army and not eligible. So the Nazis did not want him; and that was the only reference my father required. Mr. Lübeck was quite burly and ugly and had noticeably missing front teeth.

So, as I was walking around the house where Lübeck was sitting, he suddenly grabbed me, pulled me on his knees and kissed me passionately with his partially toothless mouth. After I could breathe again, I struggled with all my might to get out of his clutches to get away from him. I succeeded after what seemed like an endless time. I ran and ran not knowing where best to run, and I was too embarrassed to tell anybody. From then on, I made sure never ever again to be in his presence alone. As appalled as I was, it stirred the first sexual feelings in me, though I was only eleven years old.

In Berlin, our apartment house had a shoemaker's shop with an entrance to the street, not far from my father's corner office. The cobbler, Mr. Teske, lived behind his store with his family. We lived in the part of *Schöneberg*, where many Jewish professionals lived. Several of them took their shoes for repair to the Teskes, and had been their customers for many years. The Teskes offered to store their valuable possessions for safe-keeping, were they to be 'picked up'. . . .

Vati was also a customer of the Teskes. It did not take him long to find out that Mr. Teske listened regularly to BBC in his shoe-repair shop, located in his cellar. It was a good place, because there the piercing introductory notes of the BBC station could not be heard from outside. It was extremely dangerous to be caught listening to BBC. We were lucky that our radio was too primitive to pick up that station. Otherwise, we would have had something else to worry about upstairs. So Vati went down to the Teske's cellar almost every day.

That did not come without a price. When Vati later decided to have two rooms of furniture moved to Märkisch-Buchholz, to save them from being bombed, the Teskes saw the moving van standing in front of their store. Without asking, they added several of those 'stored' suitcases and boxes, filled with good linens and other valuables of their Jewish patrons. Vati was told after the fact. As usual, Mutti was outraged, but not surprised. Those small details never bothered my father.

That was not all the Teske's had in mind for us. They also handed Vati their dog. Onto the train my father went with the Teske's dog, a black Scotch terrier, named *Struppi*. It happened to be a pitch-black night, when my father walked with the dog through Märkisch-Buchholz. Suddenly, the leash and collar were in his hand, but no dog attached to them. Vati was looking for his black dog in the black night. Luckily, one hotel owner recognized him and asked what he was searching for. Vati explained that his dog had run away, but when asked for the name, my father said, "I can't remember." He kept calling, "Dog, come here!" The hotel owner, amazed, finally found the dog. When Vati told the story, Mutti and I could imagine what the hotel owner must have thought. We laughed for a long time, but the laughter only postponed Mutti's anger. She never liked the Teskes. That they dared send their dog to us, without her permission, was the crowning touch. She asked Vati whether he had forgotten that we all lived in one room. Now we shared that room with the Teskes' dog. Struppi, unaware of his fortune to have escaped the bombing, only missed his home. He cried all night, and nobody got any sleep.

Mutti had never shared my father's trust in the Teskes' sincerity. She thought of them as opportunists. She warned Vati – more than once – not to get chummy with those people, just because they seemed to share his political views. Most of the time, she was proven right.

Frau Teske was the neighborhood snoop. She made it her business to know everything about everybody, and she could not wait to disclose whatever she knew. For example, she enjoyed talking about 'how devastating our V2-guided missiles are for the people in London.' She knew full well how worried my mother was about her eldest daughter, who lived there. On the other hand, it was Frau Teske's nosiness and know-it-all that forewarned my parents and prevented the worst, as I learned later.

After a succession of sleepless nights, Mutti managed to return Struppi to the Teskes. How, I cannot remember. What I can remember well is that Struppi was replaced by *Flocki,* a darling puppy. He was a mixture of a fox- and wire-haired terrier. We called him *Flocki* because that was the name of Mutti's first dog.

It had been freezing outside, and Mutti's foot had slipped into a deep frozen rut on her way to town. Mutti's ankle was sprained so badly that she could only lie in bed. The pain was so severe that she could not tolerate even the lightest down-feather cover on her foot. It took weeks to heal. I often kept her company by lying next to her in Vati's bed. When she felt better, she would read to me. I remember two books, *Robinson Crusoe* and *Krambambuli,* because they were so sad. I cried for hours over Robinson Crusoe. Because, when he finally returned home, he found his mother had died. It fed right into my nightmares.

Krambambuli was the story of a faithful dog whose master gave him away in exchange for a bottle of Krambambuli liquor, from which he had received his name. That story made me sob so bitterly that Mutti got worried. She asked, "Sweetheart, why are you so upset, it's only a story?" I used the opportunity and said, "I am crying because I would like to have one of the little puppies that the Lübecks are giving away, but you won't allow it!" Mutti tried to reason. She told me about her pain of losing her first dog. (He was run over by a horse-drawn wagon when she was only a child.) She said that she could still feel the sorrow of that loss and that she wanted to spare me the pain. She explained, "Invariably, we survive our dogs and if not, it is even sadder." Whether she had believed that I cried about the sad story or for the puppy, I never found out. But I got my puppy! *Flöckchen* (little Flocki), as I named him, became a new family member. He moved into our one room like Struppi, and – just like Struppi – kept us awake many nights.

There was no room unoccupied at the Heidehof. Our Russians still lived in the guest room, happily eating all kinds of mushrooms that we considered poisonous. But they digested them perfectly. In the second guest room, next to the Russians, lived the old mother of our first caretaker, Mr. Weber. She busied herself with her spinning wheel, spinning the wool from our sheep. Then, there was Weber and his wife. Though fired and replaced by Lübeck and family, all the Webers, conveniently, had never found another place to live. How Weber supported himself and his family, I don't know. One thing was sure; in our place nobody paid any rent, because nobody seemed to have any money.

War End

The more the war intensified, the more cantankerous my father became. By then he was 67 years old. So far, his age and his intimidating demeanor must have saved him from getting arrested. As long as I can remember, I had to maneuver my father to the other side of the street, whenever somebody in uniform was approaching. I was so aware of impending danger that I became quite inventive in coaxing Vati in a different direction to avoid a confrontation.

Once, my father had laid his hat on the train seat next to him, when a young *SA-man (Nazi Sturmabteilung,* who originally were used to police mass assemblies) sat down on his hat accidentally. Mutti and I trembled watching my father's uproar, while the man kept apologizing. Fortunately, we were able to calm Vati down. Another time however, a Sunday morning at the Heidehof, it became more than a challenge.

Vati had planted small pines in the sandy soil in order to define a circular driveway in front of the Heidehof's main entrance door. Every day we had to carry water from our pump, in back of the house, to keep those little pines alive. Suddenly, one Sunday morning, we heard the unusual noise of an approaching car. It came head-on toward the front door of the house, ignoring the circle. The noise of the car engine alarmed us all. At the time, Vati was shaving with a straight razor. Lather on his face, the razor in his hand, he stepped out onto the covered balcony, closely followed by Mutti and me. We saw a man from Märkisch-Buchholz wearing a *Volkssturm*-uniform, driving a Jeep-like army car, coming straight toward the row of circular pines. Mutti and I immediately pulled Vati back into the room. He continued shaving with increased speed. Suddenly, the man in uniform walked into our room, without knocking. He demanded to know, "Why did you pull Mr. Uhlenbrock from the balcony?" The 'Why' became immediately obvious, because now we had to restrain Vati again. This time we had to keep him from attacking the man with his razor. "Because you did not use the proper road!" my father roared. "And now you entered without knocking!" he continued. Vati was so self-righteously outraged and seemingly dangerous, that the man (whom we recognized by name) suddenly changed his attitude. He explained that he was on a duty-call to pick up Mr. Weber, who had purposely avoided the *Volkssturm*. (The *Volkssturm* consisted of the male 'leftovers' formerly not eligible for army duty. Their age ranged from 16 through 70.) With that the man left, but not without threatening, "I will take care of you later for what happened here today!" When we saw him again, he 'took care of us' all right, but without realizing it. By then, things had changed significantly.

We heard a constant roar of tanks. We assumed they were Russian tanks rolling toward Berlin. I was excited because I saw the Russians as our liberators. Vati had often said that we would celebrate when the Russians came, because it would mean the end of the war and the end of the Nazis.

My parents, Frau Typke and my uncle and aunt were all at the Heidehof, when we heard the bad news that Hitler had declared Märkisch-Buchholz a *Festung* (fortress). That meant that this small town was chosen to be the 'last stand' against the approaching Russian-army tanks. Even though we never saw any tanks, Märkisch-Buchholz busily prepared for them. Wooden dams were constructed to flood the Dahme river, and *Panzersperren* (tank barricades) were built to obstruct the main streets. The bridge across the river was dynamited to make the main road from Märkisch-Buchholz to Berlin inaccessible.

Our ears were our only source of information. The roar of tanks rolling toward Berlin had long ceased. Instead of tanks, we now heard and saw only Russian fighter planes. They were shooting at anything and anybody moving below. Many of their victims were refugees from the eastern part of Germany. They had their hastily gathered belongings on wagons, drawn by horses or pulled by themselves. There were also some of the very young – newly drafted – and all those previously considered too old for army service, who made up the *Volkssturm*. Only the still enthusiastic very young attempted to shoot back at the low flying planes. This drew attention to the fact that they were still alive, but not for long. The hastily erected dams eventually served only one purpose; they stopped the many dead bodies from floating downstream.

When two anti-aircraft cannons were moved in front of our house, even Frau Typke got frightened. She commented, "This makes us a perfect target! We can forget about surviving!" When she said something like that, it frightened me. I had become very used to my father predicting our demise, but when Frau Typke did the same, I stopped believing that even God could save us.

Soon, Vati was proven to be at least partially right with his crazy gesture downward toward hell. We did not have to march downward to some place to find it – it had found us.

Not long after the incident with the *Volkssturm*-man, everybody from town was asking for shelter at the Heidehof. People fled Märkisch-Buchholz, knowing it was to become a prime target.

Many times before, we had asked Frau Typke to move back in with us, but to no avail. Suddenly, when the shelling came closer and closer, she asked me to bring Vati's bike and help her pick up whatever we could carry from her rented room. Since she lived on the other side of town, I was curious to see what was going on in our little city and agreed to help her.

We went as fast as possible, packed quite a lot of stuff on the bike and headed back.

Märkisch-Buchholz had become a ghost town. We were just through the city, heading back toward the Heidehof, when we heard heavy artillery and continuous bombing behind us. It was truly a miracle that we made it back unharmed! I felt like a hero, accomplished and brave. My mother had been missing me, and when she heard where I had been, she got the angriest I had ever seen her. In a low but stern voice, she accused Frau Typke of endangering my life and warned her – in no uncertain terms – " Do not do anything like this ever again!"

Our house also gave shelter to an army communication-unit, with a captain in charge. We watched the soldiers giving up their rifles, one by one, saying, "Sir, we want to turn in our weapons, we aren't fighting anymore!" The captain, sitting in front of our veranda, accepted the guns without comment. Then, he began to pass the time by firing some of them into the air. It was my father's turn to get furious. "We don't need you to draw attention to us, get away from here!" he said. I heard the captain explain that they were planning to leave that night. "We are trying to get through to Berlin where the Americans have arrived," he said. Their communication was very sketchy, at best. Most of the time the 'communication-unit' could only get their news by the same means we got ours. It had been reported by refugees that the Russians were killing, raping women and stealing everything in sight. I did not believe any of it; after all, they were our 'liberators' and little did I know what we had done to them! I had also forgotten what Vati often claimed, namely that Hitler had learned his methods from Stalin.

Our soldiers left that night, only to be back the next day. The unit had lost quite a few men. They reported that we were encircled by Russians. The captain was perplexed, because he had been told that the Americans had arrived in Berlin.

"Where did they go? Why would a victorious army retreat? Germany had no resistance left!" The captain said that they were going to try to get through the Russian lines again the following night. So they tried, and even fewer came back this time. They were sitting on our stairs, and everywhere on the floors. No one could take a step, without stumbling over men with listening devices. Now they talked about two circles of Russians, and the next day there were three. The circles of Russian troops around us multiplied, as the number of our returning soldiers shrank. The survivors became more and more desperate to escape the Russians. "Rather dead than falling into the hands of the Russians!" we heard them say. I am afraid most of them got their choice.

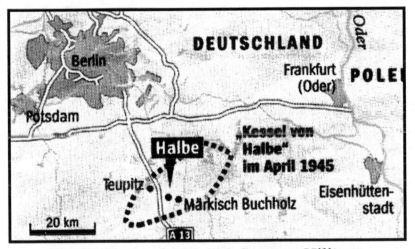

**Of an estimated 200,000 German Military
who were in the above illustrated
encirclement, barely 45,000 survived**

The bombing of Märkisch-Buchholz could still be heard, while bullets were flying all around our house. Somebody attached a white sheet with a red cross to our roof, to signify that our house was used as a hospital for the wounded. It started as a good idea, but soon it became a self-fulfilling prophecy.

Vati had men build a bunker into the side of a small hill, not far from our house. Tall thin pine trunks were used to reinforce the s a n d y top a n d sides. The end result was a large square cave in the embankment. I took cover in that newly built bunker. Even though we were packed in there like sardines, holding each other up, we were wet and cold. I had a bladder infection and had to squeeze through the frightened people to go into the woods. I was still small enough to avoid endangering others by forcing them to step out. In and out I went to my woodsy outdoor 'bathroom', which was a risky place. The bullets were whistling all around me. I saw two young soldiers hiding behind a bush. The next moment, they were hit and fell over. I could see people dying wherever I looked. There were wagon trains of refugees who had tried to run ahead of the Russian troops. Death hailed from diving planes that sprayed us with bullets. Since I had been spared so far, I got brave and ran from the bunker to the house. I entered from the back through the kitchen door. There I stepped over bleeding, moaning and dying soldiers, lying on the concrete kitchen floor – wall to wall. I could not step over them fast enough to get away from their pain. Our potato cellar, under the front part of our split-level house, was filled with people who had sought shelter. In their midst sat Frau Typke holding my puppy, Flöckchen. She asked me sternly where I had been. Then she ordered me to take Flöckchen outside, so he would not dirty up the already air-deprived cellar. Through the kitchen, stepping over the dying soldiers again, I carried my little puppy into the hail of bullets. I took that trip many times, and each time there were more cadavers outside. In front of the kitchen door the ground was covered with dead horses, foam coming out of their nostrils. They were so big that I could hardly jump over them. There were bodies as far as I could see. When I struggled back through the dead, I saw a little old lady, crying and running toward me, looking for her husband. Somebody knew him and had seen him just a little while ago. Even though she was warned not to go look for him, she was desperate to find him. We found both their bodies later, not far apart. When we shoveled them underground we were wondering aloud, whether they ever got close enough to see each other, before they got caught in the crossfire.

In the confusion, nobody knew where anybody else was. The shelling had subsided somewhat. Suddenly, I saw Mutti walking away with some stranger. I called out to her and begged her not to endanger herself. She shouted back that she had heard there was some 'butter' in a deserted army supply truck. There was no stopping her – she was already thinking ahead – because, should we survive, starvation was the next enemy.

It got to the point, where we did not know who was shooting at us. Somebody reported that he had seen Russians, and we needed to fly a white flag to show that we capitulate. Our name was called repeatedly. They needed to get a key for our room, to place a white flag in the most prominent place. That happened to be our balcony. Some stranger had just heard that the house belonged to someone with the name 'Uhlenbrock'. He kept shouting our name, but I was the only one responding. So I went upstairs with a person who attached our white bed sheet to a broom handle and then fastened 'the flag' to our balcony, indicating our surrender! We had hardly got back down to the cellar when somebody screamed, "We need the key. We need to remove the white flag! The *Waffen SS* is shooting at us, because we are never, never to surrender!" I was scared to death, because I thought if the *SS* shoots at us, they are not going to miss. I ran as fast as possible back upstairs with my key, I put the sheet back on the bed and – without thinking – threw the broomstick over the railing. With relief, I thought 'Mission accomplished!'

Mutti had returned unharmed with the butter and *Kommissbrot,* when somebody announced that the Russians had been sighted. This time Mutti was by my side, when we ventured back up to mount that white flag again – only now the broomstick was missing. Faster than Mutti could say 'no', I ran downstairs and outside and retrieved the stick. Moments later, Mutti and I waved the newly constructed white flag from our balcony. I can still hear her say, "I feel like Jeanne d'arc!" Did she feel victorious? I did not ask; we both laughed. Then a bullet hit the wooden railing right below Mutti's hand. It reminded us that we were still in the middle of a battle and not on some stage. We took cover fast.

Before we went downstairs, I saw a cow hung up on a tree about 50 yards away from us. The rope on her neck had wrapped around the tree and she was mooing for help. I was more disturbed by seeing this trapped animal, than by all the dead people I had seen and climbed over. The poor cow was helpless and could not get away, but nobody had the courage to run under the unpredictable diving planes and bullets to help. That is my most painful memory. To this day, I can cry when I think about it. It represents to me all the senseless cruelty and suffering that war brings.

In that final battle of the war, I learned how callous all of us get when our own survival is at stake. When the bullets stopped flying, we had only one worry; how to bury all the bodies in that flat and sandy ground. The May sun was getting strong, and we did not know how to get rid of the cadavers to prevent an outbreak of disease. All those lives could have been saved because Berlin had already fallen, but we did not know it!

THE RUSSIANS ARE COMING

We were now in May of 1945. We were still without a clue as to whether Berlin had been captured, and if so, whether there was anything left resembling a city. Surviving refugees from East Prussia and Silesia were telling horror stories about the Russians and Poles taking everything of value and raping women. We had not seen any Russians or Poles yet.

We decided to bury some of our valuables. There was a wooden box containing my sister Inge's silverware, a complete set for 24 persons in Sterling Silver. It came from Inge's parents-in-law, the Moslers, who had given it to us for safekeeping, just before they were 'picked up' by the Nazis.

I was sitting in bed, nursing my bladder infection. It was still bothering me ever since I had been in that cold, wet bunker. Flöckchen was under my cover, well hidden. Our little terrier was still just a puppy, but he was smart enough to stay under cover as long as my mother was around. He knew the rules as well as I did, 'No Dog in Bed!' Therefore, Flöckchen always waited until my mother left the room and then hopped into my bed. I helped him by lifting the bottom of my cover, with my feet, just high enough for him to crawl in. While I kept 'evenly warm' in bed – as instructed – I occupied myself with counting out our own silverware. We had heard that it was what the Russians liked second best, after they had collected loads of wristwatches. To pass some time, I counted out: 6 spoons, 6 forks, 6 knives and so on, from a set of twelve that we used on a daily basis. When I was finished separating the pieces, I had a good idea. I put my part of the divided set into a jar meant for conserving fruit or vegetables. I added some murky water and set it on a shelf on the balcony. The 'conserved' silverware is still with us today. Everything else was buried with Inge's silver box, as well as a portable typewriter and other stuff, all irreplaceable at the time.

The 'burying' was my father's brilliant idea. He was as proud of that, as if 'he' had invented it. Fact is, it was common practice at the time. Everybody did it – but there was one thing only 'he' did. He went to the burial site on a daily basis, just to admire it. After only one week, his daily routine ceased. The burial place consisted now of empty holes. Somebody had stolen everything before the Russians got to it!

I was really getting interested in seeing one of those much talked about 'Russians.' Then the first one arrived, riding high on a horse. He looked as if he had stepped out of a fairy tale. He was very handsome in his impeccable uniform, and he spoke German well enough to make his orders very clear. He informed us that he was rounding up all males, in or out of uniform. He warned us not to hide anyone between the ages of 15 and 65. If we did not strictly obey his orders, he threatened to shoot all of us and burn the house down!

All the men, who had taken shelter in our farmhouse, came outside. They had to remove their shirts and hold their bare arms over their heads. Those, with their blood type tattooed under their upper arms, were shot instantly right in front of us. I could not believe my eyes. Then somebody explained to me that the 'blood type tattoo' distinguished the SS from the regular soldiers.

The Russian, in our second experience, resembled the 'liberator,' for whom we had waited. We were impressed, and my father looked at us as if he were saying, 'I told you so!' This Russian seemed to be a high-ranking officer. He explained to my father, in perfect German, that the 'regular' Russian troops were subject to strict conduct-regulations and not to be feared, "But what comes behind," he added, "is under nobody's jurisdiction." He had good manners and treated us with courtesy until he was ready to leave. Then he got up, said "Goodbye!" and took our bicycle, as if it were his. There went our prized possession! He took it without a word of explanation. It was an omen of things to come.

The *Volksturm*-man from Märkisch Buchholz, whose throat my father had 'almost' slit, just a few months ago, was carrying an unconscious little girl. When he happened to see my father, he transferred her to his arms without asking, and said, "She is my grandchild, please watch over her, I'll pick her up later!" The girl was about three years old. She was beautiful with naturally curly blond hair. Mutti was upset that Vati accepted anything from a man who had threatened not long ago, 'to take care of us'. Mutti left no doubt about her feelings. She thought 'why allow this Nazi to give Vati his so-called grandchild.' She said, "I do not believe for a minute that the child is even related to him." Since revenge was not part of my father's make-up, he pretended not to hear her – his usual demeanor when she was angry.

But Mutti's good heart could not reject the little girl either. She laid her on our sofa that stood in an alcove, close to the entrance door to our room. She sat down beside the little girl, keeping watch. She wondered aloud, 'whether this child would ever regain consciousness,' and 'what might have happened to her parents.'

When it got dark that day, hordes of Russians – who had obviously never heard of 'the conduct-regulations' – swarmed all over our house. First, they collected everybody's watch. "Uri, Uri," they demanded. They were saying *Uhr* repeatedly, the German word for watch. (Most of them had their arms already covered with watches, from their wrists to their shoulders.) Their next command was, *"Frau komm!"* (Woman come!) and then they proceeded to rape everyone they could grab. We were all hiding out in our separate quarters. In our room we had only experienced the watch collection so far.

All women had made themselves look as ugly as possible, but our liberators did not have discriminating taste. The 'Mongolians' were the most feared, because they seemed the most insatiable. Their appearance resembled my conception of 'Attila and his Huns,' except for their wool-lined leather flight helmets. The news spread that one of my schoolteachers – bleached blond and well endowed – had been raped sixteen times consecutively.

I had no idea what 'rape' meant. Since we had been spared so far, I went outside to look downstairs. I was curious what they were doing and what the screaming was all about. Then I heard the same screaming noise across the hall in my uncle's room. That convinced me to follow Mutti's advice and stay as inconspicuous as possible. I heard heavy boots coming up the stairs. A Russian soldier entered, needless to say, 'without knocking.' He looked at the beautiful, 'lifeless' little girl on our sofa and hesitated. He stared in awe, and with pity showing in his face, he turned around and left. That gave Mutti the idea to approach every entering Russian soldier with a request, "Please find a doctor to help the child." When they heard that, everyone of them turned around and left. Mutti had also noticed that some of them had looked – with a certain reverence – at a crucifix on the wall. So she moved it, as well as the picture of Jesus holding a lamb (my gift from the church at my First Holy Communion) into plain view for those who entered. It worked! We were the only room spared. Eventually, to our surprise, somebody really sent a Russian doctor. He identified himself and examined the child. He explained in German, "The child is dying and needs to be moved to a cool place." He surmised that she had been too close to a powerful explosion. The pressure had caused severe brain injuries. I remember well how barbarian we felt, when we decided to keep that little girl lying in our room to further protect us!

The doctor was right. The girl did not regain consciousness. We would never find out to whom she belonged. All kinds of people had heard that we had buried a little girl. They came, week after week, telling their horrifying stories. They hoped that they had found somebody, who last saw their lost child.

I do not know how long the chaotic situation continued – we lost track of time. Eventually, everything that interested the Russians had been taken. Most of the women had been raped, and the search for alcohol and German soldiers was over. So they moved on.

My only good memory of those days was eating twelve slices of *Kommissbrot* with lard. Never before had anything tasted so good, nor had I ever eaten with such an enormous appetite. Somebody had put a huge clay-pot, filled with rendered lard, in the middle of our table. The bread had come from Mutti's dangerous foray into the battlefield. Right after I had finished eating and was stuffed, somebody claimed the lard pot as his own. He wondered aloud, how the pot got onto our dining table. He was very angry that some of his lard was missing. I only felt glee that I had finished eating before the man and his lard pot were re-united!

When the spring sun grew warmer, there was an eery stillness all around us. We were faced daily with the problem of how to get rid of all the dead bodies. Everybody was digging. It was a never-ending job. The horses were almost impossible to get under ground. The graves were never dug deep enough. Many bodies became exposed again, as the wind shifted the sand. The smell of decaying flesh permeated the air for miles around us. There was no getting away from it. That horrible, sweetish odor stayed around for years, and in my memory forever!

We later learned that we were in what was called, the final *Kesselschlacht,* the final battle where the Russians encircled us many times. That battle was still going on after Hitler had committed suicide, and after Berlin had fallen to the Allies. Three miles from us in Halbe, there is a cemetery where 22,000 lie buried – most of them unidentified – from all walks of life. Fifty-seven of them were transferred from Dallgow, where the German military court executed 15,000 German soldiers. They were the ones who had outspokenly refused to continue fighting in this hopeless war. The horror of the final battle is indescribable. The struggle to survive made us numb to the pain around us, otherwise we would have gone mad.

Märkisch-Buchholz was more destroyed than any other town within a thirty-five mile radius around Berlin. Vati had rented an old horse-and-buggy type garage, behind one of the hotels, at the central Marketplace. We had used this space to store our furniture and some valuable pictures, to save them from the bombs on Berlin. There were also the Teskes' boxes and suitcases they had added to our moving van. I remember my favorite pictures that used to hang in our dining room. The two were very large copper plate engravings. One showed a lioness with young ones and the other, a tigress with her cubs. After the war, there was hardly a house standing in the Marketplace, except for 'our' garage. Unfortunately, everything valuable – which was not too heavy and too awkward to carry off – had been stolen. Not by the Russians, but by our own countrymen, as was reported to us later. They had even cut leather pieces out of our massive armchairs to see whether anything had been hidden inside the upholstery. Those good people also helped themselves to the Teskes' suitcases and boxes.

Mutti was pre-occupied with finding something for us to eat. If it had not been for an abundance of mushrooms, growing in the woods that year, we would have been even hungrier. But then there was the cow hung up in the tree that had died so miserably. I don't know how long she had been lying there dead in the sun. Nobody was courageous enough to cut her loose during the shelling, but now everybody cut meat from her body. We made German beefsteak (known as hamburgers in the U. S.) out of it. Those 'hamburgers' were all meat, the first in years without loads of breadcrumbs. I don't understand why we did not die of food poisoning, and I cannot believe, to this day, that any of us could eat the meat from that poor animal!

Vati had managed to find a way back to what was left of Berlin, to check on his business. The compartments of the trains were open only to Russians; Germans rode on top of the coal cars, or lay on the roof of the trains. Sometimes we would just hang on the outside door to the compartment, standing on the steps. Vati had become quite good at climbing up on top of the coal. It surprised us, because one could not call him athletic in any way. We worried about him falling off. But, at least, we did not have to worry about him fighting Hitler anymore! Hitler was dead, and all the Nazis had vanished miraculously with him.

Vati stayed in Berlin for long periods of time, and we were left behind being terrorized by Polish and Russian speaking civilians. They came with horse-drawn wagons, filling them with whatever struck their fancy. We tried all kinds of tricks to discourage them. We rang our big bell that hung under the back gable of the roof. (In a much more civilized time, it had been mounted there to call the workers from the fields for supper). Now we were using it to pretend that it alerted the Russian Commandant, who supposedly protected us from these lawless invaders. It worked sometimes, more often not.

We had some boxes left that contained Mutti's beautiful linens (brand new with her initials and bundled with a bow, still from her dowry) as well as our Sterling silver tea set. Since Vati had not 'buried' it, it had not been 'excavated'. The Lübecks came up with the idea to hide these items, along with their own stuff, in the cellar under the front part of the house. They moved their cupboard in front of the door, so no one could possibly suspect that there was as much as a crawl space behind it. This hiding place lasted about as long as my father's 'burials'.

One morning, we noticed our caretakers taking all their newly acquired wealth (left behind by the many dead refugees) out of our mutual hiding place. When we asked what they were doing, they said that the stuff needed to be 'aired out.' That was timed well, because that very evening two horse-drawn wagons – guided by foreign sounding men – pulled up in back of the house. One of the men walked straight to the cupboard in the kitchen and demanded that it to be moved to expose the cellar door. Then they loaded what was left in there, namely 'our' belongings, onto their wagon. I still see myself running behind them and pleading for the return of the silver tea set. One man, sitting among the boxes in the back of the wagon, actually searched for it. He only found the tray and tossed it at me, while the wagon rolled away. That silver tray still remains in my possession. I never stopped wondering what the Lübecks gained by giving our hiding place away?

The Lübecks had profited handsomely from the war. Frau Typke, in turn, had nothing left but necessities. She had become a compulsive collector of anything and everything that was left on rubble piles, 'to start a new household.' One could not take a walk without her stopping at every clean-up pile to see whether something 'useful' was left in it.

It did not take long for my father to transfer his anger to the Russians. Now he repeated his former assertion, "Hitler learned all his inhumane methods from Stalin!" He had ample time, from his vantage point on the coals, to watch the Russian soldiers remove our railroad tracks and load them on trains bound for Russia. He had to travel back and forth on the same track. That allowed very few trains to run those 35 miles to Berlin. The joke told at the time was: *In the U.S. the trains are so fast that the telephone poles look like a solid wall, while in Germany the trains run even faster, one cannot see the second track.*

One weekend, while Vati was back with us at the Heidehof, Frau Typke, Vati and I were walking to town. A horse-drawn buggy, filled with four Russian soldiers, commanded us to stand still or they would shoot. My father continued walking. He was not taking any commands! The Russians jumped off, all at the same time, and warned him not to take another step. He kept right on walking, being his usual self! In desperation, I ran toward the Russian who was pointing the gun at my father, threw myself into his arms and begged him not to shoot my father – It worked! One more time my father got away with his behavior. Frau Typke never let me live it down. From that time on, she would tease me, "Don't complain to me about the Russians, I saw how you fell around his neck!" The boots and the sound of the voices had changed, but our fear and Vati's rebellion were still with us.

Our former manager, Mr. Weber, had been taken away by the Russians. We were told that he had collected all kinds of Nazi memorabilia, including flags. It was said that, when the Russians saw his collection, they thought him to be a Nazi, wrapped him in one of his flags, and shot him. I don't know whether the story was true, but we never saw him again. I still wonder whether Lübeck had something to do with that, too. What was he getting out of it? By now, we all wondered what was the real story concerning Lübeck's past? We would never find out.

Frau Typke was giving me private lessons in German and Math. I also continued going to Frau Hauck for English, as soon as it was possible to get there. Since she lived on the other side of the river, getting across was a real challenge. The only bridge over the Dahme had been blown up. Its steel I-beams looked as if they had been cut in the middle. Both parts of the bridge had dropped down, but were still attached on either side of the riverbank. I carefully crawled down one side, balanced over wobbly boards and climbed up the other side. Soon, I found a faster way. I would perform a balancing act over the pilings of the tank-deterrent dam, close to our house. That so-called dam never flooded any field or stopped any Russian tank, but it sure was a way to get to the other side of the river. The challenge was to get across without falling into the water and joining all the dead bodies. Those bodies looked worse from week to week. They were buoyant, blown up like balloons with eyes staring at me. I carefully balanced on my hands and knees, holding on for dear life.

As my father spent more and more time in Berlin, Mutti, Frau Typke and I were left to our fate, battling the never-ending pillage at night. We did not care anymore about losing our belongings, but we feared for our personal safety. So, we rented a room at the *Schwarze Adler,* the only hotel left standing in town, and spent our nights there. One night, all in one room as usual, we were kept awake by noisily nesting swallows. Frau Typke – for whom her rest had always been high priority – was not just disturbed, she was furious. But it did not keep her from making many funny and even risqué remarks. She kept us laughing for hours. When we left the hotel the next morning, we saw a sign on the wall. It proclaimed, *Humor ist, wenn man trotzdem lacht.* It could not have been more appropriate: 'Humor' means to laugh in spite of it all!

BACK TO BERLIN

The summer of 1945 was coming to an end, but the nightly intrusions by Russians, Poles or whatever, were not. There was not much left to take from us, but they kept coming, looking the place over. They came by ladder over the balcony, or broke the door down, if it was locked. Our nightly trips to town, to sleep in the hotel, became annoying. Frau Typke had to get back to Berlin to teach, and Mutti had enough of being terrorized. One day, when Vati came back from his week in Berlin, we informed him that we were moving home. We did not know how we would get there, but we knew we were going. All passenger trains were still reserved for Russians only. We were not looking forward to climbing on top of the coal like my father, who had become a pro in traveling as part of the cargo. Since we needed to take our belongings, we decided to walk the 35 miles back to Berlin. We even took our precious rugs with us, before they were completely eaten by mice. With one of our larger hand-wagons filled up, we started our long march home.

The stench of dead bodies, decaying in the woods all around us, was almost unbearable. The highway to Berlin seemed deserted. We had not gone far, when a woman stopped us, telling us that she knew the whereabouts of our 'excavated' belongings. Although we did not know her, she knew us by name. But since she did not want to divulge the names of the responsible persons, for fear of retaliation, she was just an unwelcome interruption. Why tell us in the first place? Mutti was annoyed.

Frau Typke – always preferring her privacy – walked ahead. She did not offer to help pull our wagon either. She got further and further ahead of us, until she could not be seen anymore. Suddenly, three Russians came out of the woods and demanded our jewelry. Mutti had managed to quickly put her diamond ring into her mouth. My father's golden wedding band did not come off. As the Russians were preparing to cut off his finger, they discovered that they had apparently lost their bayonets. Frustrated, they left.

Frau Typke was less lucky. We could only suspect what had happened to her. When we saw her again, she seemed traumatized. Her demeanor had changed. Now she stayed very close to us and even helped pull the wagon. We continued walking a road that seemed endless, until we reached the halfway point. We were exhausted when we arrived at the railroad-station at *Königs-Wusterhausen;* we could not take another step.

Königs-Wusterhausen had quite a big train station. Masses of refugees, with even more baggage than we had, were waiting to get on a train somehow. If they were lucky, they might even get into one of the covered freight cars. There seemed no hope for us to get even close enough to push our way through the crowd. Suddenly, the station manager shouted, "The tall teacher with her family and belongings comes first!" Our mouths dropped open in surprise. Everyone had to step aside to let us into a covered freight car with our stuff. Only sometime later, Frau Typke explained that her wartime-rations of cigarettes had been carefully tucked away and saved. They had been our pass for a space in the freight car. She had guarded those cigarettes carefully to be used in a dire emergency. She considered this to be one, and we were overjoyed. But the normal three-hour train ride took all night. It was like a scene out of *Doctor Zhivago.* The train would stop suddenly in the middle of nowhere, for no apparent reason, and we wondered whether we would ever move again. The first time we just waited without a clue. Then, after dark, some Russians jumped on, shone their flashlights into our faces, inspecting us one by one. We did not know whether they were searching for a particular person, or looking for women to rape. We never found out. Eventually, the train started moving, only to stop soon again. We lost track of how often we stopped and started again on our way to Berlin. When we eventually arrived, it was still dark. We lay down on the concrete station floor to get some sleep. Again, from time to time, flashlights held by Russians shone into our faces. There were so many people lying everywhere that we were lucky to find a space big enough to stretch out. Although exhausted, we had to take turns staying awake to guard our belongings.

Schoeneberg 1945

Berlin lay in shambles. The city was one massive pile of rubble. Once in a while, there was a firewall left standing, with plumbing still attached. It reminded us of my uncle Fritz, who was much more jovial than my father ever was. A few months earlier, we had joined Fritz to walk to Halbe, trying to find a train going to Berlin. We were tired, hungry and edgy. Every step had become a chore. Suddenly, uncle Fritz – reminded of Frau Typke's compulsive collecting habits – pointed to a W.C. It was still hanging on the third-floor wall of one of the bombed houses in Halbe. He remarked, "Frau Typke obviously hasn't seen this yet!" We all laughed and that made walking the final distance much easier.

We were prepared to find only half of our apartment still habitable. Vati had told us that a Nazi family with the name of Berg had moved in where Sternchen had lived before. In the final days of the war, Dr. Berg decided to shoot out of his second floor window. That caused the Russians to aim their artillery toward our house. They fired two rounds. Our three rooms upstairs, as well as the Krämer's three rooms below us, were turned into rubble. Our rooms had been occupied by the Guhrs, the bombed-out homeless couple who were assigned to live with us. They lost their housing a second time.

Not a house intact, but the streetcars were running again

My father had the wrecked part of the apartment walled off by his 'very capable help.' The wall served its purpose for the time being. The kitchen and the small room next to it (meant for a maid) were the least damaged. Since Vati would not hear of eating in the kitchen, he had moved a small table on top of the debris in what used to be his large *Herrenzimmer.* That is where he had been eating next to a hole in the floor, big enough to fall through to the Krämers below. One had to watch out not to pay them a surprise visit.

Everyone's fear had changed from bombs to lice. Most of the many refugees had acquired lice, supposedly because they had been on the road for months without hygiene. Lice were said to spread tuberculosis. My mother's anxiety level would rise, whenever I dared scratch my head. Help came in the form of delousing 'salons' that the Americans had opened everywhere. There, when the DDT-gun was pointed at your head, a white cloud descended upon you. The whole salon was snow white, since that powder landed everywhere, not just on your head. I experienced it myself, when I forgot 'not to scratch my head.' Immediately, Mutti insisted I had to get 'deloused'. I hated it, because I had to wear a scarf for 24 hours afterwards, so the lice had time to die. Everybody knew where I had been! I was getting to the age where my appearance had become important to me. I was convinced that the delousing procedure did not just kill lice, but it came close to killing all of us. Maybe, I was not too far off.

We were approaching the coldest and worst winter Berlin had seen in years. There was hardly any food, water or heat. There were no suitable winter-clothes to keep warm. The leftover clothes and blankets were worn-out or outgrown; after all they had not been replenished in years.

Mutti was very sick with a gallbladder attack – the prevalent illness of that time. It seemed that our bodies gave out after years of stress, and the gallbladder was the weakest link. Frau Typke had to take me to school for registration. (In Berlin, school had been in session for a while, even though there was no heat, and it rained through the roof.) Frau Typke and I entered the school building from the side, the only entrance not damaged by bombs. As we stepped into the building, we heard the recess bell ring. The classroom doors flew open, and young girls came storming out and down the steps like a herd of buffalo. We had to step aside not to be trampled. Frau Typke turned purple, the way I remembered her in class, when I dropped my little blackboard. She noticeably pulled all her strength together and uttered the memorable words, "So, that is Democracy!" I would often think of her outburst, when I visited my children's schools years later, in the United States.

My first day of school, back in Berlin, was more fun than I anticipated. Klärchen was anxiously awaiting my return. I felt very important, because Klärchen had already introduced me as her 'best' friend. Klärchen was not only very smart, but she

Fräulein Dr. Tangel

was also very well liked. Studying came easy to her, and pranks even more so. The school benches seated two, so the girl who sat next to Klärchen was asked to move to make room for me.

The art-hall had become our very large classroom. Bombs had leveled half of the school, so all of the remaining space had to be utilized. My first surprise was to see a girl riding her bicycle in our classroom. She claimed that she had to take it with her wherever she went, otherwise it would be stolen. I observed another group of girls busily stacking up chairs in front of the classroom door to keep it from opening.

The school bell rang and I heard banging. Klärchen explained that it was our teacher, Fräulein Dr. Tangel. She was trying to get in, but chairs kept her from opening the door. They finally came tumbling down when she managed to pry the door open.

It took quite a long time, and it took even longer to determine who was responsible for the chair idea. Eventually, Fräulein Dr. Tangel gave up, and the class began.

Dr. Tangel had been a retired university professor before she was re-called to teach in a high school. It was rumored that she had passed her *Abitur* (the examination required to graduate from high school) with special honors. It was an achievement only a few could call their own. But now, she was poorly equipped to deal with 12-year olds, who thought they had seen everything and knew it all.

All teachers, who had been Nazi-Party members, had been dismissed. Many of them were working construction jobs, cleaning up for future rebuilding. Elderly and retired university professors were called to teach in their stead. For teachers, as government employees, joining the Nazi-Party was obligatory. If they refused, they forfeited any promotion, or, in many cases, lost their jobs. Frau Typke was just lucky that in Märkisch-Buchholz nobody ever checked.

All textbooks, including the classics, had been confiscated for fear of Nazi propaganda. Most teachers dictated from their own books, if they had any left. Dr. Tangel attempted to dictate to us a ballad by Friedrich von Schiller, *Der Sänger* (The Troubadour). When she arrived at the point where the troubadour humbly refused the gift of a golden necklace, Klärchen decided to show off. She exclaimed, "I would have taken it and sold it on the black market!" Dr. Tangel was livid. She called Klärchen a *'minderwertiges Frauenzimmer'* meaning something like a 'broad with low morals'. Now Klärchen was fuming. She turned to me and explained that Dr. Tangel had implied that she was a 'low life.' I was bewildered. That compelled Klärchen to whisper the explanation into my ear. Now Dr. Tangel had enough, and she gave Klärchen a demerit. (Six demerits prompted a 'blue letter' to the parents.) Klärchen was on her way! Eventually, she got five more demerits and one of those dreaded blue letters sent to her father. We tried, unsuccessfully, to intercept the delivery. It took her father no time at all to transfer her to Catholic school. I had learned amazingly fast how to accumulate demerits, but knew how to control myself after the fifth one. – Klärchen never totally forgave me for not transferring with her.

We earned demerits by having the most ingenious ideas. There was no window glass left in Berlin. All window openings were covered with cardboard. That meant no daylight in any classroom. Many classrooms had been divided into two by a partition. That made them so small that four rectangular tables had to be placed together to make a large table and we sat around it. We had the idea to unscrew the only light bulb in the room. We then all crawled under the large table. We were so quiet that Dr. Tangel thought the room was empty, when she came to teach her lesson. She looked for us from room to room. We could hear the doors opening and closing. Then the principal, a kindly lady with the name of Dr. Wiese, accompanied her back to our classroom. We were all sitting there waiting, with the light bulb screwed back in. Dr. Tangel tried to explain, but only we believed her – we, who were stupidly enjoying the fact that we had cheated ourselves out of a history lesson. I am ashamed to admit that we were really cruel! Dr. Tangel was the most abused teacher of them all. She could not understand that we were not self-motivated and as eager to learn as she had been.

But she was not the only one who had a hard time with us. Mr. Barkow taught math. One day, we got word that the neighboring class had to be released, because the rain dripped through the damaged roof and through their ceiling. Surprisingly, our ceiling was still dry – but not for long. . . . I had seen a bucket with water in the hallway. It gave me the idea

Herr Barkow

that we could produce our own rain; all we needed was a large blackboard-sponge. It took skill to throw the wet sponge carefully against the 12-foot high ceiling, without missing a tell-tale dry spot. When Mr. Barkow arrived, the water was dripping from our ceiling. We were also released to go home where it was not warmer, but hopefully dryer.

I had become popular in my own right – not just as Klärchen's friend. Most of the girls were now thirteen, while I was still twelve. We all felt powerful and invincible. Unfortunately, this attitude and the chaos in school were reflected at home. There everybody's nerves were already frazzled, because of being perpetually hungry and cold.

Mutti was worried how to get 'something on the table.' We were still on ration cards, but now we had to wait for them to be 'called up' (validated). There just wasn't any food. Sometimes when a load of fish reached Berlin, it became a substitute for meat. Then there was as much of a run on the stores for fish, as there was for bread and potatoes. The lines were endless. Sugar and fat were seldom available. The black market flourished. UNRRA (United Nations Relief and Rehabilitation Agency) goods were given to Polish Jews who had survived the holocaust. They used them to open small stores with high prices.

Hanging on the Train

We took all valuables, like Meissen vases, to surrounding farmers in exchange for potatoes or vegetables. Masses of people headed for the suburbs. They were packed like sardines into the trains, or they hung five deep outside on the train running board. Inside you could not breathe. There were people so desperate for food that they cut bags off their handles while women were holding them in their hands. For old people, or for parents of starving children, life had become unbearable.

**Endless lines waiting for water
from the street pump**

The winter of 1945-46 was mercilessly cold. Everything froze, including the water in the toilets. There was no heat, no warm water; in fact, soon there was no water at all, because all the water pipes had frozen. We had to carry water from a pump, a block away, which was at the curbside left over from horse-and-carriage days. Now we waited in line for water, as well. We had an oldfashioned gas meter in our apartment. It used water to function. Soon the water in the gas-meter froze. As long as we had electricity, we used a hair dryer to melt it, so we had gas for cooking again. Gas and electricity were rationed like everything else. Mutti cooked with one pot on top of the other to save gas. Many electrical lines were exposed to the elements, because of damaged walls. One fuse blew after the other. No fuses were to be had, so we learned to wire around them. We were lucky when Vati got an allowance of anthracite coal for his business, and he managed to barter for a space heater. We put it into the smallest room, the one next to the large, icy-cold kitchen. The stovepipe was vented through the cardboard covered window. When we burned the anthracite in the little cannon-stove heater, its iron walls turned so red that we feared they were melting. The room became unbearably hot for a while, then it got cold. Survival became a full-time job again, as it had been during the air-raid days.

Many of Vati's irreplaceable tools were stolen. They sold well on the black market. He could not find any workmen, since most fit and able men had been killed in the war. Almost all of Vati's supply cellars and warehouses had been bombed out. He still had contracts with the Magistrate of Berlin, but it was hard to find the materials necessary to fulfill them. Some businesses were salvaging old pipes and fixtures from the ruins of bombed buildings, to use them to repair others. It was not legal, so Vati would not consider 'laying his good name on the line.'

For workmen, he hired some former government employees – former party members who had lost their jobs. They had not yet been 'de-nazified' by the Americans. ('De-nazification' had become the new household word.) My mother was angry again, even though those new-hires had probably been as harmless during Hitler-times as they were incapable now. She was even angrier that Vati wanted to keep his former office manager, Fröhlke, whom Mutti hated with a vengeance. I would soon find out why. . . .

EARLY TEEN YEARS

In that horrible winter of 1945-46, I was twelve going on thirteen. My social life consisted of visiting Klärchen after school. Berlin schools had been closed for a long time before re-opening after the end of the war. Since I had continued my schooling with Frau Typke and Frau Hauck, I was ahead of the rest of my class. I seldom had to do homework, so my study habits became nonexistent.

Klärchen, Flöckchen & I

Fräulein Dr. Tangel taught History and Latin, as well as German. Mr. Barkow, also out of retirement, repeated the same self-created lessons and tests, year after year. We all knew it, and swore that he had kept them from his own dissertation. If we could have found somebody who had taken his math-class before and was willing to pass on the tests, we would have had all the answers. Mr. Barkow seemed mild-mannered and undemanding, but he was unpredictable and even unfair, when our lack of achievement illustrated his poor teaching ability.

Chemistry and Biology were taught by Dr. Kalincke. He was still young. It was hard to believe that he had not been a party-member; he certainly seemed to have the mentality for it. He was quite short, a little Napoleon, and much disliked by all.

Our homeroom and English teacher was Fräulein Krüger. She was young and attractive and we adored her. Fräulein Schiefer was our sports teacher, a favorite in the whole school.

The following year we started French with Fräulein Dr. Ayen. She was also under fifty. She was very small, very tough, but very fair. I think, she believed that a teacher needed to be an absolute

Frl. Kruger

dictator to get pupils to learn. We were in the American Sector of Berlin. 'For democratic reasons,' the Americans ordered all teachers' desks to be put on the same level as those of the students. When I first saw Fräulein Ayen, she came in with a stack of fat books in her arms. She put them on her desk with a big thump, and placed her small wiry body on top of them. "So I can see who is cheating," she explained. Since we had a very healthy respect for her, French class assignments took priority.

(Thinking back, I am amazed that there were quite a few teachers who had resisted joining the Nazi party.)

There was no heat whatsoever in any public buildings. In our school, but for the wind, there was no difference in temperature inside or outside. We dressed as warmly as possible – with whatever we could find – and never took it off from morning to night. Klärchen and I spent all our free time together. She did not have to study either. She was an avid reader, who knew all the Karl May books from cover to cover. Karl May was very well known in Germany. He wrote about the North American Indians. It was said that, although he had never actually seen the country, he was able to describe its landscapes down to the shrubs and trees, as authentically as if he had lived there.

After Klärchen's brother returned from a prisoner-of-war camp, he brought home a wonderful game. The men had crafted it themselves to shorten their time. The game was called *Wer Da?* (Who's There?). The board game was a battle between two Indian tribes. The pieces were made from cardboard, glued together so they could stand up, unidentifiable by the opponent. Each piece had a different destructive capacity. A piece was moved in front of an unknown enemy, and the question was asked, "Who's there?" At that point, the stronger one wiped out the weaker one. There were grizzly bears and traps. The strategic positioning of the pieces were of utmost importance. I remember the day I cheated. I excused myself with Klärchen's endless stay in the bathroom reading the toilet paper. (We used neatly cut-up newspaper pieces for toilet paper.) Once I knew the positioning of her pieces, winning was easy. But there was no joy in winning by cheating. There was no joy in confessing it in church, either!

Klärchen's father was a tyrant, and a selfish one at that. We were both scared of him, and so was her mother and her brother. One day, her father had bought a ham on the black market. That was the only place to find such a treasure – and only for big money. He had hidden it behind his books in his study to keep it for himself. When Klärchen was looking for a book, she happened to see it, and she decided that we should 'share' it with him. What a situation! He must have noticed that it got smaller faster than he had eaten it, but he couldn't say anything!

Hunger was a steady companion for all of us, and finding food was like finding gold. Mutti lamented, "If one has something to put into the pot, cooking is not an art, but when there is nothing to start with! . . . " Nobody heard her; we were hungry, and we left it up to her to find something to feed us. Vati had never been a big eater. Food was not really his priority – cigarettes were. He rolled them out of dried and pressed dandelion leaves. To Mutti's dismay, he pressed the leaves by piling our Brockhaus-Encyclopedia on top. For him, the cigarettes turned out just as good as those made from tobacco, since he never inhaled and had no taste buds. He also drank a lot of *'Mookefook,'* a word that few people knew, had evolved from 'mocha faux'. It was Ersatz-coffee made from black-roasted grain. Since the war, we could not import coffee beans. Vati was the only one I knew, who claimed that he could not taste the difference. The pantries were locked in most houses, so that no one could help himself or herself early, with whatever little there was for the next meal.

In springtime, we played with dolls. I still loved playing 'house.' Klärchen would play the father, going to work with the stuffed terrier, Struppi. I enjoyed playing with my dolls, but I had a problem carrying them from my house to hers. I was embarrassed, worrying about what people might think, when they saw a girl of my age still playing with dolls. To be truthful, my concern was not just 'people,' my concern was Peter.

Peter was the most handsome boy in the neighborhood, at least by our standards. He lived across the street from us, right between our house and Klärchen's. His mother, it was said, was a Gypsy who lived with Peter and her sister. His father had never been seen, but he was rumored to be Japanese. Peter turned out looking just exotic enough to be every girl's dream, and his beautiful German Shepherd added to his attraction.

I had to be home at 7 p.m. 'and not a moment later!' Peter seemed to be as aware of that rule as I was. First, he and his dog just happened to stand outside their apartment door, when I walked home. After he was sure I had noticed him – who didn't? – he started sending his dog across the street to greet me. A week later, he came across the street himself to ask me whether I wanted to be his girlfriend. Like most German girls, I replied, "It takes years to become friends, and it doesn't happen by answering 'yes' to a question!" That did not discourage him a bit – which pleased me. The next time

I saw him, he grabbed my house keys from me. He said that he would only give them back, if I allowed him to kiss me. Even though it sounded good to me, I couldn't allow myself to be manipulated like that. I did not know what to say next, but I knew I enjoyed his attention a lot. By now, it was two minutes past seven o'clock, and my mother saved me by making her appearance on the balcony. She called *"Cisi!"* with a stern voice, since I was late for supper. To avoid that from happening again, the next day Peter walked me into my apartment house entrance. The proposition, my keys for a kiss, was the same. My mother was not fooled easily. We could hear her call me again from the balcony. A neighbor girl, hearing her, volunteered, "She is standing with Peter in the entrance hall!" It was unthinkable that I was in the hallway with a boy. After that, Mutti put an end to our rendezvous and our impending romance for a long while!

Because of Peter, Klärchen had to carry the dolls and walk on the opposite side of the street, as if we did not know each other. She did not care what people thought. She had much deeper concerns, like 'why were we not born male – men have all the power!' I cared little who had the power. I enjoyed being a girl and had only one desire, to be allowed to be outside after 7 p.m. At that age, I would have been very pleased with the way I looked, had it not been for my 'strong' legs, as my Vati called them. What made them look even worse, were the dark blue knee stockings I had knitted for myself. A boy once remarked that I looked like a soccer player with those knee-high stockings. I was devastated, although I had to agree.

When the long, hard winter came to its end, we played outside in the street. There was no traffic; nobody owned a car. One of the boys had found what was said to be a rugby ball. It had the shape of an American football, before it was flattened and somewhat torn by a tank. The ball was very heavy, made from leather, and stuffed with something resembling horse hair. Once, Peter threw that ball and it hit my nose. I was out like a light. I woke up on a sofa in his apartment that was located on the ground floor. It was the only time I saw how he lived. I can remember thinking, 'For this kind of attention, he can knock me out any time.' He was a year or more older than I. By now, he was more interested in girls available after seven o'clock at night, than he was in me.

Instead of running home to go to the bathroom, we used to run into the bombed-out houses, to save time. That was dangerous and against the law, because one never knew when the last remaining walls would tumble down. But we were young and felt immortal, so that did not worry us in the least. What worried us, was to be seen. So we always took a friend along to stand guard. One time, when I was in one of those buildings, my friend shouted, "Peter is coming!" I ran out of the rubble so fast that I did not see a piece of iron fence, with a sharp point, sticking straight up. In my hurried escape jump, I did not clear that iron point and it cut deeply into my knee. Even though blood was running down my leg, I did not want to take the time to go home. Peter ran to the drugstore for gauze, and it took the whole roll to keep the blood from soaking through. He wrapped and wrapped, so I could continue playing – though with one stiff leg. In the evening, when my mother attempted to unravel the bandage, she almost got sick. There was no way to unstick the mess. In fact, we could not get the bandage off for a whole week. I guess, if a doctor had taken care of the wound, my knee would not show a scar today.

We also dared each other to walk across an I-beam, still somewhat anchored in the remaining building-walls, high over a crater that once was a cellar. Thank goodness, our parents had no idea what foolish things we did!

Mutti said that there was nothing I could do after dark that I could not do during daylight hours. I never had a chance to find out whether that was so, and I envied those whose parents were not as strict. Once a week, on Sunday afternoon,

I had permission to see a movie. The prospect of the cinema in the afternoon was the only way I could endure the awful cold in our unheated church on Sunday morning. I felt guilty about that, but never confessed to it. I saw many American movies of the late thirties and forties, all with German subtitles. I started dreaming about Clark Gable and Errol Flynn, and wanted to become like Katherine Hepburn, Ingrid Bergman or Bette Davis.

Our *Matthias* Catholic Church played quite an important role in my life. Mutti, Vati and I went to mass regularly every Sunday. Twice during the school week, our class split into Lutheran and Catholic education groups. I also went on Tuesday afternoons to a Catholic group, led by a young woman.

Our diocese received its clergy from Westphalia. We had a Monseigneur and three priests. A Catholic 'Father' is called *'Kaplan'* in Germany – similar to the English word 'chaplain.' Kaplan Eising was our teacher in school. He was very tall and very boring. It only became exciting when I argued with him, which I did more and more. Talkback or discussion was allowed, even encouraged.

Klärchen and I went to confession every Saturday, so we could take communion on Sunday. It was our weekly moral inventory. We strove to have nothing to confess, but we never quite made it. Not 'telling fibs' – as we had downgraded our 'lies' – was the hardest commandment to keep. We often discussed that calling 'lies' 'fibs', was a lie in itself. The so-called fibs were really excuses for why we were late or why we did not do our homework. We took our confessions very seriously and we felt it gave us a strong moral backbone. I sometimes even got up early on Tuesday morning, to go to a special mass before school. It felt good when I had disciplined myself to do that.

Kaplan Köhne was the youngest one of our Fathers. All the girls admired him. He was dark, handsome and athletic. He had visited us once at the Heidehof, and had sent me a little pocket book entitled *Daydreams at French Fireplaces*. I think, I still have it; I enjoyed it so much. When we became teenagers, we were all secretly in love with Kaplan Köhne. He joined our group every four or five weeks, played the lute and led us in folksongs. Everybody in our group looked forward to Kaplan Köhne's visit. My embarrassment about my inability to carry a tune was intensified, when he was there. I recalled, when I sang at home, my father would smile kindly and lovingly tell me that he could not even recognize the song. I do not know what embarrassed me more, singing off-key or not at all. But when Kaplan Köhne visited, I chose the latter. He tried to encourage me to join in, to no avail. On our way home, Klärchen often mentioned that she thought that Köhne paid an awful lot of attention to me. "He seems to be in love with you,"she said jealously. "Everyone can see how he looks at you!" The situation came to a head, when Kaplan Köhne asked me to come to his apartment, where he would give me private singing lessons. I never went there, because I overheard two girls talking about me in our small Catholic library, through the bookshelves. I heard one girl telling another that I was the girl that Köhne liked. I was mortified, and I never went back to my group. The whole situation lessened my enthusiasm for everything that had to do with our church. I wondered whether any of it had been my fault. Köhne never gave any indication that could make me think he liked me more than any of the other girls. I never once suspected that his invitation was anything but to help me learn to sing. I still wonder today who started that gossip.

One Sunday, about a year later, I refused to go to church. I complained that it was too cold there, and that it took me all day to warm up from the one-hour mass. It was true, but no excuse for my parents – who froze there, as well. My father was especially shocked, but eventually I prevailed. I knew very well that it was a sin not to go to church on Sundays. I felt guilty but learned to live with it.

I did not see Klärchen much anymore. Now that she had been transferred to Catholic school, we had different friends. My friends were all Protestants. They seldom went to church. They had to go to confirmation class instead, for which I did not envy them. I was invited to all their confirmation celebrations, with their whole families present. Afterwards, none of them seemed to go to church anymore.

Marlene Jacobi

After Klärchen left, Marlene Jacobi became my closest friend. We both had relatives in America. She had an uncle, who was an artist, and he belonged to an artist-guild in the U.S. Through it, he collected clothes and food. He sent these items – via his relatives – to the German Artist-Guild, to which he had belonged before emigrating. Needless to say, Marlene was beautifully dressed, at a time when most girls had few clothes.

My sister, Inge, had been living in the United States since 1939. During the six years of war, we had heard from her only through the Red Cross. Her messages were seldom, and at least a year old, by the time we got them. They were restricted to a few specific words and very few sentences. Inge had not heard anything from us at all. When she found out Mutti was alive, she diligently tried to get food and clothes to us. It was very difficult. She used CARE, but those packages took at least a year. She also tried – through some friends – to use Army mail, which was illegal. But that way she managed, from time to time, to get a personal package through to us. I will be eternally grateful to her, because those clothes made me feel so special.

When we got a package, Mutti and I conspired to get the cigarettes out, before my father could get a hold of them. Cigarettes were like gold. You could use them to barter for bread, and one time, they even bought a wonderful pair of used roller skates for me. Once Inge included a jar of peanut butter. None of us had ever tasted anything like this before. We stored it in our credenza. Its pungent odor seemed to penetrate the wooden walls and when we opened it, the whole room smelled like peanut butter. Only Vati, with his lack of taste buds, could eat it; the taste was too foreign for us! One day, when a friend tried to help me lay the table, she opened the credenza and exclaimed, "There is a terrible smell in here!" Vati was only too eager to explain, "That is my butter!" My friend was impressed and surprised.

Foreign taste or not, we all learned to eat barbecued meat. It came in a can. In fact, it became a Sunday meal, because it was the only meat we had. My father would ask every Sunday, "Are we having sweet meat again?" My favorite food was the powdered milk Inge sent. With a little water, it made the best-tasting paste. Mutti needed the milk for cooking, but every time she opened the can, more of it was gone. She started a hide-and-seek game, but no matter where she hid it, I could find it. She went so far as to put it under the debris that was left in the three destroyed rooms. Though it was behind 'the wall,' I would find it. Shaking and loosening it up, would hide the fact that some of the powder was missing. This worked for a while, but not for long. Sometimes Mutti was very frustrated, because she forgot where she put it herself. But I was quite able to come to the rescue! What a crazy time it was!

Our apartment was so cold that the temperature fell below freezing. The large tiled kitchen was the worst. Mutti complained that in the kitchen she felt like being in an 'air swing.' She claimed that the wind blew through Vati's shabbily constructed wall that blocked off the *Trümmer* (rubble), even though it had been built out of concrete blocks. Mutti was right, the kitchen was not only icy cold, it felt actually windy in there. Mutti's beautiful hands had frostbite, and looked blue and swollen. In the little room, now our living room, we not only had the credenza, table and three chairs, but also a bed for me. I was the only one who slept in a heated room. Mutti would get up at five o'clock in the morning to start a fire in the heater, using broken furniture from the *Trümmer*. The window – rather the cardboard-covered opening – of the little room had a northern exposure. Many a winter day, the wind blew right into the stovepipe vent. Instead of a draft to get the fire going, the wind blew the black soot into Mutti's face, so that she looked like a chimney sweep. To remedy this, Vati had one of his brilliant ideas. Since our house still had an unused chimney, behind the gas stove in the kitchen, the thought occurred to him to use it as a vent for the space heater. But where could he find a stovepipe (one of the most sought-after items at the time) to go clear across the kitchen to the chimney? Well, he couldn't, but he could use one of his cast iron sewer pipes for that purpose. Again, his 'capable help' was used to install it. Wire loops were screwed into the gypsum ceiling for extra support, because the pipe was so heavy. Lo and behold, it worked; not really well, but it worked. Because it was installed nearly level, more and more soot collected in it over time, until very little air could flow through.

One day, while Mutti and I were standing in an endless line for bread, Vati decided to surprise us. When we came home, we could not believe our eyes. Vati had one of his 'capable' workers take off the pipe to clean it, while the stove was burning. The soot, black, shiny and slick, covered everything. We could not step into our one and only warm room. The carpet was so slippery that we would have broken our necks. It took a whole other work crew to clean it up. At a time when nothing could be replaced, we had to throw away our rug and my bed linens. It was a disaster! After that, the 'stove pipe' was re-installed with somewhat of an upward slant. Vati also had found someone to clean the house chimney that had not been cleaned in years. Now there was a better draft.

Not long after we had recuperated from the soot disaster,

the pipe came crashing down. It crushed Mutti's two heavy aluminum pots – one on top of the other – cooking our next meal. The pots and food were destroyed, but it missed Mutti. She would have never survived had she got the pipe on her head.

The *Funkturm* (the only radio tower in Berlin at the time) was located in the Western Sector of Berlin. Although the division of Berlin had been agreed upon by the Russians, the East German broadcasters made no attempt to vacate the station. Their broadcast drowned out *RIAS* (Radio in the American Sector) Their 'sit-in' at the *Funkturm,* and their sudden anti-American propaganda, were the first indications of the ensuing 'Cold War.' We could not believe our ears.

My favorite program was the *Russian Literature Hour.* I lay on my bed and listened fascinated. Many were animal stories that left me sobbing long after they had finished. They were written and read so beautifully. Mutti became very concerned, worrying about my nerves. She said, "Nerves cannot be repaired, once they are ruined!"

It was not long thereafter that she found me sobbing again. This time I felt sorry for myself, because of the seven long years that I carried a cloud over my head, not knowing who I was.

Who Am I?

It was quite a day, when I finally learned who I was. It all came about because of the Teskes – the shoemaker and his wife – who once had sent their dog, Struppi, and a lot of beautiful linens to the Heidehof. We had not spoken to them since we came back to Berlin. We learned that they had gone through our suitcases to see whether we – not the Russians – had stolen their belongings. It had been an exercise in futility, because how could they recognize what was theirs, when it had all belonged to their Jewish customers. Mutti was very offended. It only proved to her again that one should not get so chummy with just anybody. I avoided the Teskes whenever possible. I was afraid that Frau Teske would ask personal questions. I was sure that she knew the answers better than I – but would ask them anyway, just out of spite.

It was a cold and rainy day in the autumn of 1946. I was unhappy because Mutti was angry with me. I knew she would not speak to me again until I apologized. The silence at home hung heavily in the air. On my way to visit my friend Ulla, I was so preoccupied with 'how-to-apologize' that I did not see Mr. Teske coming toward me. He stopped to tell me that a letter, addressed to Eleonora Orazi, was left with them. "The mailman did not know how to find the addressee," he said. 'Really', I thought to myself, 'so you graciously volunteered to find the correct party.' It took all the strength I could muster, when I answered with a forced smile, "Oh, that is for me!" Then I swiftly walked on, feeling my heart beating in my throat.

My name – or names – had been a source of embarrassment for as long as I could remember. Everybody called me *Cisi;* nobody had a name like that. Then there was always the name 'Orazi,' like a middle name on all my report cards. I never dared to ask where 'it' came from. Who am I? Why am I Italian? Why do I have names like 'Cisi' and 'Orazi' to deal with? Mr. Teske and his letter-question was the last straw! I suddenly felt really sorry for myself. I had wondered about all of it, ever since that fateful day when Klärchen disclosed that I was Italian. Snooping in my mother's locked wardrobe had never answered anything! I had blocked out all the questions I had about myself for so many years – now, I had reached my breaking point!

I turned on my heel to go back home. I had no idea how to apologize, or how to go about asking those burning questions. The source of Mutti's anger had been, as usual, that I answered a question with a flippant 'no', in a manner that was neither polite nor respectful. Mutti then slapped me with her right hand – the one with the wedding ring. Often before, I ducked in time, but this time I had not. Her hand with the ring flew across my mouth. It surprised me more than it hurt. It bruised my feelings and made me so angry that I argued impertinently, "I did not do anything wrong, all I said was 'no'!" Then Mutti explained in French, *"C'est le ton qui fait la musique"* (It's the tone that makes the music.) I had heard it many times before, and knew well that I had spoken in a disrespectful tone. But I kept arguing anyhow, until she said, "Since you don't understand, I am wasting my time talking to you!" Then she proceeded to punish me with silence.

Silence worked. It conveyed that she was too hurt to be able to speak. Sooner or later, I felt miserable enough to apologize for my behavior – but this time I felt wronged. I felt that I was the victim, not she! Therefore, I did not really want to apologize at all. But how to break the silence?

I walked straight into the little room and sat down on my bed, while my mother ignored me. I tossed my house keys into the air, rhythmically. I practiced in my mind the most insincere - and coldest-sounding apology. I was still flipping my keys up into the air, when I finally spoke. It must have sounded so rehearsed that Mutti had to laugh. She took me into her arms. I did not expect that, and it did not help me this time. I wanted to stay angry, instead of being Mutti's little girl again, safe and protected in her arms. I remained strong by thinking, 'Either now or never!' I was very embarrassed, but I asked all the questions about being Italian, my foreign names and the Italian grandmother who sent packages with shoes and sweets for Christmas. The words tumbled out so fast that I didn't know whether I could be understood. I was sobbing and sobbing and sobbing – crying away years of pain.

If Mutti was startled or upset, she did not let it show. She spoke to me very calmly as she explained, "Your biological parents are both Italian, and presently living in Italy. We wanted to adopt you as a baby, but were not allowed to do so, because of Hitler. Since the end of the war, Germany is not considered a country, so no adoption can be performed."

Then she told me about Clara, my mother, who had become like a daughter to her, and who was so lovable and charming that she conquered everybody's heart. She only referred to my father as having been an immature boy, who let Clara suffer through those long months of pregnancy alone – in a foreign country – without so much as a letter! It was obvious to me that Mutti had felt Clara's pain and disappointment, when no letters arrived. It had made her very angry. But the one she really blamed was my grandmother, my father's mother, who had sent Clara to Germany.

I listened quietly. It was all an anti-climax. It was as if the dark cloud over me had shed its rain, and now there was nothing left - except maybe an interesting story. All my embarrassment was gone; it was a relief. Mutti did not defend herself for not telling me sooner, nor did she say, 'we love you.' There was no need. I knew how much they loved me, and I was happy they were my parents. Nothing had changed about that! Mutti made the whole scene an 'un-event.' She was not a bit dramatic, and reported it all like a documentary.

Slowly, as time went on, I learned about Mutti's life, as well. I hurt for her, as my love and respect grew even more. But only later in my life, could I realize what strength, determination and love it must have taken, to hide her persecution by the Nazis from me – for so many years . . .

PART TWO

GROWING UP

Mutti's Survival In Nazi Germany

Now that I was aware of who I was, and how Mutti came to be my mother, I learned the missing pieces of the puzzle that had been my life.

During those dreadful Nazi years, when I shared Mutti's worry that Vati would be caught and arrested because of his reckless behavior, I had no idea that Mutti's survival depended solely on his. She had found the extraordinary strength to keep it all from me: her horror and bitterness over the death of her brother; the worry about her daughter Ruth in London; her concern for her younger daughter Inge who was a stranger in America. In addition to all of the above, she lived those long Nazi years in perpetual fear of being 'picked up' to meet her brother's fate in a concentration camp. And what would have happened to me, if she had been 'picked up'? . . . I had no idea that she was Jewish, and that she could have been taken from me any minute of any day. Her only hope for survival was the possibility of Hitler's defeat before they got around to her. In a city of close to four-and-a-half-million people, it took a good while to have all the Jews checked out. What Hitler called his 'Final Solution' took time, no matter how methodical and organized he tried to be. 'Mixed marriages' (one partner 'Aryan') were last to be eliminated, but my father's business manager, Herr Froehlke, tried his best, to shorten the waiting time.

In 1937 and 1938 we were still able to take family vacations to places like the *Thüringer* Mountains, or to the Baltic Sea resorts. Thereafter, Mutti was not accepted in a hotel. Later Mutti could not even take the risk of being on a train, for fear of passport control. Everyone, fourteen years or older, was required to carry an identification. Mutti's I.D. had a big 'J' stamped on it, and she had been given the middle name 'Sara', which was Hitler's gift to all females of Jewish descent.

When Mutti was no longer able to go on vacation with me, she still insisted, "The child needs a change of climate to fight off colds and diseases during the long winter." So she asked my father to go with me alone. Vati and I went on a three-week vacation to *Binz* on *Rügen,* Germany's largest island in the Baltic Sea. Vati was very dear and not as strict as Mutti. It was fun to be alone with him. One day, when we

Vati and I at Binz - 1938

walked along the beach and out on a pier, Vati found a fellow vacationer willing to listen to his political ranting. Engrossed in his discussion, he did not notice that I had slipped off the wooden planks. Luckily my foot got caught in a diagonally nailed stabilizing board. It kept me from falling into the ocean, but I was hanging low enough that my head was submerged. I kept pulling my face out of the water to scream for help. The roar of the waves prevented anybody from hearing me. Only after what seemed like an endless time, Vati noticed I was missing. He saw me dangling and pulled me out. I was really shaken, but soon collected myself in anticipation of recounting the great adventure to my mother. (She, of course, was horrified, while I enjoyed the impact of my story).

Mutti was also forbidden to attend any public entertainment. I had wondered why she never took me to any children's performances. There were few opportunities, but those meant a lot to me. I remember a ballet of *Rumpelstielschen,* where a girl I knew was dancing. My friend's parents took me along, otherwise I could not have gone. I assumed that my parents were not in the mood, because of their worries about the future of Germany and us. I did not blame them, but I envied friends, whose parents seemed to be lighthearted and shared their excitement.

Since I had become afraid of going anywhere with Vati, for fear of encountering somebody in Nazi uniform, I wonder how Mutti must have felt? During the Nazi-time, we had seen fewer and fewer visitors. Friends and acquaintances had been afraid to associate with Jews. Mutti probably had agreed with Vati's doomsday predictions, but his behavior had made her frantic. During Hitler days, the mood at home was never happy. Therefore, to be allowed to spend time with my friends in their homes was a real treat.

When the new word 'coventrieren' was added to our vocabulary, and was used constantly in news-broadcasts, Mutti had nightmares about her daughter Ruth's survival in London. *Coventrieren* meant that the Nazis had planned to do to the rest of the U.K., what they had done to Coventry, namely 'level it'.

Frau Teske, whenever she saw Mutti, enjoyed talking about the *V-1* and the *V-2* missiles dropping out of the sky over London. Certainly she must have known how worried Mutti was. However unpleasant *Frau Teske* had been, she was ' in-the-know' and had been able to warn Mutti of impending danger.

It was the time when Vati had become a time bomb ready to blow up any time. He was totally obsessed with his hatred for the Nazis. He gave no emotional support to Mutti whatsoever, only added to the dread of what might be in store for her. Nobody in Berlin, or Germany, knew whether they would survive the next night of bombing. In addition to that, Mutti did not know whether she would get through the next day without being 'picked up' by the *GESTAPO*. She had often told me that 'I was her only joy, and her only reason for living', but she omitted to mention that I also added greatly to her worries.

125

Mutti was very well liked. She managed to receive 'a little better' cut of meat from the butcher, and the greengrocer often reserved his best fruit and vegetables for her. I wonder whether they knew of her plight and wanted to help her in some small way; or whether they just liked her quiet, friendly demeanor. – We will never know!

When Mutti suddenly moved back to Berlin and left us in Frau Typke's care at the Heidehof, I did not know that her ration-cards had been confiscated. Neither did I know that Vati's business manager, Herr Froehlke, had gone to the police to inform them that his employer's wife was receiving rations in Berlin, while living on a farm. Froehlke probably got the idea, when Vati told him that Mutti had tried to get replacements for the ration cards that were stolen out of my bicycle-basket.

Froehlke had been an ambitious, hard working and able business manager. Vati was very satisfied with him. In Vati's absence, he ran the company as if he were the owner, which sooner or later he expected to be. He was certainly aware that Mutti was Jewish. He also must have known that she was afraid to change her residence-registration to Märkisch-Buchholz, a town of a thousand 'Aryan' inhabitants. It was a known fact that it was a serious offense to be registered for rations in one place and live in another. Berliners had much higher rations to keep up their morale. Froehlke saw a perfect opportunity to expedite Mutti's demise. Therefore, he went to the police to notify them that Mutti was not living in Berlin, where she claimed her food rations. Froehlke also knew my father's temper and his attitude toward the Nazis, so he could be reasonably sure that Vati would not stand by quietly, when his wife was taken away. That would take care of both of them.

It was Frau Teske who told Mutti what Froehlke had done. How the shoemaker's wife knew that he had gone to the police, and how she knew that Mutti was targeted to be 'picked up', nobody took time to find out.

In desperation, Mutti went to her physician, Dr.Gottschalk. She told him her story and asked whether he could help. Dr. Gottschalk lived in a similar situation, and he also had been spared so far. He was Jewish, but his wife was not. The doctor knew of a possible way out, providing a large sum of cash could be raised immediately. He asked Mutti whether her husband was able, and if so, willing to pay the hefty sum of 100,000 *Reichsmark*. That was a lot of money at that time! Since Vati handed Mutti household money weekly, she had no idea whether her husband could, or would, even consider paying a sum like that. But to her great surprise, he agreed without thinking twice. Dr. Gottschalk told Mutti that a man, who would identity himself as 'Paul', would collect the money. At a pre-arranged hour, Mutti was hiding behind the swinging doors that divided the entrance from the center hall. The man was punctual to the minute. Mutti heard the dreaded sound of leather boots on the hardwood steps coming ever closer, up the eight flights of stairs, to the fourth floor where our apartment was located. She had little doubt, who wore those boots! (Since all carpeting had been removed for fear of fire during bombings, the sound was amplified.) Mutti shivered from fear.

The doorbell rang, and Mutti saw a man in an *SS* uniform through the narrow crack between the swinging doors. What would Vati do now?? . . . Would he attack him??. . . Throw him out?? . . . Then she witnessed a miracle. Vati handed all that cash over to the stranger, who said he was Paul – a Paul in a *SS*-uniform! The man took the money with a short, "Thank you." No other word was spoken as he swiftly left. Vati and Mutti looked at each other, knowing they shared the same thought: 'We are never going to see the man nor the money again.' But they were powerless – and only partially right.

Not long thereafter, Mutti was 'picked up' by the *GESTAPO.* She was taken to *Oranienburg,* the closest concentration camp to Berlin. Mutti later described vividly the many huge iron gates falling into their locks behind her, before she was led into what looked like an administration building. There were masses of people squeezed into a large waiting room, most of them women, showing fear in their eyes. Names were called, something resembling a worker's identification card was handed to each of them and a work assignment went with it. Nothing was said. Each person disappeared through a large door.

Mutti watched this spectacle of dread over and over again for twenty-four, seemingly endless, hours. Nobody exchanged a word; all were alone with their own thoughts, petrified by fear of what the future might hold. No questions, no lament, just a horrifying silence. The room emptied out slowly. Everybody had left with their papers and assignments, everyone – but Mutti. She was exhausted from anxiety and lack of sleep, when suddenly the uniformed man behind the desk, called out, "Frau Uhlenbrock!" Mutti's legs barely carried her to the desk where the voice had come from. There she was handed an identification card, like all the others, but she did not see a work assignment. Then she was pointed in the direction of a different door – the one by which she had entered. A uniformed man accompanied her through the iron gates that had been tightly locked behind her, just a day and a night before. She found herself standing outside the compound, walking away, not knowing in which direction to go.

Later, she could not remember how she got home. But only then did she dare inspect the papers handed to her. Inside the pass she saw, *'Arbeitendes Familienmitglied. '* (Working family member.) That title was usually given to 'Aryan' mothers with five or more children, or women who worked in a family business that promoted the war effort. – Paul had come through!

After that, Mutti did not risk going back to the Heidehof. Only when things became so chaotic that everybody was fully occupied with their own survival; when the bombings were incessant and the end of the war clearly in sight; did Mutti move back to the Heidehof to be with me. Vati still commuted as long as he could.

In 1945, not long after we had managed to get back to Berlin, the telephone rang. The man at the other end identified himself as 'Paul'. He said that he called to find out whether Mutti had survived. He further told us that it was very important to him for us to know that he did not keep one penny of all that money. He explained that it took all the money to bribe the needed connections. People had to be bribed all the way from the bottom to the top! Mutti asked immediately, "What can I do to help you, now that it's over?" He replied that he did not need any help, and that he was booked for emigration to the United States. He explained that he had survived the takeover with the assistance of people he had helped. They vouched for him and their relatives in the States had given him an affidavit to get out of Germany.

We never heard from him again.

The Years Following The War

Berlin was not recognizable. When it capitulated in May of 1945, a city of 4.3 million people had shrunk to 2.8 million. The toll of the final days of the *Dritte Reich* alone resulted in 80,000 deaths and 75 million cubic meters of debris, according to the Berlin Information Center.

A typical street in Berlin in 1945

Soon, one could see women cleaning up the city, or the remnants thereof. There were more and more neatly stacked bricks, the remaining mortar scraped or hammered off. Those stacks, all over the city, resembled miniature skyscrapers.

Again the radio had become a messenger of hate. Vicious propaganda was broadcast between endless heart-wrenching hours of *Suchdienst* (search-rosters), consisting of a stream of names and descriptions of missing loved ones. Most of them were children who had been lost during the final days of the war.

The target of the propaganda was the United States. At first, we were puzzled because we could not quite understand what we were hearing. It soon became annoying and unbearable. Soviet hate-messages dominated every program. There were awful stories how Americans treated their black citizens and their poor. After what seemed a short reprieve, Vati was screaming at the radio again – now because of his disdain for the Russians and communism.

Women reclaiming bricks everywhere

Soon we wondered why the Western Powers had believed that amicable relations with the USSR would continue indefinitely. How could they have neglected to secure highway and rail access to their three Western Sectors? (It was lucky for us in West Berlin that at least an 'air corridor' had been negotiated.) The animosity between the 'East' and the 'West' escalated from month to month. America's paranoia concerning communism was on its way.

Everyone in Germany was perpetually hungry. The few of Inge's CARE-packages that were not lost or stolen, took more than a year to get to us. When they finally got through, packages for hundreds of people came at the same time. As a result, Berliners lined up day and night to pick up their food packages from an American controlled warehouse. Once, close to Christmas, we had been notified that 'two' of those precious packages were waiting for us to be picked up. When Mutti and I arrived at the checkout place, we had to walk twenty minutes to find the end of the line of waiting people. Many had been standing there for two days and a night in the bitter cold. I went to see what the front of the line looked like, when suddenly the gates opened to let an American Jeep drive through. Immediately after the Jeep was out, people stormed through the open gates, pushing me ahead and inside, right where I wanted to be. Thank goodness, Mutti had decided to give up on waiting and had come to fetch me, just in time to claim the packages! We were gloating. In those days, it was truly the survival of the fittest, and in this case, of the luckiest. At age thirteen, I thought of myself as a survivor, and a lucky one at that! I only remember a moment of fleeting sadness for those people who may have had to wait another day in the mercilessly cold weather . . .

The one time when we received a package through an American military family stationed in Berlin, Mutti and I went to pick it up. I shall not forget the experience. It was another cold winter-day. We were freezing day and night, and we were worn out from trembling. The Berliners used to say, "I cannot shiver as fast as I freeze!" The American family lived in a less destroyed and one of the most beautiful parts of West Berlin. Germans had to give up their homes to allow the American occupation troops and their families to move in.

What a feeling of luxury it was, when we entered the house and felt the warmth of a place heated throughout. (It had been a long time since our whole apartment was heated!) Mrs. Warner had just opened a gift from her husband. Lying on a gift box were several soft-wool sweaters of the same style, but in different bright colors. I would daydream about those sweaters for years to come! They represented to me wealth, beauty and a comfort to hope for – maybe one day, far in the future.

The package contained clothes, besides powdered milk and real coffee. Inge had included a pair of her husband's used Army trousers. Gerry was so slender that they fit me perfectly. It took little alteration to move the zipper to the side that turned them into 'ladies' slacks'. (At that time no woman wore pants with the zipper in front.) What a fabric! We had not seen such wonderful wool in years, if ever. And they were warm! I loved wearing them, even though those slacks became an excuse for American soldiers to start a conversation. First, they would compliment me on how nice I looked, and they also were curious to know where I got 'their' Army pants. At thirteen, I had studied enough English to be able to communicate with them, which made me even more interesting. Those pants became an attractive nuisance, especially since I looked older than my actual age. There was no dye available and certainly no replacement possible. I learned to pretend that I did not understand what was said.

Many German girls and women, older than I, were dating American soldiers. It was not considered 'the classy thing to do'. The so-called 'Ami-girls', many of them widows with children to feed, received little sympathy from the public.

Later on, we were able to receive more of Inge's packages. I don't remember how they got to us, but I will never forget the cans and jars of food wrapped in the most beautiful clothes. Some fit perfectly, some were much too small, some much too large. But they were all gorgeous and like new. I loved the fabrics, the colors and the styles. A gift from heaven for a teenager! It never occurred to us that Inge had collected those clothes at her work-place, therefore the difference in sizes. We had somebody who could make one dress out of two small ones. It gave me a chance to design my own clothes. Many of us wore dresses made of a combination of colors and materials. We could not buy anything new and we were at an age where we quickly outgrew our clothes. I felt I was the best-dressed girl in all of Berlin, maybe only second to my friend Marlene. She was as lucky as I, having an uncle in the United States.

Berlin's situation became more and more desperate. We could not have survived, had it not been for President Truman and the 'Marshall Plan'. Along with other economic aid, the Marshall Plan provided hot lunches for school children. Those lunches consisted alternately of 'cheese soup', 'chocolate soup' and 'cookie soup.' Those thick soups were so nutritious that we all got fat! We were eager to volunteer for lunch-duty. It cut classes short, because huge Thermos-kettles had to be picked up from the few schools equipped with kitchens. Two girls were picked to carry one heavy kettle. Mutti was not pleased that I carried those loads. But who would not seize the opportunity to get out of class early? We then dished out the food, and scraped out the kettles afterwards. Our poor teachers were not allowed to eat any of the food. It was designated only for school children. Frl. Dr. Tangel, weighing no more than ninety pounds, was so starved that she ate the little that was left in our various dishes. We thought it hilarious and joked about it, not having an inclination how desperately hungry she was, and how tragic her situation!

In 1947 Mutti discovered an opportunity to book a hotel for a vacation in Binz at the Baltic Sea, where once I had fallen off the pier. Now, Binz was part of the Russian occupied zone, but then still accessible to private families. (Later, all resorts were exclusively reserved for Labor Unions.) I was allowed to invite Marlene Jacobi – now my closest friend – to join us. We had a wonderful, exciting time and at that age everything was fun.

Marlene and I at Binz

Marlene's mother had saved some cans from America to send along. Among them was sweetened condensed milk. In the nearby forest, people would gather blueberries and sell them for outlandish prices; but they tasted better than any of us had ever eaten before. Mutti had splurged, so we could eat them with that wonderful pre-sweetened milk. We only got a small portion at a time. The leftover berries were stored on the top shelf of the wardrobe in our hotel room. We had just gone to bed, when Marlene and I had the brilliant idea, to take a few blueberries and eat them under our bed cover. Unfortunately, we ended up with blue stains on the white bed sheets. From that day on, we rushed to make our beds before the maid discovered the spots. Every day, Mutti reminded us that making beds was part of the hotel's service, and she wondered aloud why we were so ambitious on vacation and not at home! It was even fun to stand in line for bread at five o'clock in the morning.

There were negotiations on currency-reform held in Berlin, because of the effect of the old *Reichsmark* on the German economy. Since there was no agreement with the Russians, the Western Allies proceeded on their own. In June 1948, the West de-valued its money. That meant, each person could exchange 60 *Reichsmark* for 60 *D-Mark* on a 1:1 basis. The rest of the money had an exchange-value of 1:10. That meant that all our remaining money was worth only one-tenth of its former value. Two days after the 'West's' money reform, the 'East' had one of their own.

The new money made West Berlin, though in geographic isolation, part of the Western occupied zone. It also started its recovery – although much slower then the rest of the West-Zone. It didn't take long until the money of the 'East' was worth only one-fourth of the currency in the 'West'. That brought on a migration from the East to the West. People sought work in the 'West'. Many left the 'East' for good. It spelled disaster for the economy of the Soviet-occupied part of Germany.

At the height of their frustration, the Russians blockaded Berlin by stopping all traffic through their occupied part of Germany. Soon trucks with coal and food supplies were delayed or stopped when on their way to Berlin. In order to reach Berlin by land, many kilometers of Russian occupied land had to be crossed. The transports to Berlin were easily stopped, and the designated 'air corridors' were allowed to be used by American planes only. *'Der Osten'*, the new word for the Russian occupied zone of Germany and the Russian Sector of Berlin, commanded whatever harassment they thought up on any particular day, at any particular time. The hourly radio alerts of approaching bombers had changed to how many trucks were detained and queued up at all the border checkpoints toward Berlin. Often the transports were held up as long as 48 hours by border police. Trucks lined up for miles. These trucks with food and coal were literally West Berlin's lifeline. It was quite a threatening situation for a starving city with meager rations.

It was June 24, 1948. No ground transportation from the Western Zone was allowed to pass the border checkpoints. Literally, the lights went out in West Berlin. Hospitals were hardest hit; factories had to close. There was food supply for 36 days, and coal supplies for 45 days. 'West' Berlin was held hostage. In General Lucius Clay's words: "It was one of the most brutal attempts in recent history, to use mass starvation as a means of applying political pressure."

The Americans assured the Berliners, they were going to supply them by air. How, they did not know themselves – . At first, they could only fly in 120 tons per day, where 12,000 tons were needed to keep the West-Berliners alive. But they managed to keep their promise. They built the Tegel Airfield in three months, and increased their transports by 4,000 tons daily.

I remember Mutti shaking her head. She had wondered for a long time, why the Americans were so afraid of the Russians. Why didn't they just drive through the border checkpoints with a convoy? Since that obviously did not happen, we were all scared to death of what may lay ahead with winter approaching.

Conditions worsened. We were allotted two hours of electricity per day, on a rotating basis from district to district. During those precious two hours, everybody used their vacuum cleaners, or other appliances, simultaneously. Our fuses blew and there was no replacement. At night West Berlin was pitch black again, except for the part that had its two hours of electricity.

Whenever we had electricity in the evening-hours, I stayed up to listen to the top-twenty songs on the hit parade. I was continually in love, and most of those songs were just right for my romantic dreams. (Vati was in bed, therefore we could listen to music instead of talk.) I was thrilled when Mutti stayed up with me. I was sure that she was not the least bit interested in this kind of music, but she did it anyhow. I still recall one of the songs that talked about a pair of little swallows. Those little birds realized that the year had passed so fast, and now they worried about the long winter ahead. Invariably, Mutti would say, "SO DO I !", shaking me back into reality.

America's rescue action, by way of an airlift through the designated corridors, was called the *"Luftbrücke"* (Air bridge). At first, Tempelhof was the only usable airport. It was located right smack in the middle of the city, between residential apartment houses. Every two minutes a plane landed and one took off. The roar of airplane engines was deafening. It drowned out any other sound, and certainly any conversation or radio. During that time, we were invited for coffee and cake close to the Tempelhof Airport. Conversation was impossible. It was so obnoxious that it was funny.

The *Luftbrücke* went on for eleven months, which included the winter. Sometimes there was zero visibility. A number of planes crashed, and their young pilots lost their lives in an effort to save us. (The West Berliners were very aware of the sacrifice made for them, and they were very grateful. A monument in front of the Tempelhof airport commemorates the lives given to save Berlin.) Coal, the greatest problem, was dropped directly out of planes from the air. We were very happy to see a coal mountain growing in our flat Berlin. The blockade not only failed because of the dedication of the Western Powers, it also brought about an unanticipated side effect: now the Berliners did not see the Western Allies as occupation but as their friends and protectors.

Vati was still going to bed with his hat to keep his bald head warm. In the unheated rooms, it was below freezing at night. I slept now in the *'Herrenzimmer'* on the couch. It had only a Persian rug over thinly covered springs. I could never get warm. I tried crawling under the rug that made it cold from below and heavy on top. In fact, the rug was so heavy that my legs cramped. Repeatedly, I had to jump out into the icy air, and dance around until my leg felt normal again.

For my parents, life continued to be a struggle. But I was young and happy, and my dreams were fed by the movies I was allowed to see on Sunday afternoons. They were the highlight of my life. Soon, I was not satisfied with only going once a week. It became my great ambition to see as many movies as possible, even if I had to lie and say I did homework at Marlene's house. One day I was caught. Knowing Mutti so well, I could read her face when I walked in. I decided to confess immediately. A second later, the telephone rang. Before the receiver was picked up, Mutti announced: "It's your friend Marlene, calling to warn you not to lie!" She was right. From Marlene's mother she had learned that we had gone to a movie. What a relief that I had already confessed. Then it seemed to me that everybody was allowed to go to the movies more than I, and they bragged about it. Soon the British films were the rage. The British Sector was close enough to us that one could walk there. Actors like James Mason, Margaret Lockwood and Stewart Granger portrayed British Society of another era. They were great movies. Because none of the theaters were heated, we took blankets. But after sitting still for a while, the cold crept through to our bones. Just like after church, it took hours to warm up.

Studying really had to be squeezed in or out, because now dancing lessons added another aspect to my already busy and happy life. Marlene had a cousin who was quite an accomplished ballroom dancer. She had taken lessons from Apitsch, the Arthur Murray of Berlin. At first, ballroom dancing seemed old fashioned to me, but Marlene wanted to go. Before I had made up my mind, she enrolled. I was devastated that she would go without me, since we had done everything together before. As usual, Mutti knew how hurt I was, without being told. She remembered the Apitsches from two decades ago, when they taught Inge and Ruth. She decided to pay them a visit. Frau Apitsch was delighted to hear that Mutti's daughters had been taught by her husband. She explained, that now her son had followed in his father's footsteps.

During the conversation, Frau Apitsch complained bitterly, saying that it was impossible to find a suit for her son. Mutti still had a formal suit that belonged to her brother, Alfred. She asked whether that would solve Frau Apitsch's problem. Frau Apitsch was so delighted and grateful, that all my lessons were free. That was great, because Vati was not inclined to pay for dancing lessons. We did not even have to pay for formal balls (quite expensive at the time), and I enjoyed special status from the beginning. There were dance studios at two different locations, and whenever Frau Apitsch needed extra 'ladies', I was asked. Oh, did that turn out to be fun! Now I could stay out later than that debilitating seven o'clock deadline, since lessons weren't over until nine, and the dances finished even later.

I remember my parents picking me up, always bringing along our dog, Flöckchen. They went arm-in-arm for safety, not to fall in the pitch-dark streets. One held the dog leash, the other a flashlight so they would not stumble over curbs. What they didn't see, was a thin rope with a sign warning people, not to come too close to the unstable walls of a bombed-out house. They promptly fell over it. Mutti could laugh over mishaps like that, imagining what a sight they must have been, had there been light enough for anybody to see them. They were still laughing, when they greeted me at the train station. I was very aware that only their love for me brought them into those cold and dark streets.

Mutti then was already sixty-three years old and Vati seventy-one. It was great fun for us teenagers, when the two-hours of electricity were up, and the lights went out. We danced in a large ballroom where a few candles produced only a dim light. That was very romantic.

Klaus Lukoshus 1948 on what was left of our balcony

Klaus was my first boyfriend in dancing school. He had lost his father in the war, and took his role as head of the household very seriously. At fifteen, he did everything to make life easier for his mother and younger brother. He was practical and very musically gifted. He dreamed of going to America someday, having his own band, and working in advertising as a day-job. He believed that only in the U. S. could he achieve a great future in both his ambitions. But for now, he used his creativity to connect a cable from a neighbor's bombed-out house, to obtain free electricity. I was impressed, forgetting my Catholic upbringing, but remembering enough not to tell my parents. Had they known, my budding romance would have come to a screeching halt. Klaus was tall, blond, and serious about everything. Klaus was already networking for his future. He was active in what we called the 'American Club'. (Whether or not it was the same as the USO, I don't know.)

One day, Klaus was given 50 Marks to organize a party. An American broadcasting crew wanted to interview German teenagers. His friend's parents had a beautiful villa that had escaped bombing. They allowed us to use their house for the few hours necessary for the party-interview. Klaus invited a large group of young people, bought snacks, but couldn't afford Coca Cola. It was very expensive and not necessary, since we were not used to 'soft drinks.' With the left-over money he bought a small bottle of sweet peach-liqueur. Klaus hid his bottle of liqueur for only his closest friends, because there was not enough to go around. I just wished, I had not been one of those friends and such a people-pleaser! The 'privileged' had to take a swallow directly out of the bottle, because we did not dare to use our hosts' glasses for fear of breaking them. I had little interest in the liqueur, and the thought of drinking out of the same bottle with all the others nauseated me. I did it anyway to please Klaus. The next morning, I woke up with a fever blister on my lip, the first of many in my life. I know for sure that the unappetizing bottle was responsible.

Klaus had already charted his future. Me, as his wife, and emigration to America. I had little ambition to go to America, and even less to tie myself down with promises at age thirteen. That became very clear, when I met Joachim who was a much better dancer than Klaus. Joachim was very aloof and therefore extremely interesting. We met at Apitsch' and danced together all the time. We became so good at it that we would go to outside dances and win prizes in contests. Those prizes all consisted of books, written after the war, poorly bound on brownish, recycled paper. They had another thing in common; they were all documentaries of the atrocities, committed by the Nazis, in the concentration camps. They gave me nightmares. I still have one of those books today.

When I invited Joachim to meet my parents, he was there on the dot. He came on a Sunday at 3 o'clock, the time my parents rose from their midday rest. We sat endless hours doing crossword puzzles. Joachim read the Sunday *Tagesspiegel*, the leading Berlin paper, cover-to-cover before he came to visit me. I was very impressed with how much Joachim knew. Soon my parents did not need an alarm clock on Sundays; they could count on Joachim ringing the doorbell at three o'clock sharp.

We had a huge bag of dried beans in the attic that somebody had given Vati, in payment for a job. Klärchen and I were very anxious to buy a used portable record player. (Nothing new was on the market.) But where to get the money? Then we had an idea. We stole beans out of our attic bag and sold them to Klärchen's grandmother at black-market prices. She had money but no food, and was so happy to get some beans. That fact was not good enough to make us proud of our caper, but it did not make us ashamed enough to stop, before we had enough money to buy the portable record player. To the music from that little gramophone, Joachim and I danced hours away in our kitchen. The record player had to be wound up by hand. But no matter how tightly wound, it did not make it through a 78 RPM record without slowing down at the end. It did not matter to us, we just danced slower. Dancing in the kitchen with rubber heels left many black marks. For every hour of dancing, we scrubbed an hour to remove the black lines from the blue and white tiles. School was becoming more and more demanding, and it was forever competing with my social life. In addition to English, French and Latin that were obligatory, I had the chance to study Italian. Because of my Italian citizenship, it was offered gratis, courtesy of the German government. I chose to be too busy with other things; I passed up an opportunity I have regretted all my life!

My Second Trip To Italy

My Italian father met his wife, Frieda Natali, at the university in Tuscany, where he was studying Medicine. She was an American of Italian descent from Elizabeth, Pennsylvania. After she met my father, she changed her major, and joined him in the study of medicine. My grandmother, Elfriede Antze Bacigalupo, was overjoyed with the good influence Frieda had on her son. Realizing he needed to normalize his life, he finally decided to settle down and marry Frieda, to the delight of his mother. Frieda knew Clara from prior years, and was very aware of my existence in Berlin.

My father, Bubi, and his wife, Frieda

So in 1950, Frieda initiated the invitation for me to come to *Rapallo,* near Genoa, so I could meet my Italian family. It was quite a summer! My father, known as 'Bubi' to everyone, was still in his thirties, less than half the age of Vati Uhlenbrock. The Italian Riviera was breathtakingly beautiful, especially after seeing nothing but ruins for years. Here the world was untouched by war. One evening, 'Bubi', took me dancing. The windows of the restaurant looked out over the Mediterranean Sea, making it seem as if we were floating on the water. Everybody stared, wondering who I was. The people in Rapallo seemed very elegant and rich to me. The stores reflected exclusive taste and the price tags were accordingly high.

Rapallo Harbor with my father's sailboat in the middle foreground

Massimo and Andrea Bacigalupo

Employed in my father's house were a nanny, a maid and a cook. Meals were still served with white gloves; a world apart from the world I knew! I met my two adorable half-brothers, the baby Andrea, who could ask for 'water' in three languages and an absolutely beautiful three-year-old boy who started every sentence with *'warum'* (why). Our German grandmother, Elfriede Bacigalupo, insisted that the boys have a German *Fräulein* who spoke exclusively German with them, while they had to speak English with their American mother, Frieda – I was impressed.

I shared a room with Frieda's niece, Geraldine, who was visiting from America. She was a few years older than I and so self-assured that it made me uncomfortable. She spoke English to the Italians, whether they understood her or not. She went through all the small, elegant boutiques, touching everything but buying nothing! In Germany that was not customary, and it caused me considerable embarrassment. That was a state in which I found myself easily.

My father and I on the Vagabonda

In the Bacigalupo household everything ran like clockwork. Frieda took charge; she arranged the schedule of what we were to do and where we were to go. She told me where to sit and when to kiss my father. Until I got to know what a wonderful person she was, I only felt intimidated. At eight in the morning, Frieda saw patients in her practice; at nine, Bubi saw his. Neither had to leave the house, because their examining rooms were next to their living quarters. Then house calls were made, and at eleven, everyone gathered on their sailboat, the *Vagabonda,* for the daily sail. At one o'clock sharp, lunch was served, then everyone took a nap, and at five we all met for tea in the garden-arbor at my grandparents' villa, *La Buona Terra.* There, the family got together daily.

147

Adriana and her daughters

My aunt, Adriana Taliaferro, Bubi's younger sister, would be there with her two girls, Juliana and Roberta, who were just a little older than my two brothers. Adriana had also studied medicine, but never practiced. She wanted to be with her children. Her husband, Alberto Taliaferro, was the head-surgeon at the Hospital in Genoa. He was the only one who seldom joined the family gatherings, because he had little free time. I noticed that he was very pale, compared to the others, possibly because he was seldom in the sun. (A few years later, he died suddenly of acute leukemia.) My grandmother, a pediatrician, made house calls in the late afternoon and therefore was seldom home for dinner; so joining her at teatime was very important, and a way of paying respect to her.

It did not take me long to notice that Bubi was very conscious of women's appearance; who was beautiful and who was not. I had just turned seventeen, and for the first time in my life, I felt very awkward, sometimes even like an ugly duckling. A big fever blister had broken out on my lip, which did not enhance my appearance. For a few days I hid away in my room as much as I could. One day, my Grandmother took me to an

Dr. Elfriede Bacigalupo

art show of a promising young artist, and bought me a picture of a sailboat that I liked very much. I still have it hanging in my living room today. On our way back, my grandmother asked what

I was planning to study. I said, "I want to become a psychologist, and do social work to help improve poor peoples' lives." She was not impressed. She said, "In this family we are all medical doctors. Should you decide to become one, we will pay for your education." – And that was that!

My grandfather, Massimo Bacigalupo, showed a lot of affection toward me. I felt a bond with him from the moment we met. Unfortunately, he was the only one whose German language ability was limited.

Grandfather and I on the Pasagiata in Rapallo

My mother Clara

Frieda had made arrangements for me to spend the last two weeks of my visit in Rome with my mother, Clara. I had met her only once before, when I was four years old. It was when I was urged to kiss her and refused because 'I didn't like the Italians.' I can still see Clara waiting for me at the railroad station in Rome. I knew her right away, although I had never even seen a picture of her.

I see her laughing eyes, and feel the way she took me into her arms with such joyous warmth, so much a part of her personality. In order to spend the first day uninterrupted together, Clara had rented a room in a hotel. She remembered only a little German and not much English, but we had no problem communicating. The following morning, together in an enormous bed in a very plush room, we talked a lot. She told me how much she had loved Bubi, but since he was married to Frieda, his life had become so regimented that she could not recognize the man she once had known. She seemed very amused about that. When she laughed, one

Adrian Rimoldi

wanted to laugh with her. Clara had no ill feelings toward the Bacigalupos, not even toward Grandmother Elfriede. Although she had been the one who had sent her away seventeen years ago, pregnant and alone to a foreign country, to get her and her son separated.

Clara also told me about her husband, Adriano Rimoldi, Bubi's friend, who had given up his medical studies for a career in broadcasting. Later he became an actor. I just happened to have seen him in Berlin in the movie *Carmen*. He was an air force pilot in WW II. Not long into the war, he decided to take off for Spain. He did not, or could not, come back after the war. Clara did not want to leave Rome and her beloved mother, who was living there. But she would drive yearly to Spain with her two girls, Simonetta and Donatella, to visit their father. (Later, Adriano had a woman and a child in Spain, but returned to Italy and to Clara, when he was terminally ill with throat cancer.)

While I was listening to her, we were still in bed. I played nervously with a button, dangling over my headboard. Suddenly our door flew open. It looked as if every male employee of the Hotel had rushed to our room, to take care of the 'emergency'. Clara burst into laughter, pulled the cover over our heads and explained that we had pressed the call button accidentally. All those men in their starched hotel uniforms excused themselves and disappeared. I don't know when we stopped laughing. When we finally got up that morning, I could see through Clara's beautiful nightgown, a perfectly round mole on her buttocks. I had a spot just like that, at the exact same place. It made me feel connected in some strange way. Decades later,

Momino, Clara's brother, Nicola and I

a dermatologist insisted that it had to be removed, to be checked for cancer. As I expected, it was benign. I am still angry that the spot that Clara and I had in common was taken from me.

The two-week period with Clara was a teenager's dream, and went by like a whirlwind. Rome was very exciting as well as very hot. We went everywhere possible. Clara introduced me to a handsome young man, named Nicola. From then on, he was our constant companion. We went to Naples, where I ate my first pizza, swimming in oil, with cheese stringing from the plate to my mouth. Then we went to pick up my two half-sisters from a convent-school. Every day we went to feed their huge dog, *Lione,* loaned out as a guard dog to Clara's American friends, to guard an Army compound. I never figured out exactly what that was all about. There were so many visual and emotional impressions that I had a hard time sorting everything out. We were constantly on the go, with little sleep interspersed.

Soon after my arrival in Rome, Clara took me to meet her mother, my maternal grandmother. Clara was well rounded and quite a bit shorter than I, but her mother was tiny. She looked up at me as if I were a Greek goddess. She also was very warm. She kept repeating, how happy it made her that she had such a beautiful granddaughter. How sad that we did not speak the same language, and we saw each other only one more time, nine years later.

After that really wonderful trip to Italy, there was no confusion in my mind. No matter how much I liked my biological parents, Mutti and Vati were my parents, because they were the ones who cradled me in their arms, when I was a baby; who sat with me, when I was sick; who held my hand, when bombs and bullets flew all around us and who loved me, because I was their child.

ABITUR

The train took me back from Italy to Frankfurt. The people who boarded in Basel spoke the wonderful sounds of a familiar language. The Swiss dialect made it difficult to understand what was said, but the sound of German heightened my anticipation of home. I took 'Pan Am' from Frankfurt. It was still the only airline that civilians were allowed to use through the 'air corridor' to Berlin, across the Russian-occupied German territory.

Home again, I was walking on air. The ruins of Berlin greeted me like dear old friends. Sharing my travel memories with my parents and my friends was almost as exciting as the trip itself. I was in love with love, and Nicola had added a proverbial Italian romance to my five-week holiday. However, there wasn't much time for daydreaming. The reality of serious studying was looming on the horizon.

School started with a big surprise. When I walked up the stairs and looked through the window onto the courtyard, I saw boys playing volleyball. Why did we have boys in our all-girl school? There were four of them. It took me a while to adjust to the unfamiliar sight, but it took little time to know, which guy of the four looked most interesting! I pointed him out to a classmate, standing next to me, who was as surprised as I was.

A day or two later, on our way to the washroom, this classmate noticed the very boy who had caught my eye. She said in an exaggerated loud voice, "Look, there is the one you like." I was so embarrassed that I slapped her, just so he would not think I put her up to that remark. I had never done anything like that before, and felt awful afterwards.

I apologized and eventually we made up. With or without help, I soon met the boy, Heinz, when I was recruited by classmates to become part of the schools volleyball team. Almost daily, we trained to play competitively against other West-Berlin schools. (I liked sports a lot and I loved this after-school activity). My position was left front, Heinz happened to play behind me. We had ample opportunity to get acquainted Berlin-style. We drew attention to each other with unflattering remarks. I thought it fun that co-education was now obligatory in the American Sector of Berlin, to match American schools.

Heinz Malskat

Nicola and I wrote each other using our limited English. But this great love soon cooled when Nicola explained that he was too scared to visit me in Berlin. Since the Russian Zone surrounded Berlin, he suggested that I meet him some place in the West-Zone. I was not impressed with that proposal and I knew my parents' answer to the idea, so I did not even ask.

Marlene surprised me when she decided she wanted to use her artistic talents to become a make-up artist. Consequently, instead of staying in school and working toward the *Abitur,* she opted for a three-year apprenticeship in a hair salon. I did not know about it until her mother came to school to have her released. I was so devastated that I went home, crawled into bed and cried for hours. Mutti sat by my side, begging me to stop crying. She tried to console me by saying, "Afterall I am your my best friend." I heard her words and knew that she was right, but it didn't change the feeling that I was losing the friend with whom I had shared my every day.

One of the newer girls in my class was Sigrun Eichelberg. She had joined us after she had escaped a Russian's unwanted attention in Fürstenwalde, where she had gone to highschool. A Russian soldier had noticed her because she was so very attractive. When the soldier came to her school, he explained that she had been selected to be sent to Russia. She was to study in a Russian political school for young Germans. Her teacher became suspicious. He told her to hide in the washroom. After he got rid of the Russian, the teacher told Sigrun to take the first train to West Berlin to stay with her aunt.

Sigrun Eichelberg

I had not paid much attention to Sigrun until I saw her tears. I heard her explain to Frl. Krüger, our homeroom teacher, that she had no money to continue school. Her aunt charged her 15 West-Mark a month for a space in her pantry that was the exact size of a bed. (The pantry was also the coldest and darkest room in any Berlin apartment, meant to keep food fresh.) Sigrun's aunt was of the opinion that Sigrun should find a job and not continue school. Then she would not have to accept the money of 'our government' for support. Her opinion may have been influenced by the fact that her own daughter had not continued school. Sigrun's mother had been forced to work for the Russians for very little compensation, and she was paid in East-Mark, worth only one-fourth of the West-Mark Sigrun needed. Her mother also had a younger son to support. Sigrun's father had been a school principal. He had been forced to join the *Volkssturm* and lost his life in the final battle of the war.

Sigrun seemed to be without hope. I told the story to my mother, she said immediately, "Bring her home and we will share our food with her, at least twice a week." Not long thereafter, our homeroom teacher, Frl. Krüger, offered Sigrun a room, free of charge, so she could continue school.

Our dinners together were the beginning of a life-long friendship. At first, I did not quite trust Sigrun, because she was so nice that even my critical Mutti liked her instantly. I still remember her words after Sigrun's first visit, "What a beautiful girl, one enjoys just looking at her." Sigrun started calling Mutti her 'Mutti II' and brought homemade little gifts for her. She made a pig out of a lemon for good luck. She used matchsticks for legs; on the round end she pinned a piece of curly yarn for a tail. At the opposite end, she cut a slot to hold a good-luck penny. The ears were easily carved out of the rind. Mutti was charmed. Sigrun was appreciative and caring and I soon learned that she was as beautiful on the inside as on the outside. She was smart and a good student, too. We would study together and we became closer and closer friends and she helped me a lot.

The Americanization of our school system had taken its toll. Without much preparation, we had been given a choice of which classes to take and which to drop. Many of my classmates took advantage of that freedom, but did not realize the price they would pay later.

German 'higher education' still prided itself on its introduction to a wide variety of basic knowledge. This included literature like Milton's *Paradise Lost* (in English!) and Dante's *Inferno.* Most of us much preferred *Gone with the Wind* or *A Place in the Sun,* novels exciting even in a foreign language. Subjects like Biology, Physics, Chemistry, History and Geography had been all mandatory for everyone. Now many students dropped the subjects they did not like. That resulted in only eighteen of my classmates passing the eligibility for the final examinations.

Our class had been split into liberal arts, math and science. Those that chose the latter suffered greatly under Barkow's poor teaching method. Many of us had memorized his math problems like knitting patterns, a poor foundation for calculus. While our great French and English teachers pulled us through those exams, Dr.Tangel's Latin was disastrous. During the final exams the stress factor was immeasurable. We were still paying for those 'out-of-control' years, right after the war.

Sigrun was introduced to a friend, visiting her cousin, a Walter Hoch. He swept her off her feet with chocolates and roses. He was much older, quite good-looking and accomplished. He was an assistant professor of mathematics at the *Technische Hochschule von Berlin*. If this was not impressive enough, he also owned a taxi-cab company, at a time when most people still struggled frantically to survive the devaluation of the *Reichsmark*. Walter Hoch tutored Sigrun and me in math. He was ever so amazed how cleverly we had progressed, knowing so little.

Walter Hoch may have been helpful with math lessons, but as a suitor, he was too busy pursuing his own success. It took most all of his time. When he took Sigrun back into the East Zone to meet his parents – knowing full well the danger in which he placed her – Mutti was appalled by how little he cared.

Their trip ended in an amusing story, never forgotten in our family. Sigrun told us about their return in a cab, when Walter suddenly sneezed. "It was not a sneeze, it was an explosion," she said. Telling us the story, she ended with these words, "One thing I know for sure, Georg would have never sneezed like that!" – Sigrun had not dated anybody in Berlin before Walter. When she had to flee her hometown, Saarow, she had left behind her highschool-love, Georg. (None of us ever met 'Georg.' My kids may not even know how the story originated, but they know how 'Georg' would – or wouldn't – have sneezed.) We all have learned to constrain our sneezes to sneeze as 'elegantly as Georg!'

As the days of the final examinations drew closer, the nightmare of facing the oral exams under the eyes of the school board delegation – with their golden watch chains and condescending demeanor – became more real.

We each had to submit our personal history before being admitted to the exams. I had to make a special request for a waiver, because I was not yet 18 years old. That hurdle was overcome successfully, with Mutti's help. She knew how to approach people, even stuffy ones.

With everything at stake, I pulled my lazy-self together and studied. I managed to pass the preliminary exams. Now the trick was, to have the final written examinations match previous grades. A noticeable discrepancy meant an oral examination.

I was always called on last, because my last name started with a 'U' for 'Uhlenbrock'. It made me wait until the end to find out in what subjects I was to be orally tested. That wait was a well deserved punishment for not fully applying myself all those years. When I heard my name called, "Uhlenbrock - Organic and Inorganic Chemistry - Sugars and Alcohols," I sighed a sigh of relief. That was not too bad! I sweated it out – and I passed.

PREPARATION FOR EMIGRATION

Berlin's *Magistrat*, (the government of the City), was Vati's main client. It was situated in the Russian-controlled sector of Berlin. The *Magistrat* had the jurisdiction over all of Berlin. The Soviets felt they at least should have unlimited rights in their own East Sector. Soon, the different democratic political parties were forced to move to the 'West', because communist demonstrators disrupted sessions of parliament. Then the 'East' appointed a new City Council, acceptable only to them.

The sudden division of Berlin was a big blow to Vati's business. In fact, his workers were making repairs in the dilapidated *Reichstags*-building – located right on the East-West border – when the division of Berlin became official. They managed to escape with our irreplaceable tools that they had been ordered to leave behind, through the windows facing the West Sector.

The newly established West-Berlin government had very little money. It had to bargain-shop for everything. That made it very tough for Vati. He had a hard time competing with the prices of younger contractors, who used old pipes from bombed-out buildings, defying danger and the law. Plumbing supplies were very difficult to find and expensive. Over and over, Mutti tried to convince Vati to sell his business, while his name was still worth money. She thought it might bring enough money for us to survive financially, if he also collected his Social Security pension. But, it was in vain. Vati could not imagine a life without his firm; after all, he 'was' his business! As far as 'collecting Social Security' was concerned, it was not a consideration and best not to be mentioned. Only needy people claimed Social Security! As usual, Mutti's advice went unheeded.

Inge had not seen her mother in thirteen years, so she invited her for a visit to the United States. Mutti would not hear of it, unless I was included in the invitation. So Inge took steps to secure a visa for both of us. The processing for a visitor's visa took a long time. The required thorough background check had generated a long waiting list. Though our family had been scrutinized already, when Inge applied for a job with the Central Intelligence Agency, we had to wait like all the others.

While we were waiting for our visas, Inge suggested, we should apply for immigration. "You can always go back, but I think, there is a much better future for *Cisi* over here," she said in her letter. Vati was only too happy with the plan. Without any mouths to feed but his own, he could plough every penny back into his business and hang in a while longer. He said, "When I can't make it anymore, I shall follow you. I have always wanted to see the United States."

I was not enthusiastic at all. I was in love with Heinz. He was still in school, because he was six months younger and a grade below. In fact, he had an additional school year ahead; the requirement now was 13 years! To make my parting easier, I concocted the unrealistic idea in my head that I might be able to find a job in the United States and earn enough money to put him through university. – 'What was economically impossible in Germany, just might be possible in America' –

Immediately after graduation, while we were waiting for our visas, I enrolled in a business school to study accounting, typing and English shorthand to make myself marketable. I hoped it would pay off, and it did. In fact, it got me a good job in Berlin.

Employment was scarce in Berlin. Employers with jobs, could pick and choose whom to hire. They even required an *Abitur* for selling shoes. I looked through the newspaper and saw an ad by Becker, a crane-manufacturing company. I recognized the name because I had seen the owner. He drove a big Chevrolet, very conspicuous at a time when hardly anybody owned a car. Certainly not such a gas-guzzler!

As requested, I mailed in my personal history, all my report cards, and a cover letter. I was surprised to get an interview. I remember sitting nervously in the 'inner sanctum,' waiting for a moment of Herr Becker's time. While I was waiting, I heard him shout at everybody as if they were deaf. Later, I saw that he had been using an intercom. Listening to him made me certain that I would never get the job. All my previous anxiety had dissipated by the time I got to meet him. He bellowed only a few questions at me, and I was dismissed. I thought that was that, but to my surprise, I was called back for a second interview! Being used to shouting from my father, it did not impress me much! I said what was on my mind: "I wonder, Herr Becker, why you are always shouting. When I first met you, I thought you disliked me. Now, that you called me back, you are still talking to me in such a loud voice?" He asked me, somewhat calmer, whether I had anything else to say. I answered, "No," and found myself dismissed again. A day later, his secretary called to tell me to report for work the next morning.

For my first month with that company, I did nothing but return applications and report cards with a letter of regret. I wondered why I had been chosen. Maybe because of my business school, or maybe he was impressed that I found the courage to talk back to him.

My job was very boring, and the hours passed slowly. I did not know for what he was paying me. But, it became more interesting when I was sent to his other business ventures, like his Real Estate Co. It took me six months to realize that I was being trained to become Herr Becker's administrative assistant. A very pleasant Fräulein Rose, who had been friendly and helpful to me, held that job but she never let on what they had planned for me. When I found out, I felt awful.

I had purposely not mentioned my intention to emigrate to the U. S., knowing full well that it would have prevented me from being hired. I will never forget how embarrassed I was, when I finally had to tell them!

The labor law in Germany required a minimum of four weeks notice, prior to the first of the month. Therefore, after I had told them, they could not fire me immediately. Instead, they sent me to the accounting office of their crane factory, clear across town. I bicycled daily for one hour, only to be greeted with open disdain. When I mustered the courage to ask why I was treated like an enemy, I was told that several long-time workers felt that I had stolen their job opportunity. They had been aware of my job designation, long before I knew it. I left a week early, because I could not handle their animosity any longer.

Packing up for the U.S. was hard. We took some dishes, crystal and some smaller rugs, among other things. Everything was packed into crates. I sat on the floor looking through old letters and mementoes that had been tucked away for years. One of them was a *Meissen*-cup with a gold inscription. Translated it said: 'For his Father's Pride and his Mother's Joy, Today Alfred leaves his first year behind!'The cup was for my Uncle Alfred's first birthday. It belonged to the same Alfred who had been blind and killed in Auschwitz. I sat on the floor, looked at the cup, and cried for a long time.

I also found an old letter. It was written in 1933 in the old German script. In that letter somebody, with the name of Margarethe, wrote how happy she was that Hitler was now our *Führer,* (leader) and how good that was for Germany. I read it a few times and then asked my mother, "Who in the world is the Nazi who wrote that letter to you?" Mutti said that it was her stepdaughter, Grete, whom I was to meet in London a few weeks later.

Leaving Germany – A New Start

It was the first day of October 1952, and my last day in Berlin. I stayed overnight with Ulla, and it was the first time that I ever spent a night at a friend's place. It also was the first sleepless night of my nineteen-year-old life. I was crying, not knowing how to say 'good-bye' the coming day. It amazes me now that I never questioned how Mutti felt, who was leaving her home after a lifetime. I was in such emotional pain, I could not think about anybody but myself.

Assi and I

The second of October was a day without daylight. Berlin was soaking in rain. The city seemed to be crying with me. We took a cab to Tempelhof Airport. I had just said 'good-bye' to Assi, my German shepherd. How could she understand that our dear and caring housekeeper would be her new family and promised to take good care of her from now on?

I had not recuperated from my first good-bye, when we went through the gate at the airport, and Vati was standing there waiving *"Auf Wiedersehen."* I somehow knew that I would never see him again. I seem to remember that Heinz came just before we took off. By this time, sadness had overwhelmed me and had left me numb. When the plane lifted off into the grey sky, I felt that I was being carried away from everything I loved. Mutti said nothing; she showed no sign of emotion. I left nineteen years behind; she, sixty-seven! I cannot imagine how she must have felt!

Inge had everything arranged. She had even sent us the tickets for the *Maasdam* of the Holland America Line. She left from Southampton and was to arrive in Hoboken, New Jersey. But first we stayed two weeks in London. My sister Ruth welcomed us with the excitement and the warmth I remembered so well from our vacation in Italy and her visit to Berlin in 1948. She did everything possible to make our stay enjoyable.

Ruth and Walter

Ruth had a one-room flat at Westbourne Court, near Kensington Gardens. There she lived very modestly with Walter, whom she had married in 1946. Their flat consisted of a livingroom-bedroom combination. Across the hall were kitchen and bathroom. They were divided only by a freestanding wall, which allowed outside air to come in from the bathroom window to the kitchen. In the kitchen there was only standing room for one. Although very small, everything was meticulously clean and looked inviting. Ruth was a vegetarian since childhood. Whether it was the soil of England or her cooking, she prepared the best vegetables I had ever eaten before or since.

Mutti did not care much for Walter. Walter with his Austrian-German dialect had the sweet mannerisms that seemed so affected to Prussians. Instead of 'How do you do?' he would say, 'Kiss your hand, Madame,' and actually do it. He had a hunchback, which made him shorter than Ruth who was barely 5'2". But she loved her Walter dearly and they were very happily married – penniless but happy. I guess the 'pennilessness' was Mutti's main complaint. Walter had been a film director in Prague. He lost his first wife and everything he possessed because of the Nazis, and he had no luck starting over with any sort of job in London. Ruth's secretarial work sustained them.

Mutti and I slept at the 'Kowalski's.' Their dark rooms and even darker furniture were an inspiration to write ghost stories. Once in bed, I did not dare open my eyes until daylight; I was afraid of what I might see. The curtains, as well as the fabric on the chairs, all had a dusty appearance.

When Ruth first came to London, she had worked for the Kowalskis, cleaning their flat. (Maid level jobs were the only jobs immigrants were allowed to hold.) Ruth became like a daughter to them and they remained friends throughout the years.

I knew from Ruth that the Kowalskis wanted very much – and succeeded – for their only daughter to marry into British society. That was no easy task for refugees and Polish Jews, but they succeeded. Mercedes Stappenbeck, a classmate of mine, had been looking for a job, where she could improve her English. It so happened that the Kowalskis', now well situated daughter was looking for a nanny for her two boys. Unfortunately, she believed in raising her kids 'free-style'. The boys were never told 'no'. Taking care of these boys turned into a nightmare.

During our stay in London, we were invited to dinner at the beautiful villa of the Kowalski's daughter. Half through the formal meal, something like a fire alarm went off. Everybody in the household scrambled to the front door, including Mercedes. Soon it became obvious that the disturbance was caused by their boys, who did not wish to be kept waiting. One was ten, the other twelve years old, and they entered the dining room like wild horses. They jumped up to sit on the sideboard, ignoring the chairs that were waiting for them. When they leaped back down, I was surprised that the crystal did not come tumbling down after them. From then on, everything was a blur. Those boys were so loud and unruly that no conversation was possible, and nobody said a word to admonish them. Mercedes had been told never to punish the boys, even when they tore off her eyeglasses and broke them. It became very clear to me how not to raise my children.

That experience colored Mercedes' view of London. She explained that London's mental institutions are filled to capacity, therefore there are so many crazies walking the streets. (I often thought of my classmate and London, when I saw the many homeless and hopeless street-people in Washington. They all seemed to have shown up during – and ever since – the Reagan Administration.)

Mutti Passport picture 1947

My first impression of any city was related to how much was – or was not – destroyed by bombs. In 1952, London seemed fully intact to me. I was surprised to see no missile damage, when my sister's young friend Heinz took me sightseeing. Mutti had met his mother, when both were waiting for an 'inter-zone' passport. Heinz' mother also was anxious to travel to London to see her son, whom she had not seen for many long years. She was Jewish, her husband was not. To protect him from the Nazis, they had sent away their only child to be raised in England.

After seeing many of London's historical sights, I especially enjoyed Hyde Park with its eccentric public speakers, literally standing on soapboxes. I could have stayed there for hours listening, as each presented his or her provocative agenda.

And then there was the evening when we visited Grete. She was quite short and round but not fat. She was bubbly and full of energy, warm, hospitable and generous. I felt close to her immediately, as if I had known her all my life. She was industrious and ambitious and had always earned good money. She spoke French and English fluently and, of course German, her mother tongue. She served us lobster tails – something I had never eaten before – but I got used to them real quickly.

Grete was also peculiar. Before we ever sat down at a beautifully laid table, she informed us that we had to walk very carefully, because she had china plates under her rug. Questioned why, she explained that she lived in the same house with a 'prostitute', whom she suspected of having keys to her place and nosing around in her apartment. Mutti and Ruth did not seem to be as surprised as I was, because Grete was known for her crazy stories. A little later, during our dinner, we heard a car honk in front of the house. Grete ran over to the window and shouted to us, "There he is!" Mutti asked who 'he' was. Grete explained that it was the man who picked up the so called prostitute. Mutti pried further, "How do you know who was being picked up by the man in the car?" Grete was caught unprepared, "Well, I know her boyfriend; he comes every night!" "If that is so, I don't think that she is a prostitute", said Mutti. We all laughed but Grete did not find it funny and was not about to change her story. Walter had not come with us, because he said that he was actually afraid of Grete and therefore avoided her. I learned through the years that he knew what he was talking about, and that he was not exaggerating.

After two weeks in London, we continued our journey to Southampton, where the 'Maasdam' was waiting for us. It was only her second voyage across the Atlantic. It was an indescribable feeling to see a ship of that size and luxury. She was bigger and fancier than any hotel I had ever seen, with swimming pools and sauna, playgrounds, movie theaters and a never-ending dining room.

SS Maasdam

The Atlantic Ocean lay like a mirror in front of us. There was not a ripple to be seen. The first evening, when the sun set, it looked like an unrealistic painting. It was so quiet that one could not tell whether we were standing still or moving; even the ship's engines were not audible. Time seemed to stand still, too. I walked around the ship in a daze. There were some French soldiers trying to talk to me, but I had a hard time understanding them. I had already forgotten all the French I had studied. Mutti and I went to the movie theater on the ship. They showed one of Jerry Lewis' films. That was my first indication that it takes more to understand a country than just to know the language. I wanted to laugh like the others, but this type of comedy did not seem at all funny to Mutti or me.

It was our third day on the ocean, when suddenly there was a strange industriousness. The crew and the staff scurried around. Tables and chairs were bolted down, and ropes were strung everywhere. I had no idea what was to come.

It got stormier and stormier. Nobody was allowed on deck; they would have been blown overboard. Doors to the outside were bolted shut. People were seasick wherever one looked. It did not take me long to join them. I, who had suffered motion sickness in a bus, learned fast about real seasickness. Until almost the last day, I could not get into a vertical position. I dreamed about a piece of earth that did not move. But there was no such place in sight. My mother, who seemed immune to seasickness, started counting the people left in the dining room. There were fewer every day and then, she and a very old lady were the only ones left in that huge diningroom.

Lifeboat Drill

The day before we docked at Hoboken, the ocean finally calmed down, but not my stomach. I had not eaten a bite in six days. I was so exhausted, that I could hardly get up on deck to see why everybody was singing, "God bless America, my home, sweet home!" We were passing the Statue of Liberty. It was a moving experience, and I was envious that so many people were actually coming home.

It was the morning of the 28th of October 1952, when our ship pulled into the harbor. My stomach was still very queasy. We waited hours, until all the luggage and crates were unloaded and separated for customs inspection. I stood there in my thick-soled and high-heeled shoes (similar to those worn again forty-six years later). Some time during that day, we finally got to meet Inge and Gerry, and an eleven-year-old neighbor-girl, Sharon. Prior to our arrival, Inge and Gerry, having no children of their own, had used the opportunity to spend three days with Sharon to show her New York City.

By the time we were through customs, it was evening and we were exhausted. Little did we know what lay ahead. Inge and Gerry had planned to drive us back, that very night, to their home in Virginia. At the time, the trip took at least seven hours, including one milkshake stop at Howard Johnson's. The Woodrow Wilson Bridge, stretching over the Potomac from Maryland to Virginia, was still a dream, realized only a decade later. So we had to go the long way through Washington, D.C. It was a very cold night, and we were freezing and very tired. Inge explained to us that their car did not heat well in the back; therefore they wanted the neighbor-girl to sit on the bench seat in front, between Inge and Gerry. There was only English spoken in the car, 'so Sharon could understand what was said!' It was not a good way to get re-acquainted after thirteen years of separation.

I got carsick on top of my lingering seasickness. It seemed to me as if we were driving straight through to California. I had no idea of the distances in the U. S. I was too sick and befuddled to take notice of how peculiar Inge's behavior had been, but Mutti cried herself to sleep that night. I had never known her to cry, except for the time she received the notice that her brother had died, or better said, had been murdered by the Nazis. I felt lonely and scared of things to come.

Learning About Life In America

The first day we spent admiring the immaculately kept Mosler home. There were two bedrooms and one bath upstairs. On the first floor there was a living-dining room combination, as well as a small kitchen with a screened-in porch in the back. Everything was like new; the hardwood floors were polished and without a scratch. The house was located about a mile south of Alexandria, Virginia, in the Huntington Subdivision.

Inge and Gerald Mosler

Inge introduced us to her world by starting every sentence with, "In America . . ." as if it were the uncontested norm. She said to me "In America, girls your age wear their hair short; nobody wears long hair like you." Soon we were familiar with everything from the pressure cooker to the refrigerator and, of course, the television. The TV was still something of a novelty then – in black and white only – and three channels. There was little conversation in our new home. When we mentioned anything about our 'previous life,' Inge walked out, as if nobody had spoken. She did not want to know about our years in Germany. She did not ask how we had survived or how Vati was doing, and – in turn – did not have anything to say about her life. Her work was an enigma to us, and after work she wanted to watch TV. 'After all, she had been away from home all day.'

On the second day, after having been by ourselves for twelve hours again, Mutti and I mentioned that we would like to walk to Alexandria, where we could see something. Inge warned, "In America people don't walk much, and for goodness sake, do not go into a stranger's car, should you be offered a ride." We did not consider that a problem, because neither of us was looking for a ride, just a place where we could walk. There were some sidewalks in the immediate neighborhood, but very soon there was a fence where the development ended. Everywhere else there were only paved roads for cars.

After so little stimulation at our new home, we became adventurous. We walked the two blocks to Huntington Avenue. There we turned left and walked to Route #1, and then left again to go north on Richmond Highway (Route 1) to Alexandria City proper. We had fun because it made us feel somewhat self-reliant again. Since leaving England, we had only been transported by ship or automobile.

We had a good time getting acquainted with Alexandria. We stopped at the King Street bakery and decided to wait in line for a piece of cake. When it was our turn, the saleslady called, "You girls are next!" I stepped up to the counter when Mutti held me back and argued, "She did not mean us! She couldn't call me a girl!" But, she had called us. – We had our first lesson in American culture.

We were on our way back and had just reached Richmond Highway again, when it started raining. We soon were cold and wet. Cars traveling south toward Fort Belvoir splashed muddy water on us. Every so often, somebody stopped to offer us a lift. "No, no, thank you," we said heeding Inge's warning. As we were walking on, we got muddier, more soaked, and more uncomfortable. We had noticed that most of the cars that stopped had a young man, in army uniform, at the wheel. Finally our resistance wore thin, and we decided to take a chance. We reasoned, 'after all, there were two of us!'

The next car that stopped just happened to be driven by a very kind, and equally persuasive, young man; so we accepted his offer. He took us straight to Inge and Gerry's house. Before we could say 'thank you' and 'good-bye', he asked whether he could make a date to show me Washington, DC. Mutti got very nervous and told me in German that I could not go with a stranger. It did not take a linguist to understand what she was saying. The young soldier immediately offered to take her along. When Mutti saw that I was interested in going, she very reluctantly agreed. I guess, we both thought that the way things were going, this might be our only opportunity to see Washington, DC.

Punctually the next day, the young man arrived to pick us up. He explained that in the rear seat of his car he had a 'buddy', whom he had promised to drop off at National Airport. He explained further that the airport was located on our way to Washington.

We crawled into the automobile. I sat in the middle of the front bench and Mutti to my right. When we came to Huntington Avenue, our driver turned right instead of left. We were going in the opposite direction we had walked before! Mutti said to me in German, "I have not seen this area before." I had to agree, but it did not worry me, and I chose not to answer. Five minutes later, Mutti made a similar remark, while she was getting noticeably more worried. The third time was the charm. This time she added, . . . "And I worry about the man in the back. He could easily hit us over the head!" There was a moment of silence, while I was feeling very uncomfortable. I have to admit that I had started wondering myself where we were going. I was also very embarrassed that Mutti spoke in German, so we could not be understood. – Suddenly a very nice and calm voice from the back seat said in perfect German, "You don't have to worry, Ma'am, my friend is honorable, and I wouldn't think of hitting you over the head!" I turned bright red, which lasted the entire sightseeing date. Every time I calmed down, I would hear the voice of the 'buddy' in the back seat again, although he had been dropped off a long time ago. We learned a very important lesson: Don't speak German and assume you wont to be understood. Might as well whisper, which is similarly rude!

Inge suggested that I look for a job as soon as possible. She said that all the department stores were hiring extra help for the Christmas season. She was right. I went into Woodward and Lothrop in Washington, DC and was hired immediately for wrapping Christmas gifts. Boxes, paper and beautiful cloth ribbons were all included with the smallest purchase. To my surprise, people bought the most impractical gifts, as if they did not know what to do with their money. I got a real insight into America's wealth. I had great fun making pretty gifts out of insignificant purchases. With my discount, I could send Christmas gifts to all my friends and pay Inge the fifteen dollars per week that she had requested as soon as I was hired.

Mutti offered to prepare evening meals so that when Inge and Gerry got home, they could sit down and eat. On her way home, Inge bought groceries in the old Giant store in the northern part of Alexandria. She planned and organized all the meals and never failed to mention that if Mutti did not feel like cooking, it certainly was no necessity. "After all, I have done it myself for thirteen years, and can easily keep on doing it," she said. It may have sounded considerate, but it only contributed to Mutti's feeling of total uselessness. Before dinner could be served, Inge and Gerry would make themselves comfortable and sit down to watch favorite shows like *What's My Line?* or *The Dinah Shore Show*. While Gerry was always friendly and hospitable, Inge barely spoke a word. After dinner, Gerry liked to watch boxing or baseball. I enjoyed watching whatever was on, because it was new and interesting, and I could improve my English word-recognition. But Mutti grew more and more withdrawn. She had lost all appetite and spoke rarely.

Inge claimed that she had forgotten her mother tongue, but remembered it perfectly when German colleagues were visiting. It did not take long for us to realize that her job required her to use German all day long. When Mutti once asked why we never had any conversation, Inge told us that she was not allowed to speak about what she was doing. She also explained that 'The Agency' preferred her to associate only with people, with whom she worked. The ones we met were all Germans, still speaking German fluently.

The exception was the neighbor family, who occupied the other half of their duplex home. They were the Peters, parents of Sharon, the girl who had come along to Hoboken, when we arrived. Sharon had a new baby sister. Inge 'adored' her, and made a lot of fuss over her. The Peters were all born and raised in Alexandria and had a lot of relatives in the area. Mr. Peters was a bus driver for the A B & W bus line. Soon I would meet the whole Peters clan, when Inge insisted that I go bowling with them, which they did on a weekly basis. There I met their nephew, who had just been discharged from the Navy. He invited me to go dancing. We went to a dimly lighted dance hall, with a huge dance floor in the middle. It was furnished with long picnic-style tables and benches on two sides. It was all very new to me. It was customary for patrons to bring their own bottle of alcohol, while the establishment served 'set ups' for highballs. I learned that this was because Virginia was a so-called 'dry state'. The music was great. I was chauffeured in a brand-new 'Hudson' automobile. Never have I had a date with someone who owned an automobile. It was exciting! I made a flying entrance into the dance hall, by missing the steps leading down to the tables. Those who could not see me entering certainly heard me. It was another embarrassing situation! But my escort didn't mind; he was attentive and nice, and happy that I was not hurt. We danced the hours away and had a good time. In a foreign country, everything was a learning-experience.

I loved the romantic songs of the fifties. They could be heard on the streets of Alexandria when played very loud in Murphy's Five-and-Dime Store at King and Washington Streets. Every restaurant featured jukeboxes. The voices of Eddy Fisher, Patty Page, Teresa Brewer and of so many other vocalists, were sounding everywhere. Those romantic lyrics fed the imagination and dreams of a nineteen-year-old; but my mother had no dreams, just nightmares of what the future would hold.

The man of the hour was Eisenhower! His election was in full swing! Nixon was the number-two man. I seemed to have read about him first, in connection with the Joe McCarthy communist-witch hunt. I disliked Nixon from day one, but I felt quite different about Eisenhower. Eisenhower was very respected and well liked by Germans. He was considered the victor of the war in Europe and credited with freeing us from the Hitler regime.

Every night we sat in front of TV to follow the election-process. I had no idea what the two-party system was really like, nor did I know the platform of either party. But it was the excitement of learning about the American elections that kept me spellbound and made me forget my homesickness.

It was also the time of the Rosenbergs' spy-trial. I tried to read as much as I could about it, always thinking they were unfairly accused, and I was hoping for a break for them.

I was young and full of hope, but Mutti was getting sicker and sicker. She had lost thirty pounds in one month, her blood pressure was sky-high, and every night she cried herself to sleep. Her hopelessness for a future, as well as her disappointment over the loss of closeness to her daughter, seemed too much for her to bear. It added to Mutti's sadness that Inge had only unhappy childhood memories from her days in Germany. Mutti felt accused and hurt. She had raised her two girls alone for four years after their father died in 1916, and before she married Vati in 1920. Mutti saw no future for herself living with Inge, but had neither the means nor a plan to return to Germany!

"In America I do not feel too short; here I have learned that all men prefer short women," Inge proclaimed one night at the dinner table, targeting me because I was taller than she was. This time Mutti surprised me by answering, "That may be so, but who is interested in all men?" Inge was forty and I was nineteen. She had not liked me as a child, and now she blamed me for her bad relationship with her mother. Inge had been jealous of her older sister Ruth, as well. She claimed that Ruth was always the center of attention, when they were young. "Therefore, I had never considered helping Ruth to come to the States, even in those years when Ruth was alone and in need," she told us.

I noticed very soon that being young in America was considered an achievement in itself, quite a contrast to Germany! There I remember young people being constantly scrutinized, as if asked, 'what have you accomplished so far?' and 'what are you planning to do with your life?' I enjoyed the difference!

In those days, there were not many foreigners in the Washington DC area. When people heard my accent, most became interested in talking to me. Everybody was extremely friendly. Not so to my mother. Many persons inquired about her – right in her presence – as if she were deaf and dumb. Mutti had learned English in school many years ago, but still could understand and speak enough to answer. My school-English served me well. I was always thrilled when somebody thought I was British, because I had learned the British pronunciation in school. (Unfortunately, I think that my German accent became stronger over the years.)

I was constantly worrying about Mutti's health and unhappiness, and the increasingly bad atmosphere in the Mosler home. The lack of public transportation to and from Huntington was no joy either. Buses north- and south-bound to Ft. Belvoir ran only every fifty minutes, and hardly at all at night or on Sundays. Nothing was ever timed with any other bus connection. To travel seven miles from Washington DC to Huntington could take as long as two hours. November and December 1952 were rainy and cold. The bright headlights of on-coming traffic were blinding, on the then very narrow Huntington Avenue. There were no sidewalks; when two cars passed each other where I walked, they had to come to a complete stop. I learned to hate that road. Often my tears ran down my face, only camouflaged by rain – my nightly companion. I wondered why people talked about the heat in 'sunny' Virginia. I had to wait six months for it, but then it came with a vengeance.

Inge's boss, also quite a close friend, had found a stray cocker spaniel. He gave the dog to me, because he already had one. I did not want the responsibility, and was still mourning my German shepherd. It was traumatic for me to reject a dog and to deprive her of a home. I remember being embarrassed because I cried so bitterly in front of Inge's friend. Thank goodness, Irv had pity on me and agreed to keep the dog. I was relieved that I got out of this situation. It did not last long. To everybody's surprise, the cocker spaniel gave birth to numerous puppies not long thereafter. Inge, now wanting to help her friend again, decided to give me one of the puppies for Christmas. What was I to do now? I was furious but couldn't say a thing.

The dog, which we named Spotty, became poor Mutti's challenge. How could we house-train him without damaging Inge's impeccable floors? Mutti took him out constantly and even made the ultimate sacrifice to put him on her bed, to keep him off Inge's precious floors. At least, there she could observe him, because he was still too little to jump off. Thank goodness, later when we left the house on Arlington Terrace to move to Alexandria proper, Spotty became Inge and Gerry's baby, and lived out a very pampered life with them.

That first Christmas was very lonely and foreign to us. Inge and Gerry decided to introduce us to an 'American Christmas' by visiting people, they hardly knew, and we had never met before. With the next-door neighbors, we went from place to place all Christmas Eve. We did not know what they were talking about and did not understand their jokes. When Gerry took it upon himself to translate one, I was thankful that I had not understood them. Mutti became more alienated than before. She could not understand why we did not spend the first Christmas Eve together as a family.

After Christmas, I had to look for a permanent job. Through an employment office, I took a job in the offices of 'Shirley's Food Stores,' not in existence any more. I had the boring job of addressing envelopes; the days were endless! At least the office manager – the only male there – was extremely nice to me. Not so the women who worked with me. They openly disliked me. One day, to my surprise, they asked me to join them for lunch. It was my first experience with Chinese food, in a dingy restaurant on King Street. The food was awful, but the lunch was an eye-opener. Listening to my co-workers' conversation, I understood that they were in competition for the attention of our boss. I don't remember how I got out of that job, but I still have bad feelings about it.

Inge was a 'foul-weather' friend. She was very capable and efficient, and did not get discouraged easily. "In America," she assured me, "It is advantageous to change jobs." She sent me to a private employment agency and told me not to worry, "In America, there is a job just waiting for you."The agency sent me to the American Security and Trust Co. If they liked my work for the first three months, my employer would pay my fee. I was thrilled!

After I got the job.

Mutti came with me for the interview. We ventured to 15th and Pennsylvania Ave. in Washington, DC, where the main office of the American Security and Trust Co. was located. It was across the street from the Treasury Building and not far from the White House. A very distinguished looking man, a Mr. Grimes, interviewed me and told me to come back to take a test at two o'clock. Three others were also there looking for the job. I walked down to my waiting mother and said, "It's no use, I'll never pass the test, there are three Americans applying for the same job." Mutti said, "It's alright if you don't pass. Who will know about it? Just don't worry." At two o'clock, I marched back up. I was the only one who passed the tests, and a long, happy working relationship ensued. The same Mr. Grimes, who was vice-president of personnel, was also the real estate officer for whom I worked for many years. I could tell from the start, he liked Germans. It was the first time it occurred to me how hard it must be for people to suffer negative discrimination all their lives.

For Mr. Grimes, I could do no wrong. I learned to operate a Burroughs bookkeeping machine and did the accounting for the Real Estate, Mortgage and Insurance Departments. We managed properties for wealthy customers with large deposits, and also real estate held by the Trust department. My business school in Germany had not prepared me for all the new terms. For months I couldn't think of anything else but my job and that monstrous machine!

I was very happy those twelve years I worked at the bank, and I guess it showed. When I quit to raise Steven, Mr. Grimes said to me, "Eleanor, I am aware that everybody is replaceable as far as their work is concerned, but I'm fully convinced that I shall never find another person with such a cheerful attitude!" I cherished that compliment and I never forgot it.

MEETING YOUNG AMERICANS

Inge was nagging me, "In America, every young person does volunteer work, and you need to meet Americans." She went on to tell me that I could be lucky enough to marry an American, instead of waiting for my German boyfriend. I thought, 'this is not a compliment to Gerry!' I'm sure she thought that an American husband would beat having a German one. As far as the volunteer work was concerned, she suggested the USO in Alexandria. It was chaperoned, and I could go there after work. I needed to commit to only one evening a week. I was not a bit interested until she told me that the nephew from next door could not go there. I liked him, but he had become so interested in me that he was already talking about marriage. I had no intention of getting married, and had run out of excuses as to why I could not go dancing with him every weekend.

So every Friday after work, I ventured to the USO in old-town Alexandria. Inge was right. It was an easy volunteer job. Often, I ended up watching TV with the guys, but when it came to dancing the jitterbug, I was no match for the cute, pin-curled American girls.

The very first day at the USO I found a friend named Aaron Kreme. His parents were German and Jewish. Aaron had learned to speak German at home and enjoyed practicing it with me. He also happened to be one of the very few guys who owned a car. It was a 'Willis', a very nice small car in which he stuffed four buddies and me to take me home. But first we always stopped at the Hot Shoppes on North Washington Street in Alexandria.

One Friday, there was a new 'buddy' with an attractive accent sitting in the back seat. Later he sat across from me at the table with his hamburger and milkshake. I took a closer look at him. There was something very attractive about him. As we walked out, I noticed his interesting walk, and that he was very slender and sinuous. I could guess that he would be a good dancer. (I had always been aware of how people walked.) After we scrambled back into the Willis, the newcomer asked Aaron, why I didn't sit in the back. Aaron explained simply that he happened to own the car, and therefore, it was his choice where I sit. Before Aaron dropped me off, the new buddy with the name of Clemente Pereda and the South American accent, asked whether he could pick me up from where I live on the following Friday. That certainly beat waiting for that rare and often tardy bus.

Clem and I at Inge's party to initiate her newly built recreation room

The following Friday, Clemente came in his 1942 Ford, and introduced himself to my mother and sister. When we arrived at the USO, he acted as if he owned me. I found him charming and exciting, but his possessiveness was against the rules of the club. The minute I danced with someone else, Clem disappeared for a long time. Asked where he had been, he said he walked around the block to cool off. He was 'disgusted' because I danced with another guy. I could not quite place that word, but it gave me pause. I had no doubt that his behavior was absurd, and that I had done nothing wrong. I could not understand why he was so upset. As soon as I got home, I looked up 'disgusted' and cried heartbroken. I could not explain to myself or to my mother, what was wrong with me? Mutti liked him, she told me she thought he looked and acted like he came from a good family, but she had a very reasonable question, "Why do you care what he said, since you are in love with Heinz?" That question bothered me, too! When Clem called early the next morning to apologize, my world brightened up. But Inge did not like him, and was annoyed that he dared call so early in the morning.

Heinz wrote regularly about our school and that he did not like to be stuck with a thirteenth school year, by American decree. When I addressed his coming to America, he said that his father insisted, "A man never makes himself dependent on a woman." He was to study in Germany, and then he could do whatever he wanted. Well, I looked eight years down the road, and imagined all the women he would meet and I thought to myself, 'better an end with horror than a horror without end!'I admit that my resolve was strengthened, and my disappointment lessened, because of my infatuation with Clemente. Little did I know then that I would make the same decision, concerning Clem, just six months later.

As usual, Mutti was right. Clem came from a 'very good' family. He was born in New York City, while his father was Dean of one of the schools of Columbia University. Being an American citizen by birth, Clem was drafted right after graduating from Columbia. Because of his obvious dislike of the Army, and because of his cocky manner, he was not offered a commission, although he held a Civil Engineering degree. His father was already retired at age forty, and spent his time translating 'Kant' from German to Spanish. His parents must have been quite wealthy, because they donated enough money to build a Catholic church in Caracas, Venezuela, where they lived.

I liked my job at the bank and I looked forward to my weekends with Clem. Once a month we went dancing in the *Madrillon* Ball Room, a place where a South American band took turns with a North American band to provide dance music. Like so many Latin Americans, Clemente was a great dancer. He was also a lot of fun and very generous, as long as his meager corporal's salary would last.

Our fun became serious when Clem wanted to turn our relationship into a sexual affair. It was not so unusual, I suppose, and I could have been tempted. But I knew better. My Catholic upbringing, and knowing that he would have never married a girl who had been accessible before marriage, made me stand fast. It caused many break-ups in our short time together.

I kept my commitment at the USO on Friday evenings. I did not like to go when Clem was not there. But there was always my friend, Aaron, with whom I socialized and even got a ride home.

Al Erickson 1953

During one of those many break-ups, there was a blond, nordic-looking guy sitting in an armchair close to the entrance. I noticed that he did not seem very involved in the whole social scene. I liked his boyish look. I had just walked over to Aaron, when he surprised me by saying, "I would like to introduce my friend, Al Erickson." When we walked over to where Al was sitting, he jumped up as if bitten by a tarantula and said, "I am glad to meet you!" and returned to his former position in the armchair. Once during the evening he asked me to dance. I had the feeling that he did it only to have a chance to talk to me, certainly not for the joy of dancing.

My situation with Clem had not changed, but he showed up at the USO the following week. It made me feel more miserable. Al Erickson was there again, too. He had changed. He wanted to dance every dance and acted as if he had known me all his life. When he offered to take me to an Italian restaurant, with the help of a motorized friend, I thought it was a good opportunity to get away from Clem.

Al was different from most Americans I had met. He was interested in everything, as if always anxious to learn something new. He also seemed to know quite a bit about a lot of different things that made conversation interesting. He was good company, but I don't think I was. I was only half-heartedly there.

Mutti at Great Falls Park, Virginia, 1953

The situation in Inge and Gerry's home had not improved. Mutti had become scarily silent. On Easter Sunday, Inge and Gerry decided to take us to Great Falls, Virginia. That was the first and only outing we had with them. Exceptions were invitations to meet Inge's German colleagues. Those times were unhappy, too, because Inge would tell Mutti of the invitation at the last minute. Mutti felt treated like a child and told her daughter that if it happens again, she is not going. That worked, because the reason for the invitations was for the hosts to meet Inge's mother. Inge seemed to dislike me more and more, as she blamed me for her strained relationship with her mother.

When Inge and Gerry took a vacation in Florida, I used the opportunity to look for an apartment. Apartments were hard to find at the time. I explained my situation openly to the manager at the 800 South Washington Street apartment-complex in Alexandria. She felt sorry for me, and put me at the top of the waiting list. In July of 1953, we were able to rent a one-bedroom basement apartment for $75.00 per month. I earned $60.00 a week. We bought our groceries for no more than $10.00 dollars a week. Mutti did all the shopping and cooking for us. She commented, "I don't think anybody has to starve in this country, where all the staples are so reasonable!"

Mutti revived after we were on our own. After living in Inge's tiny room on the second floor, without so much as a fan, this basement apartment was luxury! Inge was angry when we moved out, but she agreed to keep the dog. She also came weekly, to give some money to her mother.

Finished table and chairs that started it all

After the Italian dinner with Al, he was anxious to see me again. "How about the following weekend?" he asked. I explained that my mother and I had moved and had been lucky to get an old table and four chairs from our janitor for only ten dollars. The janitor had found the set discarded in the basement. We were planning to refinish it that weekend. Al insisted on helping us. He explained that he had been away from home for so long that just being with a family was special. I did not know how to discourage him. He showed up in the morning and we worked all day in the sizzling July temperature – air conditioning was unheard of at the time. I had never met such a capable and hard worker. In the evening, when we walked around the block to cool off a bit, he tried to kiss me, but I told him that I was still in love with Clem. Even though Al knew Clem well – they both taught 'Soils' at Ft. Belvoir – he did not tell me. He did not mention how much he disliked Clem, and that he found him sneaky and deceitful. But he did tell me that he was going to be discharged in August, and that he planned to go home to Iowa.

By that time, Al and I had become good friends. Al wanted to learn German, so he often came and stayed to eat dinner with us. Mutti liked him very much and vice versa. Shortly before his discharge, Al asked me to go with him to Iowa. I told him that I was not in the habit of traveling with men. He clarified his position immediately, "I certainly mean, as my wife!" That took me by surprise! I thought he was not for real, and I said, "But you don't even know me!" He said he knew me well enough to take the chance – gladly.

A Home In America

It was July of 1953. I had sold Mutti's diamond brooch, a 1.5-karat diamond set in platinum, to get some money to buy furniture for our empty apartment. I was offered sixty dollars from a German jeweler on 15th Street in Washington, DC. He said that the diamond had an old fashioned cut and therefore only little value. I was stupid enough to believe it. But the proceeds bought us an almost new sleep sofa with two matching chairs. After that we got brave and bought some new things from the Kline Furniture Store in Alexandria. Gerry knew Mr. Kline, who was willing to give us credit. Our apartment, with our rugs from Germany, looked warm and homey.

Inge had given to her half-sister, Grete, an affidavit to immigrate to the United States. Grete, Mutti's stepdaughter from her first marriage, was the same one we had visited in London. When Grete arrived, she moved in with Inge and Gerry – but not for long. Then she moved in with a schoolteacher in the same apartment building where we lived – but not for long. "Inge was too stingy," she said, and "The schoolteacher was too ignorant. She did not know whose statue was standing in the middle of Trafalgar Square in London." Grete considered herself very knowledgeable. When I said my apartment was 'un-orderly,' instead of 'dis-orderly', I received a lesson in English, which did not end for years. Grete had low tolerance and never failed to get into conflict with others. After I got to know her better, I came to the conclusion that fighting with people gave Grete energy, the same way other people are energized by being in love.

When our rent was raised by five dollars per month, we thought it prudent to move. Close by was a large efficiency apartment available for only $65.00 per month. The price was right, but unfortunately we did not know about 'cross-ventilation.' There was only one large window. We learned pretty fast the significance of 'cross ventilation', at a time when air conditioning was still a thing of the future. I do not know how Mutti stood the hot summer. She never complained. The bank building, in which I worked, became hot too. But its thick walls kept the heat out longer. I also had a fan blowing on me all day long.

The first year in Virginia, I woke up every morning with a sore throat. Eventually it became full-blown tonsillitis. Thank goodness for penicillin, and my refusal to have my tonsils removed. I had not worked long enough to have health insurance or sick leave, something we had taken as an 'inalienable right' in Germany. Unfortunately, Mutti was uninsurable for the rest of her life, because she was over sixty-five when we applied.

I had gone to work with a fever, because I was afraid to lose my job. A co-worker noticed that I shivered so much that I could not keep my fingers on the keyboard. He insisted on driving me all the way home to Alexandria. I remember how g r a t e f u l and appreciative I was.

Ursel and Colonel Tharp

Soon after I began to work at the bank, I met a wonderful German girl, Ursula Gierloff. We became friends and still are. While I was home, miserable and worrying about my job, Ursula brought a basket of fruit and put it in front of our apartment door. She did not have a car either, but her sponsor and friend, Colonel Tharpe, drove her. She will never know how much her thoughtfulness meant to me, at a time when I felt so alone and powerless. I had to miss a whole week of work, but they kept me on and paid for sick leave, something they did not have to do.

My second big scare was when I went to Gerry's dentist for just a regular check up. It had been nine months since I had been to a dentist, but it was hard to believe that this dentist could find twelve cavities. At six dollars a filling, it was more than a week's pay, not to mention the scare that all my teeth were going bad. The next day during lunch with Ursel in our bank cafeteria, I told her of my tooth-plight. She recommended her dentist for a second opinion. Dr. Hagan had his practice nearby, on the top floor of the Westory Building, at the corner of 14th and F Streets. He checked my teeth and said, "No cavities," and when I told him of my previous diagnosis, he took X-rays. "No cavities," he said again. When I asked, how much I owed him, he said, "Nothing, I don't charge for good teeth." I could not believe it. I was still worried about my twelve cavities, but now I was very willing to wait and see. (By the way, I have not had twelve cavities since!) Needless to say, Dr. Hagan was our dentist until he retired.

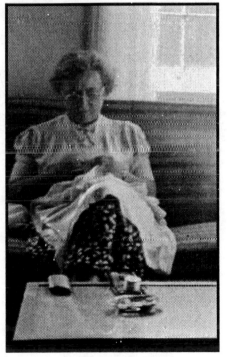

Grete visiting

Our life was happy again. We had weathered the tonsils, the teeth and Mutti's stomach-flu. She had caught it the day after I had talked her into trying the hamburger-milkshake combination of which I had become very fond. Needless to say,

Mutti never ate that combination again, especially since she did not like milk in the first place!

When Inge and Gerry came to see us once a week, their demeanor left no doubt that it was a sacrifice. They came in the evenings unannounced and their visits were strained. But they were never as strained as the time when Grete happened to be visiting. I had my tonsillitis and was suffering on my sofa bed in the dining area, when the doorbell rang. We all knew it was Inge and Gerry. Grete disappeared into our walk-in closet, obviously to hide. There was no use saying anything, so Mutti let Inge and Gerry in, not knowing what else to do. She nervously conversed with them, all the while hoping they would not stay long. Well, they stayed too long for Grete. She suddenly decided to come out of the closet, holding a coat on a hanger in front of her. That hid her from view, except for her shoes. Could she have believed she wouldn't be recognized? Whether she had decided to entertain us, or wanted to cause another fight, nobody ever found out. Inge and Gerry did not take the bait, they said, "Goodnight" and left. It could easily have caused even more damage to Mutti's relationship with Inge. But I guess by then, Inge knew Grete well enough not to get into a fight with her.

When Inge started her weekly visits, she would put twelve dollars into Mutti's hand. Inge soon said that they could not afford that any longer and reduced it to ten dollars. It was all done in such a demeaning manner that Mutti hated the position in which she found herself. The chasm between Inge and Mutti kept growing. Whatever Mutti said angered Inge, and whatever Inge did hurt Mutti.

Clem and I had resumed dating for the umpteenth time. When Clem became aware that Al was interested in me, he stepped up his efforts. His first idea was to get the 'only' theater tickets available for *Oklahoma,* and they happened to be for a Friday night. I accepted the invitation and asked Mutti not to tell anybody where I was. (By that time, several people missed me when I skipped a Friday at the USO) On that particular Friday, Al called Mutti repeatedly, worried that I was not at the club. Mutti commented later, "This young man is really caring!" She already related to him then.

Al was discharged from the Army in August of 1953. He left shortly thereafter to return to Council Bluffs, his hometown in Iowa. I was sad that he was leaving, but looked forward to the three-day Labor Day weekend to go dancing with Clem. Suddenly there was a change of plans. Clem had to go to New York to settle his younger brother at Columbia University, his alma mater. He had the opportunity to drive with an Army buddy in a 'highway-worthy' car, which he did not consider his old Ford to be. He asked me to join them. Well, that was out of the question. My heart sank. I knew that his former girlfriend from college was still living there, and I was jealous. After declining his invitation, I settled down into one of the most miserable weekends in all of my twenty years. I do not think that I ever was so jealous – before or since. I contemplated what life would be like in Caracas with Clem, if I married him. I knew that the Madonna prostitute syndrome was still alive- and well in all Latin countries. I could see a life of jealousy ahead. He had already mentioned marriage. It troubled me at the time that he had not asked, but simply stated, "You will be just right for me, when I marry you!" That statement bothered me a lot. I thought, 'don't you ask me first?' 'how will I be right then, if I am not now?' To be stuck in another country without knowing the language, and being dependent on his German-speaking father, was a scary thought. All this went through my mind on that endless Labor Day weekend. I never even thought of Mutti and what she would do, if I left her behind. I decided I had to put an end to this potential torture right then.

Tuesday, the day after Clem had come back, he called me an hour later than usual. That intensified my anguish and strengthened my resolve. When I finally heard his voice, I pulled myself together and told him that it would be better if we went our separate ways. He did not believe that I meant it. He argued with me and told me that I would regret it all my life. I stood fast, but it was not easy. As a matter of fact, it was awful. He was not the only one who could not believe that I meant it; it took a good while before I could believe that I meant it myself!

Al and I had stayed in touch by mail. He had written that he was planning to go fishing with his father in Minnesota. In my letters I reported whatever I thought of interest about people we both knew. I also told him that I had broken up with Clem.

Al's 1953 Chevrolet heading East

It was not long before I learned that Al's mother had forwarded my letter. Al returned home immediately, took his brand-new Chevrolet, and drove day and night back to Alexandria to be with me. He found himself a room and a job, registered at George Washington University for evening classes and spent every available moment with me. At night, Mutti would usher him out at eleven o'clock. He frequently offered to help in the kitchen, but Mutti would say in no uncertain terms, "At this hour of the night, we don't do dishes!" Eleven was the deadline, whether I had a visitor or a date. Al was well aware of it, and so was everybody else who had dated me. It had never presented a problem, except when Al asked me to join him for a picnic soon after we first met. He was still in the army then, and did not have a car. His Chinese friend, Ray Wong, offered his car and his companionship. We were to buy the hot dogs and whatever, and then we were to pick him up from his army kitchen-police duty. Al and I had all the picnic supplies, and we sat waiting in Ray's car for an endless time. We did not know what to do with our perishable supplies, so we kept on waiting and talking. When Ray finally came, the picnic had become a midnight snack. Mutti did not speak to me for two weeks. (Only now, after having children of my own, do I understand her worries.)

After Al's return from Iowa, the room he rented was in a house at the West end of Alexandria, while we lived at the East end. That did not keep him from picking me up early every morning to drive to work, nor from picking me up in the afternoon in front of the bank. Often, on a very hot day, Al would drive my mother and me to Mt. Vernon and back to cool off a bit. The green trees on both sides of the beautiful Mt. Vernon Parkway provided shade and lowered the temperature by a few degrees.

Al taught me how to drive in his spanking new car, his prize possession. Nothing is free though; the price I paid was that the teaching never ended! From time to time, we had to stop, turn off the lights to save the battery, while Al tried to explain over and over again, how to shift gears without grinding them. (It also gave him time to collect himself, being a perfectionist with little patience.) We chose to practice driving on Ridgecrest Drive, at that time, a deserted street with few houses, paralleling the Parkway. While we were standing there with the lights turned off, a policeman pointed his spot light directly into our car. Then he came around to alert me to the dangers of being alone with a young man on a deserted road. I was so embarrassed that I turned red, wondering what the policeman thought we were doing. As far as the warning was concerned, only the gears of the car were in danger!

Our second Christmas in America was very different from the first one. I suspected that Al wanted to give me an engagement ring. I discouraged it, I did not want to get married. As we were lighting our Christmas tree on Christmas Eve (for the first time, as customary in Germany) beautiful traditional German Christmas music filled the room. Tears ran down my cheeks, when I heard all the familiar music sung in German. I was in heaven. I was surprised and moved that Al had made such an effort to order the record from England, because it could not be found locally. He also gave me a record player and quite a few other records. He had remembered all my favorite songs. I was overwhelmed. I knew he had little money, and everything was expensive.

Another six months had gone by, when one evening after a drive-in movie, Al was much more serious than usual. He said, "I cannot stay here much longer just waiting for you. I need to continue my education. That forces me to go back to my home state, Iowa, where I qualify for reduced tuition. I want to marry you and take you with me." I answered, "Go ahead and get your education and then come back. I cannot go with you. You know my circumstances, I do not want to leave my mother here alone". Al replied, "I love you, but if you do not marry me now, I will never see you again nor write to you. I know you'll find somebody else, and I don't want to set myself up for a heartache. But if you go with me, we will take your mother with us. I promise I will take care of her until the end of her days."By now, It was hard to imagine losing him! Al had been with us every day and had become part of my life. He was also my best friend, and as Mutti said, "He has a shoulder to lean on. Most women don't have that in a man!" I loved and respected him, and it was a scary idea, not to have him around anymore. But I had never given marriage to him serious consideration. – I had made up my mind that whatever I did, it had to include my mother. She could not emotionally survive in this country without me, and it was not possible for her to go back to Germany.

Vati had given up our apartment in Berlin, when the three destroyed rooms were finally rebuilt. That brought the apartment back to its original size and it became very expensive. At this point, being almost seventy-seven, Vati had looked to share a place with somebody who would keep house and cook for him. The offer was attractive to East-German refugees who still had no eligibility for housing in Berlin. A war-widow, in her forties with a young son, took him up on his offer. Vati provided the rent and household money. (My father was stingy when he was well to do. I can only imagine what he must have been like with little money.) Needless to say, the arrangement did not work out well, but little could be done about it.

I really was not ready to get married, but Al's marriage proposal was an offer hard to refuse. Neither Al nor I had money, but I never thought about that. Al said that if I married him, we would never go hungry. He would always find work someplace, be it in a gas station or paving roads. He had done it before, and could do it again if he had to. I knew that whatever he did, he did well. I did not worry about any of that for one minute. I also knew that I would do my share, and together in a country like the United States, we could and would do fine. I knew Al to be very pragmatic and reasonable. I liked that! But I would have liked it more, if he had also been a little more carefree and fun sometimes. But I was already aware that one rarely finds everything in one package.

MARRIAGE

We got engaged on my birthday in 1954, and were married in the First Presbyterian Church in Alexandria on the 18th of July of the same year.

Running from church to avoid the rice

We had looked into being married in the Catholic Church, but when I was asked to sign for not using birth control, my days in the Catholic Church were over. Al had warned me, after studying in a Jesuit university in Omaha, but could not prepare me for our interview at St. Mary's in Alexandria. America's Irish Catholic Church seemed to be a century behind, compared to my Matthias Roman Catholic Church in Berlin.

Knowing we were penniless, and starting with a family of three, 'no birth control' was not an option. When we refused to 'sign', we were given an unsolicited education in all possible methods of birth control that we were not allowed to use. I was embarrassed and appalled. To sign something that only Al and God could know, was an offense in itself. Agitated, I said to the priest, "We cannot afford twenty children." He condescendingly replied that twelve would be enough. I was so angry that I couldn't remember what followed. According to Al, I replied, "I regret to inform you that you have just lost thirteen Catholics – me and my twelve children!"

Our wedding cake

Inge was so delighted with my marriage plans that she changed personality. She even offered to have the wedding reception in her home, as long as I provided the cake and champagne. She very creatively cut salami and cheese into squares, and stuck them on toothpicks into grapefruit halves for finger snacks. She also served a fruit punch. I had bought a beautiful wedding cake from 'Clements', the Washington bakery that supposedly baked for the White House. It was an investment for me, but I wanted my guests to have something they could enjoy. After the ceremony, I was too nervous to eat and therefore never tasted my own cake. When we returned from our three-day honeymoon, Inge had generously – and generosity was not one of her virtues – given the remaining half of the cake to her close friend and boss. She explained, "Because his two boys can always eat sweets." I was furious!

Our wedding guests were few. They included Mr. Grimes, my boss at American Security & Trust Co.; two other co-workers of mine; my dear friend, Ursel Gierloff; and Marlene, my high school girlfriend from Berlin, who was now living on Long Island and Grete who came from New York. (Grete had just moved there, after returning from London. There she had unsuccessfully attempted to resettle, when she thought she had enough of life in the U.S.) Then there were, Inge, Gerry and Mutti, of course.

My fifteen-dollar wedding dress was made of white nylon, and looked fine for the occasion. (It was cheaper than the cake!) I remember all my expenses at that time, because I did not have much money to ' hold together' (Mutti's term for being frugal); just enough to be able to distribute it carefully. That was a challenge I enjoyed.

**My family at the wedding – from l to r:
Inge, Gerry, I, Al, Mutti and Grete Jacobsberg**

Al had bought himself a suit (on credit). His parents decided not to come to the wedding, because we were going to meet them soon in Iowa. The money they saved by not attending, they sent to us. It amounted to $300.00 that we used for our honeymoon.

Gerry was a partner in a wholesale boys' clothing company, and did a lot of traveling. He recommended Rehoboth Beach, Maryland, as a nice place to go. He reserved a room for us in a motel in Salisbury, MD, for the first night, and then a place in Rehoboth by the ocean.

On the way to Salisbury, we stopped at a little diner. The ambience was not very inviting, but we thought it good enough for something like a sandwich. I did not feel very comfortable after eating, but Al felt good enough at the motel to indulge in some more of the champagne that Gerry had insisted we take along. Well, the following morning, I thought I had lost Al to the bathroom. I found out soon, there was no need to worry. He made a miraculous recovery, when a huge breakfast was set in front of him.

Our motel room in Salisbury had the luxury of a window air conditioner, most welcome in July. It had only two positions: 'too hot' and 'too cold.' We were almost frozen for posterity. What a relief when we had a nice ocean breeze at our place at Rehoboth Beach.

Gassing up on Route 1, Alexandria, Iowa bound August 1, 1954

The following month, we packed all our belongings into the smallest U-Haul trailer we could rent. All those long hot twelve hundred miles to Iowa, our Chevy pulled that trailer. Because Mutti's neck was painfully stiff, we dared not open the windows of our non-air-conditioned car, for fear a draft would make her worse.

When we arrived in Council Bluffs, Al's mother was ironing. She asked me to sit next to her to get acquainted. I liked her instantly, although I was surprised that she continued to do her housework. One of the first stories she told me was about Al's love for his pony that he had named 'Sailor'. When he first got the horse, he trained it for riding. It took a lot of effort and patience, but it also made him bond with his horse. Then a year or so later, the horse was diagnosed with encephalitis (sleeping sickness). Soon Sailor could not stand up anymore and could not be saved. The then ten-year-old Al sat with his horse night and day. He held Sailor's head to keep him from banging it on the ground in frustration when he tried to get up. That story moved me to tears and I knew then that I had married a kind human being, with a 'shoulder to lean on', as Mutti had told me before. At dinnertime the whole family gathered, except Eldon, Al's next-younger brother who was in the Marines. He was stationed in Virginia, where I had met him. There was Andrew, only seven, as well as his sisters

Marilynn, eight, and Celia, thirteen. At the head of the table sat Al's father, just home from a twelve-hour workday.

I had suspected that Eldon, a patriotic Marine, was not delighted to have a foreigner in his family. Al's father acted as if I had come from Mars. He did not seem to understand a word I was saying – but he liked my mother. She said little, but he seemed to understand her. His own mother had lived into her late nineties. Al's father had moved his family back from Denver to Council Bluffs, to live close to her.

Al's mother, a registered nurse, tried to help Mutti's neckpain with a heat lamp. Unfortunately, it was only the beginning of Mutti's years of suffering with deteriorated discs in her back.

Al's mother had a list of 'fix-it' jobs waiting for him, when we got to Council Bluffs. Lots of things needed to be done, from electric wiring in the attic to a new barn roof. Also, new Formica was to be installed on the kitchen counter. It seemed impossible to do it all in two weeks' time, but Al got it done. I felt lonely. Between working for his mother and trying to please his father, I seemed forgotten. I learned soon that Al was able to do just about anything, and work was always the priority. Unlike him, I need people with whom I can share. Marriage was not an easy adjustment for me. It helped to have Mutti.

After the two weeks with Al's family, we moved to Ames, Iowa, where Al was enrolled at Iowa State University. Our next challenge was to find housing – close to impossible – especially for three. Mutti had the idea of going to the newspaper office before the papers hit the street. The plan worked. We found a furnished apartment in the middle of Ames. Unfortunately, it was also right at the main intersection with a traffic light that stopped cross-country truck traffic.

Our landlady was in her eighties, and sat in a chair most of the time. She kept it very warm downstairs, making our third floor apartment bearable only with the windows wide open. The fresh air was wonderful. At night though, the air brakes and engine revving of the overland trucks were deafening. Al would wake up, jump up saying 'unkind words' and then go right back to sleep. I, in turn, lay in that sagging double bed waiting for the next truck, and my husband's next outburst. I got increasingly angry. What good is swearing about a situation that could not be changed?

I had been lucky to qualify for a job in an animal-husbandry laboratory, as an assistant to doctoral students working on their research projects. This was the second time my knowledge of chemistry helped a lot. (The first time helped my graduation.) Everyone in Ames seemed the same age. All had little money and looked desperately for a job; the competition was fierce. Al received $135.00 a month from the G.I. bill, and I started with $1.10 an hour. Tuition and books had to be paid for out of that. Sometime later, Al got an additional $60.00 a month for overseeing a soils lab, where he could also study. We needed little and could stretch what we had. There were three supermarkets in town, and the highlight of the week – our only outing together – was running from one to the other, buying the specials at each. They made up our menu for the following week. After shopping, we rewarded ourselves with a banana split from Dairy Queen. We were grateful that we never had to worry about rent or food. We just never spent more than we had. We even managed to put away just a little money at a time, regularly. It added up to a thousand dollars over the two years in Ames.

Iowa and married life created a difficult transition for me. Young mothers with children stayed home and made friends with each other. Women, who worked, socialized in the evening. I did not belong to either group. I stayed home after work to keep Mutti company, because she had been alone all day. Al worked and struggled to get the best grades possible. He was so stressed out after a six-day week that he spent most Sundays nursing a bad headache. I have never been prone to headaches – neither were my parents nor anybody I had known in Germany – so I was not as tolerant and compassionate as I should have been. The fact is, I complained that I must be the cause of his headaches.

In January of 1955, I was pregnant – certainly not planned. But we did not spend one moment worrying about how to take care of another mouth to feed. At the Ames clinic a monthly checkup was two dollars. For that money, I was assured that everything was progressing as it should, and that I was a good patient for not gaining much weight. In those days, women were told that every pound gained over fourteen would stay there after the baby was born. When I was hungry, I filled myself up with peaches by the crate-full. That year in Iowa we could get the tastiest peaches I had ever eaten. Later I paid the price for the dubious achievement of gaining so little weight. I became very skinny after Catherine's birth. All those peaches had ulcerated the lining of my intestines, giving me a chronic pain on the right side of my lower abdomen, always exacerbated by eating raw fruit or vegetables. It took many years until it was finally diagnosed. It taught me: 'everything in moderation – even peaches!'

The moment we told our landlady we were expecting a baby we lost our apartment. She had already made an exception with Mutti; a crying baby was out of the question. We got on the waiting list for campus housing for married students. The housing was corrugated-steel army barracks from World War II. We were lucky to get in quickly. The thirty-five-dollar-a-month rent, and short drive to school and work, helped our budget considerably.

Pammel Court 1954 – Ames, Iowa

The single oil-fired space heater in our new quarters handled the cold pretty well, but the summer was unbearable. There was no relief from the heat at work either. The laboratory, where I worked, was on the second floor of a temporary building. Heated ovens, for drying our beakers and other lab glassware, were on all day long. Being pregnant made me feel the heat even more. I was also bothered by the strong odors. One doctoral student had a grant for cattle-feed evaluation. For that purpose, a large round hole had been cut into a cow's stomach and re-closed with a wooden plug. When food was taken out of the cow 's stomach for testing, the odor was indescribable. My job required that I get up often during the night to take care of timed experiments. It was interesting work, but physically demanding in my condition. I didn't complain; I was happy to have a job where jobs were in high demand, and I was looking forward to my baby. A cold shower at night and an occasional visit to the Student Union were the only places one could cool off. The latter was actually airconditioned and sold ice cream cones, a great treat. The Iowa summer of 1955 was unusually hot. I remember the cows crowding under the one lonely tree in an endless field. When I saw that, I felt so sorry for them that it made me forget how hot I was myself.

Eventually, we broke down and bought a reversible window fan from Montgomery Ward. How exciting to have a fan, in a house where the sun beating on the steel outside made the walls hot to the touch inside. The fan was a big investment for us, but the joy over it can never be replicated. A vacuum cleaner was another such investment. Until then we had still been using a brush and a dustpan to clean our rugs.

Everything in Ames was 'list price' because there were no competitive businesses. But, from time to time, Montgomery Ward, the main retailer in Ames, would give incentives like some 'free underwear with the purchase of a vacuum cleaner'. Oh, how upset we were over buying our vacuum cleaner a week too early – and missing out on the underwear!

The student-housing area was called Pammel Court. Its cinder-covered roads prevented us from opening the windows. Whenever there was a breeze, it stirred up the cinder dust turning everything black inside the house. But we were young and were looking forward to our baby with so much anticipation that we felt fortunate and – Mutti never complained.

Al putting up the antenna for our precious one-channel TV

We had brought our television with us in our U-haul trailer. It had been acquired by standing in line the better part of a night, in order to be early for a 'Washington's Birthday Sale' in Washington DC. For $30.00 we laid our hands on a used TV that actually worked when we got it home – a happy surprise! But now, here in Ames, we could only receive one of the two available channels. We were unaware that a knob in the back would have easily pulled in the other channel. We did not dare tinker with the precious set, for fear it might then require a repairman. Mutti and I watched whatever was on that one channel, while Al went to his soils lab to study without distraction. We saw a lot of 'Wrestling from Chicago', which actually became great entertainment. Mutti exclaimed every few minutes, "No, that cannot be!" "How is this possible!" "It is unbelievable!" – and what we saw, certainly was!

In those first years, Al and I had a few nasty fights. Before we got married, I never knew that he had such a bad temper. Now, Al was so keyed up, that it did not take much to set him off. I exacerbated the situation with my 'sarcasm', at least that is what Al called it. Bad temper or not, Al never said an angry word to Mutti – as he had promised.

BEING A MOTHER

Our practical 'can-do' little girl managed to be born right on Al's twenty-seventh birthday, October 1, 1955. She became a continuous birthday gift for him. He was still in the midst of his studies and anxious to go on a field trip that was planned for October second. Catherine Ruth Erickson arrived in time to greet her father before he had to leave.

At two o'clock in the morning, the Ob-Gyn nurse rang our home phone to tell Al that he was the father of a little girl. He slept so deeply that Mutti had to shake him awake. Being a mother, she had not slept a wink and had a hard time understanding that Al could sleep so soundly, knowing his wife was in labor.

When they rolled me out of the delivery room, I felt like a newborn baby myself; it was the most wonderful feeling. Al arrived in the room where all the new mothers of that night were temporarily stored. My cleaned infant had been placed into my arms. Immediately, Catherine took my little finger and held on to it tightly. I was overjoyed. Al said she was beautiful which I thought a bit exaggerated, looking at her elongated head with a lot of stringy, pitch-black hair. In my happy excitement I could have celebrated all night, but Al was anxious to leave, to get some more sleep before his class trip.

There was only one visitor allowed per new mother. Because Al was out of town, Mutti came in his place. When she saw our baby in the nursery, she could not keep from laughing. Catherine looked different from all the other babies and made the funniest faces, as if she were entertaining us. Mutti, who

211

did not laugh often, could not contain herself. She laughed and laughed. The other babies either slept or cried – as babies do – but Catherine's expressions changed constantly. Mutti apologized for laughing!

Al with our 14 day old Catherine

I was back to my weight of 125 lbs. when I left the hospital. It pleased me a lot. Eight months later, when we left Ames, we sold our refrigerator to a nurse, who remembered me from working in the hospital's baby ward, when I took my baby home. Even though the hospital in that studenttown resembled a baby factory, she recalled the nurses commenting at the time that I looked like Gina Lollobrigida in my black knitted dress that showed my big bosom and my totally flat stomach. –

It was a short-lived joy! A month later I had lost ten pounds and looked awful. My hands were shaking, and I had lost my appetite. The latter I had in common with my baby. Catherine would never drink more than two ounces at a time, although I practically drowned her in mother's milk. She slept through the night from the day I brought her home; maybe because she was never hungry. She did not cry either. Al's mother worried that she would not develop her lungs.

Our little Catherine brightened up our lives and made it very difficult for me to go back to work a month later. But my loss was Mutti's gain. It gave her a new reason for living and made her feel a working part of our family team.

I suddenly realized that Inge claimed Mutti as a dependent on her income tax return although she did not contribute a penny. I informed her that from now on, we would be claiming Mutti. That resulted in an audit by the IRS. They could not believe that four could live on such small income. Our case was easily proven. We were under the poverty level, and we were reimbursed all our taxes. We used our sixty-dollar reimbursement to order a German baby buggy, the kind I had already admired in Berlin as a teenager. The buggy was difficult to get into the car, but it doubled as a crib and could be rolled outside. It had a cover with a windshield to protect the baby from wind and rain.

Catherine sleeping in her insulated buggy in the fresh air   **Catherine's baby buggy**

Our last year in Iowa was saddened by the awful news that Al's mother, at age forty-eight, had terminal ovarian cancer. Her Blue Cross insurance, to which she had paid premiums for thirty years, dropped her instantly. (It was before Kennedy had signed a bill, prohibiting insurance companies from dropping clients, who have catastrophic illnesses.) The doctor, whom she had assisted as a nurse in prior years, attempted to remove the cancer.

After she had recuperated from the surgery, she came to Ames and spent two wonderful weeks with us and with the one and only grandchild, she lived to see. She was a lovely person. We played many board games, and she made everything fun. We laughed a lot in our short time together.

When she said goodbye at the train station, she told us that she had spent the best time ever and that she had never been so spoiled before in her life. It made us realize how little she expected for herself, and how modest she was.

Al, I and grandmother Erickson with 3-month-old Catherine

Eldon and his wife, Lois, visited us in January of 1954 shortly after Al's mother had left. He wondered aloud why anybody would have a girl, where he was looking forward to a whole football team of boys. He ended up with four girls of his own, all of whom he can be very proud.

Al graduated from Iowa State University in June of 1956. Al's mother and his two sisters, Celia and Marilyn, came to help us celebrate the occasion.

Before we went back to the Washington area, we spent two weeks in Council Bluffs. We gave Al's Mom the opportunity to go on a fishing-and-camping trip with her husband and his friend. Al took care of his

Eldon, Al's next younger brother, and new wife Lois

father's boat-and-motor shop and his adjoining service station. Al's Mom ended up doing the cooking, and the ones who lucked out were the men! I don't think we did Al's mother a favor.

l to r: Celia, Mutti, Marilynn, Al with Catherine and his mother

It was late June, when we left to drive back to Washington. Al and I, Mutti and little Catherine – who was sleeping in a car-bed on the back seat – drove away from Al's home on the narrow country road. None of us spoke for a long time. We had just said a heavy-hearted 'good bye'. We all knew that we would never see Al's mother alive again. I think she knew it, too. She died in May of 1957, not even a year later. Andrew, her youngest son, was only nine, Marilynn was ten and Celia a mere fifteen. It was tragic.

Vati Uhlenbrock died in September of 1956. The hospital did not know how to notify us. My letter in Vati's pocket had our old address on it. – He finally had to give up his business. He had bought himself into quite an expensive senior residence. I sent small, but regular payments every month from Ames. It was not long before he could not get along at the residence either, as he got progressively more difficult and confused. He had complained about his memory for quite a long time. Now it had become so bad that he couldn't find home, and did not even remember his address. Somebody found him lost, couldn't deal with him and put him into the psychiatric ward of a nearby hospital, where he died shortly thereafter. I was so sad that I never saw him again, after that rainy October morning in Berlin, and that Al never had a chance to meet him.

Al took a job with the Army Corps of Engineers in Washington, DC, which offered an eighteen-month training program. During that time, he transferred from branch to branch, and was able to pick whatever interested him most. It was also the safest employment to choose. The government was

215

the only employer that offered more than 2-weeks vacation per year and accumulative sick leave. With our uninsured Mutti, we thought we might need time-off some day to take care of her. Mutti was now seventy-one. 'What would we do, if she became seriously ill?' That thought was always hanging over us like a heavy cloud.

Al never regretted his choice to go back to Washington. After the initial period, he chose a dynamic boss, mentor and later, a good friend. The branch was 'River Basin Planning', a field in which Al had already done graduate work. Their big project was planning the improvement of the Potomac River for flood control, recreational use, water supply and water quality control.

It was only a short time after we got back to Washington, when Mr. Grimes of the American Security and Trust Co. called me. He asked me to please come back and head the department where I had worked before. Although I had hoped for some time off, I was happy to be back with my former colleagues and friends. The first time they ordered doughnuts for a break, my appetite returned in full swing and has not left me since.

Mutti had her job cut out for her. A baby was a lot of work, but she did it with great joy. She gave all her attention, love and wisdom to our little sunshine, Catherine.

Return Trip To Europe

We spent five happy years in our two-bedroom apartment in Belle View, located just about one mile south of Alexandria, VA. Mutti could walk to the supermarket, the kindergarten Catherine attended and even the pediatrician, if necessary. She would take Catherine to the neighborhood playgrounds, where she compared notes with young mothers about their kids. She felt in charge of her life, because she could walk to places. If it had not been for Mutti's suffering with the deteriorated disks in her back, and a child that was never hungry, everything would have been perfect. For seven years, we took Mutti weekly to a chiropractor, who could not help her much.

We pampered ourselves with investing in two window air-conditioners, one in the dining area and one in Mutti and Catherine's bedroom. The charge for electricity was 54 dollars per season; reasonable considering that our 99-dollar rent per month included utilities. So we could put some money away, enough to plan a trip back to Germany.

The German Club in Washington offered charter flights with the 'Flying Tigers' airline. In July 1959, we were all packed and ready to go when I got a phone call at the bank. The FAA had withheld its authorization for the charter. After that shock, I spent a long time in the washroom drying tears that kept running down my face. I finally composed myself enough to call Al, who surprised me by saying, "I don't care what it costs, find a regular commercial flight!" It was not easy on such short notice. At the Air France office, I was lucky. Their agent happened to be a Berliner, who could feel my pain. He said, "Lady, you have a flight, I am going to make it happen!" After a stressful waiting time, he came through. Very excited, and with a little leaner budget, we left on the day of our 5th wedding anniversary, on July 18th. No commercial jets were in use yet, so we flew in a propeller driven Super Constellation. We sat over a well-traveled wing, with oil seeping out of the engine. It added to my nervousness and convinced me that we would not make it back to Europe – but we did. It was a long trip, twenty-four hours. We had stops in Paris, Strasbourg and Frankfurt, before arriving in Berlin. Each landing and each take-off made me more motion-sick. By the time we stepped off the plane in Berlin, I was wiped out. Neither Mutti nor Al had any problem and Catherine was fine, until a last minute orange juice came up as fast as we were descending – and all over Al's new suit!

**l to r: Joachim Pohl and wife,
Catherine, Mutti, Frau Typke and I**

We stayed at the apartment of Ulla's parents', where I had

spent my last night in Berlin, almost seven years ago. I was so emotionally exhausted that I couldn't wake up the next morning. But Al had no mercy; he could not wait to see all the places I had talked about.

In an unusually hot summer in Berlin, we walked more than we had in the last seven years. Al kept asking, "Why did you complain about the heat in the U.S.?" We met all my old friends, like Frau Typke, Klärchen and her parents and even Joachim, my dancing-school partner. Berliners sounded so different from what I remembered. Never before could I hear how strong the Berlin dialect was.

After two weeks, we went on to Frankfurt, where my sister Ruth and her husband Walter greeted us. We had invited them to join us. We rented a car and all together drove south to Mayrhofen, a beautiful little town in Austria, with mountains all around. There we had reserved hotel rooms for two weeks for Mutti and Catherine, as well as for Ruth and Walter, while we were driving on to Italy.

**l to r: Fr Haedenkamp & daughter,
Ulle, Ruth, & Mutti in Mayrhofen**

When we saw how beautiful Mayrhofen was, Al and I wanted to stay a couple of nights. We could only find a room in the home of a sculpturer and cheese-maker. There, a life-size sculpture of Jesus greeted us at the entrance. I had so much fun with Al, who returned the greeting. Our room had several crucifixes, but the largest one had been over our bed. It was now only represented by an outline on the wall. Al was convinced it had fallen on some previous unfortunate occupants of the room, and doubted they had survived. In the morning, bright and early as always, Al disappeared down the hall to find the washroom. He had hardly left, when he returned shivering. "These Austrians are fresh-air-fiends," he declared disgruntled. The small bathroom had a large window that was left wide open all night. The cold mountain air blew Al out as fast as he went in. Still half frozen, he tried to wash himself with the water in a carafe on the dresser. "The water is icy cold, too," he whimpered, when he heard something at our room door. He opened it and found a pitcher full of boiling hot water. By this time he could not think clearly anymore. He said, "First the water is icy cold, now boiling hot, how can one wash oneself?" That gave me a good laugh. "Maybe you should mix the water in the large basin, don't you think?" I said very amused. It was only the beginning of a nice day. We spent it with family and friends, good home cooking at the inn, and lots of laughter until late in the evening.

We got back late to our temporary abode in a very good mood, and a little tipsy from the wine. We were not only greeted by Jesus – still standing at the entrance – but by a very pungent odor that permeated the whole house. Now we remembered that our hosts were not only wood-carvers, but also cheese-makers. Al reminded me that he was never crazy about dairy products; but that smell was too much even for a dairy lover. It could surely only be endured by a cheese-maker. Al assumed that was the reason we still got a room there, while everywhere else was sold out.

Al and I left the picture-perfect scenery of Mayrhofen to drive further south to Rapallo. I wanted to introduce Al to my Italian father, his American wife Frieda, her mother Nona Mary, as well as to my two half-brothers and my grandparents. It was interesting for Al to experience the elegant lifestyle my father and his family lived.

l to r: Al, my grandmother and grandfather and I

There was still daily sailing before lunch, and afternoon tea with my grandparents in the grape-arbor of their villa, *La Buona Terra*. After our stay in Rapallo, we stopped in Pisa. (We were still allowed to walk up the stairs of the Leaning Tower; quite an experience.) We continued on to Florence on our drive to Rome. That is where my Italian mother, Clara, and her two stunning teenage daughters, my half-sisters, lived. When we went to the seashore, they were in skimpy bikinis, while I looked like their grandmother in my black one-piece American swimsuit. Clara's warmth was as welcoming as I remembered from my last trip, nine years ago.

We all went to visit Clara's mother, my grandmother. Neither Al nor I will ever forget it. We could only get to her condo via the roof of the neighboring house. My grandparents previously owned the building where my Grandmother Orazi lived. A tour-bus company

My sisters Simonetta and Donatella

had forcibly acquired it, but grandmother refused to move and stayed in her condominium. The bus company occupied the whole street floor, which cut off her entrance. That prompted that peculiar, treacherous approach to her place. We had to crawl from the neighboring roof to her roof and go down one floor by elevator. How she got in and out, we never understood. However, we can say we have been on the roofs of Rome! – I am sure glad I did not take that roof-journey by myself; otherwise I would have thought I had dreamed it. – (Thinking back now, I realize that the members of my biological families were all very much attached to their mothers and to their homes. I am no exception.)

On our way back we visited Venice. We saw Venice over and over again because we got so very lost. We had a marathon walk, and thought we would never find our hotel again. It was the only time that Al had asked me for help with directions. I enjoyed that, even though I was no help, but a policeman finally was.

We packed a lot of stops into those five weeks. With Sigrun and her husband, Paul, we took a boat trip on the Rhine river to Bonn, and finally they accompanied us through Neuen Ahr to Frankfurt. In Neuen Ahr, I had the most delightful dinner of my life, fresh water trout with local wine, and the company of everyone I loved best. – Ruth and Walter were still with us. – No one wanted to leave, but our early morning flight from Frankfurt forced us to press on.

Last but not least, we spent five more days with Walter and Ruth in London, before we flew home to the United States. They still lived in the same small apartment at Eastbourne Court, not far from Kensington Gardens, which I had liked so much before. Hyde Park still had the same crazy people giving speeches. But this time, it was much more fun, because I could share it with Al.

We brought home wonderful memories of those five weeks. I was thrilled to have been able to have Al meet my relatives and friends, and show him a bit of the country of my birth.

Back in Virginia, I realized I had left my homesickness behind. I was happy that the United States was now my home.

MUTTI RECEIVES SOME MONEY

Grete had been working for some time for a lawyer in New York City, whose specialty was suing Germany on behalf of his German-Jewish clients. Needless to say, Grete found her niche with that job! She became very astute in suing. She was already receiving monthly reparations from Germany, but she decided to sue General Motors of Germany, where she had worked until 1939. GM was afraid of bad publicity by one of their former Jewish employees and paid her, justified or not.

Grete also sued for Inge, who ended up with a sizeable monthly pension, especially when the *Deutsche Mark* increased in value compared to the dollar. (Without it, Inge could never have covered her ever-increasing expenses at the Nursing Home, where she struggled for the last five years of her life.) Grete also sued for Inge's husband, Gerry, whose parents were both murdered in a Concentration Camp.

After that, Grete insisted on getting some money for Mutti. She asserted that Mutti had suffered through twelve horrible years in Germany, and her husband, Vati, had lost a fortune in warehouse supplies. Grete worked with her German lawyer, who blamed Mutti's high blood pressure and back-problems on all those years of stress. Mutti never believed that she would see a penny! To her surprise, there was a provision called *Lastenausgleich* (Financial-loss-equalization). Financial assistance was given to those who had lived under hardships, greater than average, and could prove their losses.

In 1960, Mutti was awarded a small monthly payment and a lump sum for back pay. The payment grew over the years, because the value of the German Mark increased. In addition, whenever Germany had a cost-of-living increase, it went to reparation-recipients in foreign countries, as well. After a few years, Mutti could pay for her doctor-visits and medication. We were very lucky that she had no major illness.

Mutti had always been generous, no matter how little she had. For example, she helped us buy our '59 Chevrolet, using most of the $2,000 she had received retroactively. But she knew 'how to hold her money together' – her favorite expression. After doing just that, she could buy a nice dress for Catherine in one of the more expensive stores. Sometimes she would buy something for us that she knew we would not buy for ourselves. So, while growing up, Catherine thought of her grandmother as the wealthy one in the family.

Catherine, Mutti and I at summer camp

In 1967, Mutti unwittingly sent Catherine to an exclusive summer camp in upper-state New York. Catherine's girlfriend, at that time, was her teacher's daughter. Her teacher's family went to that very camp every summer. Little did Mutti know that the teacher had a horseback-riding concession there. Just to outfit Catherine became an expensive experience. Catherine learned riding and sailing, while camping in a log cabin. She loved it and never forgot it, and we did not regret sending her.

When Catherine turned thirteen, she was dreaming of a 'live' band for her birthday party. Since this 'live band' were schoolmates and affordable, Mutti promised to hire them. All her friends had been invited, but the band cancelled at the last minute. Now, other live music had to be found, which cost much more than anticipated. Of course, Al and I always made up the difference.

Mutti gave Catherine a thousand dollar gift for her sixteenth birthday in 1971, so she could buy herself a car. Catherine's dream came true when she found a 1969 Mustang! – Again Al and I ended up with the 'fringe' expenses. But again, it was worth every penny. It gave Mutti a position in our family, not just an existence. We never wanted her to think she was a burden – and I know we succeeded.

OUR FIRST HOUSE

In 1961 we had a house built just up the hill from Belle View. We were excited because we thought that we had got a very good deal. Mutti understood our joy, but she would have much preferred to stay in our apartment in Belle View. She felt isolated and afraid in a house with 'four doors, all leading to the outside.' At age seventy-six, she was also much more aware of the energy needed to keep up a house. One day, I asked her what she thought of our big new home. I shall never forget her answer, because as I grew older, I understood her better and better. "My honest answer is," she said, "I would want a maid first and then a house." (I did not smile then, but thinking about it now, I understand what she meant.)

6703 Beddoo Street, Alexandria, Virginia after shrubbery was established

I left my job in 1964, just before our second child was born. I had enjoyed those working years. Work had become a home-away-from-home, and I knew I was going to miss my good relationship with my colleagues. But I was also looking forward to my new life. I thought that maybe now I would have time to share barbeques in our backyard with neighbors and friends. I also looked forward to staying home with my baby, a luxury I could not afford the first time. Mutti had turned seventy-nine and her health did not allow her to take care of a new baby, in addition to the eight-year-old Catherine.

With little notice, Steven demanded to be born in the afternoon of the 23rd of March 1964. Al had gas-peddle trouble when driving my little *Renault-Caravelle* home from work. When he finally arrived to pick me up, Mutti and Catherine were in a panic. I don't know how long we had waited, because my labor pains had progressed to a point that I could not move anymore. But it never occurred to any of us to call an ambulance. Instead we raced to George Washington University Hospital in Washington, DC, while I was trying to hold back the baby. It was a long, tough ride, but ended with the happy surprise that it was a boy this time.

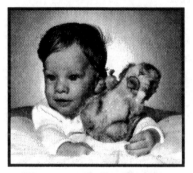

Steven at 3 months

Steven Thomas Erickson was a strong baby; in fact, he could already turn his head from one side to the other before we left the hospital. In contrast to his sister, he ate well but slept a lot. In December, he suddenly came down with a high fever that turned into a low-grade temperature that he could not shake for months. There were no symptoms but swollen glands and the need for a lot of sleep. The doctor said that tonsilitis could cause swollen glands for a long time after the infection, and could also cause his high white-cell count. But we became increasingly uneasy. Even though his health improved in summer, the next winter the lowgrade fever and high white-cell count returned. All that time, Steven looked healthy and grew stronger. Over and over again, Al kept saying that he must have mumps. When I took him to be diagnosed again in October 1966, a pediatrician suddenly shared my worry about leukemia. He immediately admitted Steven to Children's hospital. We had to wait the longest twenty-four hours of our lives until the cells taken from his hipbone were evaluated. As we drove home that night, I heard again in my head what Dr. Gold had said to me. "Leukemia in children is always terminal, but one in a hundred fools us!" I could not understand why everybody kept on doing what they did before. I thought the world should stand still, because it felt like it had ended for me. I had no hope, but Al said I must wait and not give up. But he himself worried so much that he had one of his terrible headaches the next morning. I sat alone waiting in the hospital at five o'clock in the morning. At ten a young Colombian intern came into the room and said, "I can't stand to see you suffer any longer. I looked at the cells, and they did not look bad to me. No matter what the findings of the other doctors, you must promise never to tell what I just said to you, or I'll lose my career." – I will be forever grateful to him. Without his kindness, I don't think I could have made it through the following six hours. Finally, Dr. Gold came in to tell me that five doctors had come cautiously to the conclusion that our worst fears had not become reality. Now, no one knew what caused Steven's symptoms. – The following spring his pediatrician advised us to have his tonsils removed, just in case they were the cause. He was right; it put an end to the fever.

At the same time, Mutti's one remaining eye with vision had become a great concern. Many years ago, she had lost her eyesight in one eye due to glaucoma. Now the other eye had high pressure, in addition to a cataract. To treat the glaucoma with pupil-constricting drops would have rendered her ninety percent blind. At that time, surgery was not an option because of her age. So, she was given an oral medication to reduce the pressure. It made her so ill that it impaired her thinking. On the other hand, she did not dare stop the medication, while her ophthalmologist was on an extended trip to Japan. The longer she continued the medication, the more mentally disabled and depressed she became.

My dreams of leisure times had turned into a nightmare of worries. Once the doctor returned, and the medication was stopped, Mutti regained her mental capability. Unfortunately, the worry about losing her eyesight hung over her until her death.

My Relationship With Inge

When we returned from Iowa in July of 1956, the re-union with Inge was strained, and her relationship with Mutti was as bad as ever. Inge spoke mostly to Al and me in English, caring little whether Mutti understood what was said. In addition, Mutti was very sensitive to the fact that Inge had not said a flattering word about our little Catherine, which would have meant so much to her. It would not have taken much effort because Catherine was very cute and also a good little girl. (Inge liked children, but had consciously decided not to have any of her own. She said she did not want to put a Jewish child into a world where discrimination never ceased.) Unfortunately, Inge did nothing to regain a relationship with her mother. Each get-together only intensified Mutti's backpain and heartache.

Grete was living in New York City, when she came up with one of her 'great' ideas. She thought of showing Inge that she could afford a voyage for Ruth to visit, even though Grete had been in the US for only three years. Inge had little interest in seeing her sister Ruth, so she had never invited her. The scheme behind Grete's generous gift was not obvious to any of us until later.

Ruth was arriving at Hoboken, New Jersey. We were very excited about picking her up, but money was short. We thought we could share the expenses with Inge and Gerry and drive together. I remember well what Inge said, "I have not seen my sister for twenty-one years and I can wait a few extra days!" We were very disappointed. We pleaded with her but to no avail.

After picking up Ruth, we returned home late at night, too late to call anybody. The next morning, Inge called demanding to speak to Ruth. After that conversation, a surprised Ruth told us that her sister had used strong language she had never heard her use before. In fact, Ruth wondered whether Inge was drunk. Inge must have been very angry that we had not called her earlier. She ended the conversation by saying that she didn't want to see either her mother or Al and me ever again.

To be with Ruth, Inge and Gerry picked her up in front of our apartment house. They took her to their home for a visit, and then dropped her off where they had picked her up. (To this day, their behavior is a mystery to me.) A very hurt Mutti did not know what hit her. She got very angry, even ill, over the inexplicable behavior of her daughter.

Grete's plan had worked. She was aware of Inge's lifelong competition with her sister. She also knew that Ruth did not have the means to come on her own. In addition, she knew of Mutti's fragile relationship with Inge. Grete, never married and alone a lot, jealously tried to cause trouble in other people's relationships and frequently succeeded.

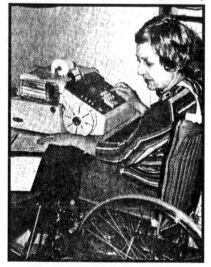

Inge doing data entry work by referral from the MS Society

We had not heard a word from either Gerry or Inge, for at least two years, when Ruth wrote to us that Inge had not been well and was scheduled for a hysterectomy. Being a mother, Mutti wanted to be with Inge during her surgery. I called and could only talk to Gerry, who promised to convey the message. We were never called back.

Ruth had kept in touch with her sister and was aware that Inge had been diagnosed with multiple sclerosis. Inge's illness was chronic-progressive, without remission. After about two years, Inge was confined to a wheelchair.

In 1966, Mutti was eighty-one. This time, 'we' invited Ruth. We would have preferred that Ruth not see Inge, because it upset Mutti so much, but Ruth insisted.

A sad goodbye to Ruth at Dulles Airport (Mutti 81)

Considering her sister's illness, she wanted very much to bring about reconciliation between her mother and Inge. I agreed with her. Inge needed help badly. Now Inge was very willing, but Mutti had endured so much that she was reluctant, afraid to be hurt again. It took a lot of convincing before she gave in.

I hoped that a reunion would give Mutti some diversion, and Inge some company. Twice I took Mutti to spend the day with Inge, then she refused to go again. She explained that Inge was detached and inhospitable. She did not even share the doughnuts, Mutti had brought. The closeness that had been between them, years ago in Germany, had been lost forever.

For the following eleven years, caring for Inge fell on my shoulders. I exercised with her in our pool and took her to an indoor wheelchair-accessible public pool in winter. I took her shopping and drove her to her various doctors. – It was long before parking for the disabled was available. Many people honked impatiently, when I had to stop outside a parking

Gerry & Inge in fromt of their house – 1967

space. None of the spaces were big enough to accommodate a wheelchair at the side of the car. It took a lot of strength to lift a wheelchair in and out of a trunk, and even more to lift Inge from the car onto the wheelchair and back into the car.

Inge's husband, Gerry, was happy that we were a family again, and that he got some help with Inge. Gerry was a handsome man, slender and sinuous, and seemed to be in wonderful physical shape. Their marriage had suffered under Inge's long illness. Inge was as ambitious as ever, and pushed Gerry hard to do the things she could not do. When he complained about being tired, she grew impatient and accused him of being lazy. She never allowed herself to give up hope that one day she could walk again. She exercised, kept herself immaculately clean and did all she could do to stay as fit as possible, under the circumstances. She was still very capable, and did whatever she could from her wheelchair.

Gerry, as a wholesale distributor for boys' clothing, took a lot of short trips, to see clients in neighboring states. In November of 1968, while on one of these business trips, he did not wake up in his hotel-room bed. He had suffered a massive heart attack in his sleep. He was only fifty-eight.

Inge was left with her government annuity, a ten-thousand-dollar life insurance and a five-thousand-dollar beach lot in Delaware. She was very frightened. A former colleague, and now a real estate lawyer in Alexandria, invested her money in second mortgages. He knew his mortgage clients and their ability to pay, so she received high interest with low risk. Eventually she had enough money to have a wheelchair-friendly house built in Severn, Md.

Lillian Levy, my close friend, kept up with the latest trends. Always supportive, she was aware of my growing concern about Inge's health. She gave me the name of a doctor who specialized in vitamin therapy. Twice a year, Inge's condition deteriorated so much that she needed to be pumped full of cortisone. She was willing to try anything that would make her feel better. The mega-vitamin therapy gave her a new lease on life and kept her out of the hospital. She was very disciplined and followed her doctor's diet precisely, even though it became more and more restricted. While Inge did well, her Dr. Woidich, on the same diet, seemed to waste away. On our trips to and from McLean, we commented on it.

Years ago Inge had helped a German girl, who had worked for a diplomatic family, to remain in the United States. Her name was Annemarie and she was very loyal to Inge. Annemarie married, had a son and subsequently settled in Severn, Md. When the property next door to her became available, she suggested that Inge move there. She offered to help with daily tasks that had become increasingly harder for Inge to manage alone.

We knew of a builder who would build an affordable custom house for Inge. Al had upgraded the kitchen in her well-kept Huntington house and it sold immediately. Inge was sixty-five when she moved to Maryland in 1977. I had a welcome reprieve from having Inge every Sunday for dinner and driving her everywhere; Inge looked forward to her new home. We spent many happy hours buying new furniture and decorating the house. My relationship with Inge had healed. I visited her at least once a month and brought along dinner and whatever else she needed. Annemarie was a good friend to Inge and served her diligently. In the beginning, Inge would reciprocate by paying for the paving of Annemaie's driveway, or for a new fence, or for other improvements. Eventually, Annemarie even had an intercom installed between her house and Inge's, in case of an emergency.

In 1981, now sixty-nine, Inge began having the type of neck pain that her mother, our Mutti, had experienced at the same age. Inge went to the hospital to be diagnosed. After several tests, she was transferred to the Maryland University hospital's orthopedic ward, where exploratory surgery was recommended. On the 18th of July 1981, the orthopedic surgeon came out to tell us that Inge had bled so profusely during surgery that they had to close her up. They had not been able to remove, what he thought to be, a malignant tumor. She was not expected to be able to move her head again, or to live more than six months. After two weeks of localized radiation treatment, she was advised to go into a Nursing Home. She refused, and hired the private nurse, who had assisted her in the hospital, to take care of her in her own home. The two became very close and, like a miracle, Inge recuperated. After a few weeks, she was able to move her head again. Her neck pain had stopped, and after repeated check-ups, her diagnosis was eventually changed to 'multiple myeloma.' She lived twelve more years, and died at the age of eighty.

Inge became so infatuated with her vivacious and charming African-American nurse that Annemarie could not do anything right anymore. Annemarie became very alienated, especially when she overheard a conversation on the open intercom. But since the nurse had to go home every night to take care of her retarded daughter, Annemarie's help was still needed in the evening. Annemarie insisted that Inge fire the nurse or Annemarie would be out of the picture. Inge had no choice but to comply. She never forgave Annemarie and vice versa. After the radiation treatments, Inge had lost a lot of the strength in her arms, so she needed help, at least twelve hours a day. Inge was very demanding, and for the minimum wage she paid, it was difficult to get reliable and competent help.

Inge's house was built so that another person could move in with her and help her. I found several nice ladies who were interested, but they would refuse after they met Inge. She could not bear the thought of giving up any control of her house, and people felt her attitude.

When I had to have potentially serious surgery in 1988, Inge decided she could not continue to maintain her house without my help. I had been looking for a long time for a nursing home, where Inge could have a private room large enough to negotiate her wheelchair. I found a place in Laurel, Maryland, that satisfied Inge. So, the day before I went into the hospital, Al and I moved Inge into the Laurel Nursing Home.

In 1991, Inge had severe pain on her right side. It was diagnosed as a gallbladder attack. The tests were inconclusive, and Inge refused to have her gallbladder removed. I mentioned her previous health history to Dr. Weltz, an oncologist, who then re-diagnosed her with multiple myeloma. After giving her radiation treatments, he enthusiastically prescribed Interferon-B injections. Although very expensive, her insurance company covered them.

Dr. Weltz was very interested in seeing whether Interferon B would treat both, Inge's cancer and her multiple sclerosis. When the radiation helped her pain for a while, Inge became very hopeful that the injections would accomplish what the doctor had promised her. When the pain recurred after many months, radiation treatments were repeated. But this time, there was no relief, and Inge refused the torture of being transported to the radiation lab, and eventually refused the Interferon injections, as well. That put an end to the doctor's research. The charming, and seemingly caring, Dr. Weltz was so angered that he never came to see her again. Inge was very hurt, and felt used like a guinea pig. (I never stopped wondering whether the massive doses of vitamins had caused Inge's cancer, similar to overfertilizing a plant.) On the 15th of April 1993, five years after Inge had moved to the Nursing Home, she died holding on to my hand. She had fought for forty years, and had never given up hope to walk again some day. – Why does anybody have to suffer that much? What a waste of an energetic, intelligent and capable person! Her struggle, and the futility of her life, left me with a deep sadness.

THE STORY CONTINUES . . .

In September 1973, Catherine had successfully finished high school, and was all packed to be taken to Virginia Polytechnic Institute & University at Blacksburg, VA. It was very painful for Mutti not to be able to accompany her. She was 88 years old, very thin, and she had lost all energy.

In the morning of the first day of October 1973, we found Mutti lying in her bed unconscious. In the hospital, she was presumed to have had a stroke. In reality, it was a seizure caused by dehydration that resulted in her collapse. It was due to more than twenty years of 'Hygroton', a diuretic prescribed for her without a potassium supplement. When she came home from the hospital, she was so weak that she could not walk or even stand up. She asked me so many times, "Why didn't you let me die that morning of October 1st?" The following six months in bed were hell for her. With her mind as clear and bright as ever, she not only witnessed her own decay, but also was aware of my pain seeing her die a little more every day.

I was forty years old when Mutti died in April of 1974, but I felt as if I were her age. The last six months had been so sad that it left me emotionally numb. All my fears and nightmares about losing her, from childhood on, were suddenly erased. My feelings resembled a blank and empty desert.

The day we laid Mutti to rest was the brightest April day I had ever seen. The trees were blooming, and the sky a cloudless blue. My children and I were surrounded by friends who stood with us at her graveside. David Bumbaugh, then the minister of the Mount Vernon Unitarian Church, was with us at National Memorial Park, Falls Church, Virginia. He said,

"Her life has been a hard climb up a mountain, but now that she has arrived, her spirit will soar off that mountain and live on forever, through the people who knew her and loved her." I don't remember anything else, but that metaphor stayed with me.

Earl Levy made all the arrangements. He and his wife, Lillian, stood by me through that horrible time, as they had done for years, and only the best of friends do. Al was in Europe representing the United States at a United Nations Water Resources Conference. Though he was not present at the funeral, during Mutti's lifetime he had always been there for her and he had respected and loved her as if she had been his own mother.

Often life writes stories stranger than fiction, and here are three examples:

Summer of 1974, the year of Mutti's death, Lillian and I had planned to spend two weeks at our beach house at Ocean Pines, Maryland. There, I had planned to start this book. Steven's friend, Keith, had just lost his father to a heart attack, and I had agreed to take him along to give him some distraction. After a few days, Lillian became ill and had to go home. I stayed with the boys because of my commitment to Keith's mother, but I was so depressed that I hardly managed the strength to do the most necessary daily chores. Even Steven noticed my condition, and invited me to go biking with him and his friend.

Toward the end of the week, on a Friday with drizzling rain, I forced myself to get out of the house and drive to nearby Salisbury. There I walked back and forth through the mall. The Hecht Co. department store had a bathing suit sale. When I looked though the suits, I saw a beautiful bikini with a matching jacket. I went through the motions of trying it on, because I really needed a swimsuit. Even though it fit me perfectly and was quite flattering, I didn't feel like spending the money. I heard Mutti's voice saying, as I had heard so many times before, 'Get it while you are still young enough to look good in it.' When she really liked something on me, she would add enthusiastically, 'Go ahead, I'll pay for it!' I could feel the love that had been mine for so many years and tears ran down my face. I bought the swimsuit, but was not a bit excited about my find. Having no phone in the beach house, I called Al from a phone booth that evening. It was so dark; I could hardly see to dial. When I finally heard his voice, I guessed I had interrupted a good TV show. But I wanted to keep him on the phone for a while, to have some company, so I told him about my shopping trip. He suddenly said, "By the way, here is a letter for you from the German Government." I said, "Please open it. What could they want from me? I have sent them all the necessary notifications!" When Al opened the letter, he found a check. According to the accompanying letter, this money was still due Mutti – it covered the cost of the swimsuit!

After Vati died, a lawyer notified us that he had left a will. In it, I was named his sole heir. Mutti and I were surprised that Vati had thought to make a will, and wondered why I was his only beneficiary. The lawyer advised us not to have it probated, since there was nothing to be inherited but possible debts. (The Heidehof was not accessible to us at that time, since it was located in the Russian Zone of Germany.) Consequently, we were never sent a copy of the will.

In 1989, when the wall between East and West came down in Berlin, the Heidehof could be claimed again. I went to Berlin to see about my father's will. It did not take much searching. Vati Uhlenbrock's testament was properly filed away and easily found. When I saw it, the answer to both questions became immediately clear. The will was drawn up long ago, in 1942, and sealed with a big Nazi stamp. It said that everything Vati possessed at his death would go to his foster child, Eleonora Orazi.

In my mind, I could hear Mutti pleading with him to make a will, reminding him that if he were to be arrested by the Nazis, she would be picked up immediately, and I would have nothing in addition to nobody. After all, she had just seen what had happened to her brother, when his 'Aryan' wife had suddenly died of a heart attack.

In 1991 my Italian sisters, Simonetta and Donatella, came from Rome to visit us. They brought a beautifully decorated box that contained letters that Clara, our mutual mother, had written to her mother, our grandmother. They were written while she was pregnant with me, and living with Mutti and Vati Uhlenbrock in Berlin. During that time, Clara had written seventy-two letters to her mother, all numbered. Not all of them were still around after six decades, but enough to learn, through Clara's written words, how much love and care she had received from Mutti and Vati. Everything Mutti had told me of her time with Clara, was recounted exactly. Clara wrote her mother over and over again, "If you were not the best mother in the whole wide world, Mrs. Uhlenbrock would surely be the best mother anybody could have or want."

Mutti truly was the best mother, and that never changed. I was very lucky. Still today, I believe that all that is good in me, came from her. Clara had a lot of warmth, enviable *joie de vivre,* and one had to like her instantly. But there was only one mother for me – and that was my Mutti.

Post Script

Now that I am too old to fool myself, time seems to pass increasingly faster, and I realize that there are not so many years left.

I have many reasons to be thankful. Both my children seem happy. They each have a child, Steven a boy, Catherine a girl. Al is always optimistic, still industrious and always helpful when needed. In our lifetime together, we have been spared bombs and famine and fears for tomorrow. Life became better and easier for us, as the United States became more prosperous. For more than forty years, we have remained in, what has now become, a modest home in a quiet little spot, not far from commuter traffic and shopping.

My wish remains that our children and their families will never forget that they can find support and encouragement right here, where they grew up – as long as we still live.

The United States has been gracious and generous to me; allowing me to immigrate, to build a life and to exchange my Italian citizenship for that of the United States.

For all that is my life, I am grateful . . .

A P P E N D I X

Biographies:

Mutti

Vati

Ruth & Inge

Drs. Hempel & Bacigalupo

Clara Orazi

Bubi

Last not Least, Al

MUTTI

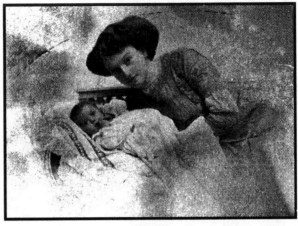

1910

. . . Only very gradually did I learn about Mutti's life – about the forty-eight years before I was born. From early on, I understood that Mutti was a very private person, and I carefully avoided any questions that I thought might make her uncomfortable. But it seems that I was always aware of the fact, that she had lost her mother when she was very young. Although she seldom talked about it, I vicariously shared her pain.

Mutti never mentioned her age. Throughout my childhood, I had no idea of the year of her birth. I only knew that she was born on the 8th of February . . .

Mutti was born in 1885 in Hannover, Germany, to Meta Catzenstein and Moses Frankenstein. She was named Bertha Erna, but used her middle name Erna. She had a brother, Alfred, seven years older, and another brother, Erich, who was four years younger. Mutti's father tailored uniforms. He was a successful and respected businessman. There were no financial hardships.

The Frankenstein family lived across the street from the Bahlsen Bakery. Mutti remembered that when she was a child, she could get a whole bag of broken cookies for just five pennies; that impressed me no end, when we were always hungry.

Mutti was just eleven when her mother became bedridden with chronic Bright's disease, a progressively debilitating and incurable kidney ailment. Her mother died when Mutti was fourteen years old. She had just been enrolled in dancing school, then customary for young ladies and gentlemen. In addition to ballroom dancing, they were also taught social graces in dealing with the opposite sex. Mutti was called out of her very first session, and got home just in time to be at her mother's bedside, when she died. The trauma of that moment, and the pain of growing up without a mother, stayed with her all her life. While other young girls enjoyed their teen-age years, Mutti was dressed in black, mourning the death of her mother.

She formed a close bond with her brothers. Alfred, already twenty-one when his mother died, became a surrogate father. Erich, only ten, clung to his sister as if she were his mother. Soon after the death of his wife, Moses became involved in many liaisons, some of which became painfully known to his children.

After Mutti had finished the Elite School for Girls, what was then 'higher education', she decided to look for gainful employment. That was considered *avant garde* for a girl in her social class. Mutti wanted to get away from her father, but it was not easy for a woman to find a job at the turn of the century. A diploma from a school of higher learning could not compete with a completed apprenticeship.

Julius Jacobsberg, a cousin by marriage, owned an insurance agency. He was much older and well established. When Mutti asked for help, he offered her a job in his company.

She was delighted. She learned fast, was well organized and very soon earned the respect of her co-workers. When Julius sold his business, not long after Mutti had started to work there, his successor asked her to stay on.

Julius Jacobsberg was going through a scandalous divorce. He had been incapacitated with a broken leg, when his wife (Mutti's cousin and the mother of their three teenagers) boldly allowed her lover into the house. Already suspicious of his extremely attractive wife's conduct, he forced himself to get out of bed and dragged himself into the sitting room, where he surprised the lovers. He sued successfully for divorce, and was awarded custody of their three children, Edith, Hans and Grete.

l to r: Erna, 'Bua' with Ruth and Julius Jacobsberg

Soon thereafter, Julius Jacobsberg fell in love with Mutti, who was 21 years younger. They were married in 1909. With that, Mutti became stepmother to her own three second cousins. She was only seven years older than her eldest stepdaughter, Edith.

Julius Jacobsberg was well read, entertaining and had a good sense of humor. He adored his young wife and she returned his love; indeed, she was gloriously happy.

Their first child, Ruth, was born in 1910. The family moved to Hamburg, where Julius had acquired a cigarette factory. Besides actively participating in the management of his business, he became involved in advertising the newly invented telephone. He was extremely successful in all his ventures. In 1912, a second daughter was born; they named her Ingeborg.

The three teenagers from Julius' first marriage, Edith, Hans and Grete, quarreled incessantly. In fact, they hated each other. Edith and Grete shared a room with an outside entrance, quite distant from their parents' bedroom. Edith was an extremely beautiful young woman and – like her mother – had an affinity for men. Once, without her parents' permission, Edith had made arrangements for an evening rendezvous without a chaperone. She sneaked out, after getting her sister's promise to let her back in. But when Edith returned, Grete (vindictive and envious) ignored her sister's frantic knocking. Only after a considerable time, Grete 'suddenly remembered' that her sister had gone out. She said that she thought that an intruder was trying to get in. Edith, exhausted by anger and fear of being discovered, would not accept Grete's incredible excuse. She furiously threw her metal hairbrush at her sister. (Fifty years later, Grete still claimed that she had had a 'memory lapse', and insisted that her sister had tried to kill her.)

The only thing the girls could agree upon was playing nasty tricks on their brother. Once, when their parents had gone out to dinner, the girls were asked to look after Hans. He had severe indigestion from eating too much of his favorite almond candy, *Marzipan*. His sisters supposedly encouraged him to eat more 'to get better'. When Mutti and their father returned home, they had to take Hans to the emergency room to have his stomach pumped out. The girls blamed everything on their brother's stupidity. But Hans ended up a very well to do businessman. He became CEO of the Israel Department Store in Berlin, before he had to immigrate to Chile because of Hitler. He also did very well there. In the early 1960's, he feared that Chile, sooner or later, would become communist, because of the disparity between the rich and the poor. He then chose to come to the U. S., sponsored by his sister Grete. To our surprise, he transferred his investment money to Germany instead of bringing it to the United States; and he managed to time it just right, before the German *Mark* more than doubled in value.

Exasperated with his children's behavior, Julius Jacobsberg decided to send all three, from his first marriage, away to different, private boarding schools in Switzerland. Their excellent multilingual education paid off.

At age forty-six, and after having been married for only a year, Julius had his first severe heart attack – the first of several. Mutti lay awake at night, worrying and listening to his breathing. With each heart attack, Julius' condition worsened, and each time the doctor warned that he would not survive the next one. Thus Mutti's happiness was marred by the fear of losing him. When Julius' heart finally gave out, he was in his factory. A friend was helping him into a heavy leather coat, when his heart stopped. It was 1916, the middle of the First World War. After seven years of marriage Mutti's world collapsed for the second time. Her children were still small, Ruth was five and Inge only three. Neither Ruth nor Inge were old enough to remember their father, the man their mother had loved so much.

Julius had provided well for his family. He had set aside a trust of 100,000 *Mark* for each of his five children. There was a house in Hannover, as well as the house in Hamburg, where they were living at the time. But that did not lessen Mutti's grief. She was so devastated that she did not want to live. The two small children had a governess Frau Buhrmeister, nicknamed 'Bua'. She eventually succeeded in convincing Mutti that she had to go on living, for the sake of her children.

Bua suggested that Mutti move to Berlin, where she could be with Alfred, her older brother. Alfred's glaucoma had taken most of his sight; therefore he did not serve in the war. Erich, her younger brother, had just finished his one-year obligatory service, when the First World War began. He was sent to the front lines immediately.

Mutti and Ruth – 1914

Mutti followed Frau Buhrmeister's advice. Unfortunately, before she moved to Berlin, she made the mistake of selling all her real estate. (All the money was lost in the inflation of 1923.) She then took her two little girls to make a new home in Berlin. Bua accompanied her but left soon thereafter, because she was needed to help her only son with his children. Ruth and Inge were very sad to lose Bua – they loved her like a mother – and Mutti felt a great loss, as well.

Mutti rented an apartment in Zehlendorf, then still considered a 'western suburb' of Berlin. As an attractive young woman, she soon realized that her new status as a widow made her 'fair game'. She was even propositioned by men, like her attorney or her doctor, no matter how reserved she was. It was so different from the respect she had enjoyed as the wife of Julius Jacobsberg.

The war took its toll. Food was scarce as the First World War was nearing its end. The loss of resources and loved ones touched everybody. Mutti experienced the misery of war first hand, by volunteering to care for wounded soldiers brought back from the front.

Erich, Mutti's younger brother, had survived four years on the front lines. But in 1918, when Germany capitulated, he died miserably in a prisoner-of-war camp in France, at the age of twenty-eight. When the flu epidemic raged throughout Europe, no medical help was given to prisoners. When Mutti was notified of her brother's death, as next of kin, she received the never-to-be-forgotten message that ended with, *"Der Dank des Vaterlands sei Dir gewiss "* which meant, 'You can be assured of the gratitude of the fatherland.' She would repeat those words with bitterness, twenty-one years later, when she was notified by the Nazis of Alfred's death in Auschwitz.

By that time, Mutti's life had become a never ending horror in Nazi Germany, and her grief and outrage over the murder of her second brother was nearly unbearable.

Alfred had introduced Mutti to Friedrich August Uhlenbrock, still a bachelor at forty-three, who had returned alive and well from the war. From the minute they met, he courted her. It wasn't long before he asked her to marry him. He was ready to settle down. He even seemed to enjoy the prospect of having a 'ready made' family. He was very kind and attentive to Ruth and Inge. Mutti had the impression that he would be good to her children. – She accepted his marriage proposal.

l to r:
Inge, Mutti, Ruth & Vati - 1922

Friedrich August Uhlenbrock was a Catholic. While he was not too devout a Catholic, he could not imagine being anything else. To marry Mutti would have meant excommunication for him, so Mutti agreed to take lessons in Catholicism in order to be married in the Catholic Church. Though raised in the Jewish faith, she was an agnostic. I often heard her quote, "Blessed are those who believe." Much later I found out that she was not a believer, and certainly not in a personal God.

Mutti had grown up with all the traditional Jewish rituals of a Kosher home. But after her mother's death, her father did not practice the traditions of Judaism any longer. Mutti's first husband had been a 'dissident', one of the few who was registered as such on his official papers. He disavowed belonging to, or believing in, any conventional religion. He considered himself a 'free thinker,' ever searching and philosophizing. Though interested in all religions, he accepted none. I still have a poem he wrote about his thoughts on religion.

Mutti had promised Clara to raise me as a Catholic and never broke a promise. Mutti did not like to discuss religion. After I knew about her Jewish background, I realized that she was very proud of her Jewish heritage and its old culture. I once heard her say that she believed the Jewish people had an inner life and a higher cultural standard than most ethnic groups. I became convinced of that as well, probably because she set a good example.

On the 20th day of November 1920, four years after Mutti's first husband had died; she married Friedrich August Uhlenbrock in a Catholic ceremony. He was to become my 'Vati' in 1933.

VATI

1930

Friedrich August Uhlenbrock was born in Barmen, North Rhein-Westphalia, on the 3rd of November 1877. His parents owned a hardware store, and being good Catholics, they had seven children. Friedrich August was the oldest. Their two daughters died of leukemia when only in their thirties. The others were sons, who all died of cancer as well, except Vati.

Vati went to Berlin to study at the *Technische Hochschule*, Berlin's well-known Technical University, majoring in hydraulic engineering. He had the fondest memories of his university days in Germany's capital. He described Berlin as 'a city full of excitement and international flavor.' It was around the turn of the century. Berlin was growing by leaps and bounds, culturally as well as in every other way.

He specialized in design of water supply systems, customized for the particular needs of each client. He opened a successful business in Berlin in 1909. His customers were wealthy landowners, north and east of Berlin, who wanted running water on their estates.

Vati loved talking about his bachelor years and always included his 'happy' war experiences. As a 'water supply specialist,' he was treated exceptionally well in the army, offered a commission from the start and became *Hauptmann* (Captain) very soon thereafter. Before the Nazi times, it was very prestigious to be an officer in the German army. Most of them came from well-to-do families. Officers' pay was comparatively small and needed to be subsidized by their families. German officers had the reputation of having impeccable manners. Before a commission was offered, their family-history was scrutinized. – I don't know whether any of this applied to Vati, but it helps explain the pride he had in his rank. Furthermore, Vati's 'expert' status, in a sought-after profession, gave him privileges usually only enjoyed by older men in higher ranks. He was chauffeured around and given a horse for his private use. Vati also liked to talk about the good food in the officers' dining facilities. That was not Mutti's favorite subject. She recalled her brother's perpetual diet of potato soup, the fare for soldiers in the trenches. Therefore, when Vati enjoyed reliving his war memories, Mutti would take the opportunity to express her hatred for war. She thought that the leaders, who declared war, should be the ones to fight in the front lines.

In 1918, Vati had returned from World War I, unharmed and honored with the *Eiserne Kreuz*. (The Iron Cross haunted us later, when Hitler insisted on exchanging it for his version with the swastika.) As before, Vati was in the right place at the right time when the First World War ended. He had more clients than he could handle. With little competition he could set his own fees. He designed water systems and employed his own construction crews.

After so many years as a bachelor, the adjustment of being a family man and sharing his time and money, was not easy for Vati. He was very 'frugal' because his money was always 'needed for his business.' After the wedding, he moved into Mutti's beautifully furnished apartment in Berlin-Zehlendorf. He commuted by *Stadtbahn* (elevated train) to *Friedrichstrasse* in central Berlin, where his office was located.

Vati was not married long, when Germany's rapidly escalating inflation became disastrous. Prices soon rose so high that it took millions of *Deutsche Mark* to buy anything. In January of 1919, eight *Mark* equaled one dollar. In May of 1920, the *Mark's* value had deteriorated to the point where it took thirty-five *Mark* to buy one dollar. On the 20th of November 1923 – exactly three years after his wedding day – the *Mark* hit bottom. One dollar was the equivalent of 4.2-billion *Deutsche Mark*. It took two people with a large basket to carry the money to the store to pay for one loaf of bread!

Mutti and Vati lost all their money. All the Trust funds of the Jacobsberg children became worthless. Everyone bartered for necessities. By then, most of Berlin's population enjoyed the convenience of running water. When in need to keep their taps running many of them called on Vati; that is how his business managed to survive.

The monetary situation created a lot of tension, but there were other problems plaguing the new Jacobsberg-Uhlenbrock family. With money scarce, Vati was plain stingy. Mutti claimed that he counted every bite that went into the mouths of her children. She fed them extra food in the kitchen, before they all sat down at the dinner table. They no longer had a fulltime maid, and Vati had difficulty revising his bachelor habit of leaving everything to be picked up by someone else. Mutti liked 'order' in the house, whereas Vati 'could not find a thing' when everything was put where it belonged. He also kept forgetting that Mutti did not run a restaurant, where he could order a whole variety of food for every meal. Both Vati and Mutti had small appetites, but Vati liked many different dishes. Preparing meals was not an expression of creativity for Mutti; it was only a daily necessity. Her meals were basic and nutritious, but never elaborate. She said that she envied people who could really enjoy food; she was also convinced that overeaters were not born, they were trained. She believed in the motto, 'We eat to live, we do not live to eat,'

Ruth and Inge were not happy with their stepfather. The four years before Vati came into their lives, they had been the focal point of their mother's attention. Inge was especially affected. She started walking in her sleep, a great concern when she headed for the window. The family tried everything to discourage her. They even placed a water bucket in front of her bed, which she skillfully avoided even in her sleep. Then they tied Inge to Ruth, so she would wake up and take charge of the situation when Inge started her antics. It eventually took care of itself.

Vati found it difficult to think as a family-team in any situation. His business continued to be his number one consideration, just as it had been before he got married. When he became angry, he shouted so loud that everyone was frightened. Mutti was embarrassed that the neighbors could hear him. He did not use profanity, instead he shouted *"Himmel Donnerwetter"* (heaven thunder-weather) before hollering about what ever displeased him. His voice level allowed the whole neighborhood to participate. Mutti, not used to such behavior, was mortified by his tirades. She would hurriedly close all the windows. The louder he got, the more quiet she became. Vati never seemed to notice his wife's hurt feelings and his anger was forgotten as fast as it had flared up. Mutti often said, "A hard block needs a hard wedge!" But this realization came too late – she was neither!

On the other hand, Vati had to compete with the ghost of a 'perfect' first husband; impossibile for nearly anyone. As time went on, Mutti's marriage with Vati did not get easier or happier. Vati was either uninvolved or so upset that he did not mind making a scene, wherever he was. It was the opposite of Mutti's quiet and elegant demeanor. One day they were both waiting for the train to Berlin. No delay had been announced. As Vati waited, he became more and more agitated. He got into such a long argument with the station manager that he missed both the train's arrival and it's departure. Mutti had pretended not to know him, stayed close to the tracks and got on the train. She could not stop laughing all the way into the city, and the other passengers looked at her strangely.

Vati Uhlenbrock did not like the daily commute from Zehlendorf, so the family moved to Berlin to be closer to his office. First they lived on *Nickelsburger Strasse* and then they moved to *Kaiser Allee*. Both were large, fancy apartments in elegant residential areas. (Some years later, I was born in the private clinic of Dr. Solms. *Kaiser Allee 9* renamed *Bundesallee*.)

Vati had a passion for traveling any place where a train would take him. He did not care to stay at any one place very long, therefore Mutti preferred not to accompany him. He raved about his breakfasts in the train's dining car, while he was watching the rising sun. He traveled back and forth to Italy – where he had a branch office for a while. But most of all he enjoyed traveling to the Arabian countries. He was quite a good photographer and his pictures of camels and Bedouins, as well as the 'grave of Jesus', filled our albums. They were all lost in Germany.

When he left on his adventurous travels, Mutti did not hear from him for months. She wondered what had happened, even whether he was still alive. Then he would suddenly re-appear with new friends, many stories and new ideas. One time, he had developed an interest in tropical fish. He arrived home with fish tanks; not just one, but many! Mutti was neither skilled nor interested in keeping tropical fish. She would have preferred a plausible explanation of why she had not heard from her husband for such an extended period of time. Her problem with the fish was that they kept dying for no apparent reason. Vati then hired 'Helmig', one of his unmarried workers, who was always in financial straits. He became the fish-keeper and, in turn, was allowed to live in our extra storage room. Mutti always ended up entertaining Vati's newly acquired travel acquaintances. They were as colorful as the fish, many of them quite eccentric.

Vati had his own eccentricities. When money was collected for newspaper delivery, or utilities, or delivery of milk and fresh rolls, Vati would complain about the high cost of those services. The deliveryman wondered whether he was going to be paid. On the other hand, Vati did not mind paying enormous sums in monthly rent.

One day, Mutti recounted what the clerk had said when she registered her new married name at the police station. He had questioned, "Does your husband happen to be related to the 'honorable' Uhlenbrock, who was a Secret Counsel to the Kaiser?" Mutti did not answer, but was bothered by the question. Not encouraged, the man continued, "This fine gentleman is known to be so stingy that he had argued with the barber about the cost of a haircut." He supposedly 'had wasted his valuable time' investigating the price of haircuts, only to discover that he had been undercharged! Mutti was not amused, especially since she saw some similarity in her husband's behavior.

Marriage to Vati meant that life was in constant up-roar – not unlike the political situation of that time. . .

RUTH AND INGE

1924

Clara was preparing to leave Berlin, after she had given birth to me. She invited Ruth to come with her to Rome, and Ruth accepted eagerly. Ruth fell in love with Italy and with Clara's parents. When she returned from her visit to Rome, she realized how much Germany had changed after the Nazi takeover. Not kidding herself, she knew it was important to get out as soon as possible. It was hard for her to leave Mutti and Inge behind, but she took advantage of Clara's invitation, to live with her and her parents in Rome.

In Rome, Ruth was welcomed with open arms by the Orazis and was treated as part of their family. She wrote in her letters to Mutti, "The generosity of the Orazis is legendary." Ruth, young and attractive, adopted Italy as her country of choice and Italy reciprocated – at least for the first few years. After a year of learning the language and getting acclimatized, Ruth felt the need to make it on her own. She started by giving German language lessons. She rented a room from a young couple, who became her lifelong friends. Ruth loved life. She was optimistic and confident, and it did not take her long to find employment with a publishing company.

**Clara and Ruth,
Venice 1933**

After Ruth established herself, she convinced Inge to join her in Rome. Inge tried it for a year, but she was very attached to Mutti and felt lonely and homesick. In addition, Ruth and Inge had very different personalities. Inge had always felt overshadowed by her older sister. She thought that Ruth was more attractive, and stole all the attention with her extroverted and generous personality. So Inge was only too anxious to return home to Germany.

Vati was furious with the direction Germany had taken politically. His anger escalated every year, as the Nazis revealed more of their hateful mission. Although it looked as if Germany was recovering economically, through government-financed public works and rearmament, Vati predicted doom. He talked about an ensuing war, because money was printed *en masse,* without resources to back it up. He complained daily, "How come England and America are ignoring our factories gearing up for war at frightening speed?"

We had moved to the apartment on Prager Platz 4. At that time, Inge had fallen in love with a young man with whom she worked. The escalation of anti-Jewish sentiment was brought home, when Inge's boyfriend was afraid to continue the relationship, because she was

Ruth and Inge

Jewish. Inge was heartbroken. Mutti suffered with her – as she did with all of us – but this time it was different! Mutti knew she was running out of time, to find someone to sponsor Inge to get out of Germany.

A year later, at a soccer game, Inge met the man who was to become her future husband. He was Jewish, as well, and found himself in the same predicament, namely not knowing how to get out of Germany. Although he had wealthy relatives in the United States, they did not offer their German family any help. (His name was Gerhard Mosler, and he was related to the owners of the Mosler Safe Company.)

Gehard Mosler, Berlin 1940

In Berlin, on the ninth of November 1938, almost 200 Synagogues were burned down, hundreds of store windows were broken and the Nazis destroyed thousands of businesses, belonging to German Jews. After the horror of the *Kristallnacht,* there was little doubt in anybody's mind what lay ahead for Germany's Jews.

Mutti remembered that her father's business partner had emigrated to the U. S. many years before. After a lot of research, she managed to locate him. With all the persistence she could muster, she talked him into giving Inge an affidavit. (An affidavit meant having the means and vouching support for individuals entering the U. S., in the event they were not able to support themselves.) Nobody was allowed into the United States without an affidavit.

Not long after we had moved to the Rosenheimer Strasse apartment, Inge left for the United States. She was twenty-seven years old when she was forced to leave her home. She had no idea what lay in store for her in the United States, but she felt sure that she would not see her mother or her fiancé again. Inge never overcame her hatred for Germany. Toward the end of her life, she told me, "I worshiped the German soil I stepped on. I can never feel indifferent toward Germany, and therefore, I can only hate it!" This hatred festered like a cancer and poisoned the relationship with her mother years later.

Inge's first years in the United States were lonely and difficult. The old gentleman, who had enabled Inge to come to Baltimore, was neither helpful nor caring. At the time, to be German and Jewish encountered a lot of discrimination. But she was practical and very capable. She could sew very well. When she got a sewing job in a factory, with endless hours for little money, she did well. Years before, when Inge had wanted to become a designer and learn sewing professionally, Vati would not sign for her, because he considered an apprenticeship not classy enough!

As soon as Inge could find her way around and spoke English well enough, she set out to find the relatives of her fiancé. After locating them, she went to their elaborate home, and begged them to give an affidavit to their nephew to get him out of Germany. But she had to threaten to sit on their front steps with a picket sign, telling the world why she was there, before they were willing to help.

Gerry left Germany in 1941, on a transport to Lisbon, Portugal. There he waited nervously. Inge had sent him enough money so that he was able to pay the $35 fee, the Captain required, to get on one of the last passenger ships to the United States. Many were left behind. Gerry's parents were not helped to get out of Germany, and they were gassed in Auschwitz.

Mutti received the bad news that now Ruth had to flee from Italy. Persecution of the Jews had followed her. Even though it was known that the Swiss government gave no refuge, Clara accompanied her to Switzerland. The two women, dressed in ski clothes, with skis placed conspicuously on top of Clara's automobile, looked as if they were on a skiing vacation. Just before they crossed the border, Mutti joined them to be with Ruth one more time. The Catholic nuns were the only ones who let them stay overnight; no one else was willing to take the chance. The following day, Mutti waved good-bye to them with a heavy heart, as they drove off toward the border.

When they arrived at the checkpoint, Clara immediately got involved in a conversation with the border policemen, who soon were interested in joining the young women on their vacation. They paid little attention to their passports. (Fortunately, Ruth had left Germany before 'Sara' was added as a middle name, and before a big 'J' was stamped onto her passport.) So the two young women crossed the border with good wishes for a happy holiday and without further questioning. They were so relieved, that Clara did not pay attention to her driving in the snow and slipped into a ditch. Now the border guards had to come to help them out of their predicament. Ruth and Clara held their breath, wondering whether the policemen would get wise to them. But Clara could laugh at her own stupidity so whole-heartedly that they all laughed with her; even Ruth forgot her fears for a while.

After a few days, the two women had to say good-bye to each other. Ruth felt afraid and lost, more than ever before in her life. Mutti had given her some money. Clara insisted on giving her every penny she possessed, in addition to the bundle she brought from her parents. But who knew how long the money would have to last? How could she find work without proper papers? Switzerland was careful to preserve its neutrality, and German Jews were deported as fast as they came in.

Where, why and how Grete had managed to live in Switzerland during that time, I do not know, but Mutti had given Ruth the address of her half-sister. After Ruth had located Grete and moved in with her, Grete made Ruth's life a living hell. (That was Grete's specialty throughout her life!)

Desperate to get away from Grete, Ruth decided to move out. Trying to rent a room in a private home, made Ruth realize that nobody was willing to rent to her, and that there was no place on earth where she could go. When she was stopped and asked for her identification, she ended up in court. There she lied under oath. As she testified, her heart beat so strongly that she had to hold her hand in front of her neck, so the judge could not see the pulse-beat. He told her that she had twenty-four hours to produce proper papers, or would be handed over to the Germans.

After leaving the courthouse, she stood in the middle of the street and cried bitterly. A man who had been watching, approached her. He wondered why she was crying. She told him about the hopelessness of her situation. He then invited her to his home for tea, and said that he might be able to help her. Having no other choice, Ruth accepted. When she arrived, she was introduced to a British colonel in his sixties. Before the day was over, the Englishman had offered to take her with him to England.

" He was the kindest man I ever met," Ruth told us later. He managed to get the papers that would allow her into his country as his companion. In London, he found her a job cleaning the house of friends. Ruth was not used to physical work, but she was meticulously clean like Inge and Grete. Later Ruth would say, "I pitied the Kowalskys," meaning that her cleaning left a lot to be desired. However, the Kowalskys must have been satisfied. They became her friends, and their home became her second home.

Ruth lived in London for more than twenty years. She became a British subject and never failed to hail her adopted country as the 'kindest' in the world. She said that England was the only country that gave asylum to refugees from all over Europe. Ruth described how well-to-do Englishmen stood lining the gangplanks – from the ships onto British soil – to hand out money and jewelry to the homeless, persecuted and emotionally-devastated refugees. She knew of that first hand, because the man she married in 1946 was one of those refugees. His name was Walter Schorsch, a Jewish film director from Prague, who had lost everything; his family, his career and his home.

Walter died of pneumonia in 1963. Ruth moved back to Italy where she had been so happy before. After several bouts of diverticulitis, Ruth decided to move back to Germany in 1979, because she could not afford the doctor and hospital fees in Rome. It was a hard decision to return to her homeland – but Germany won her back. She moved to Kleve, a city located at the Dutch border, where our oldest friends, Frau Haedenkamp and her daughter, Ulle, and her family lived. Even though Ruth was already sixty-nine at the time of her return to Germany, she got a job immediately. She went into the Kleve Police-Station, stated her age and said that she was Jewish. She added that she was returning to Germany, spoke three languages fluently and needed a job. She got a great position as a Court interpreter. She was picked up by limousine from her apartment, driven to the courthouse when needed, and was returned home afterwards. From the minute she left her house to the time she returned, she was paid a hefty hourly fee. She had free healthcare and many other privileges. She said to me,"This period in Germany was the only time in my adult life I did not have to worry about money!" Unfortunately, she only lived seven more years in Kleve.

Ruth, a vegetarian from birth, was always slender and still beautiful at seventy-five. She died in 1986 of a rare form of intestinal cancer.

Dr. Hempel And Dr. Bacigalupo

In 1921, Ruth had become very ill. It appeared to be scarlet fever, a dreaded disease. Mutti was frantic. (In those days there were no antibiotics.) She called her pediatrician's office in Zehlendorf and was told that her doctor had died, and that the practice had been taken over by another physician, a Dr. Hempel. The new doctor promised to come to the house to diagnose and treat the ten-year-old Ruth.

The doorbell rang, Mutti opened the door and a lady, close to her own age, introduced herself as Doctor Alma Hempel. Mutti did not know how to hide her surprise to see a woman physician! Who had ever heard of a female medical doctor? Mutti had absolutely no confidence in this new doctor's ability to treat her sick child. That, combined with the stress of the situation, made for a very strained relationship between the two women. Rapport became non-existent when Mutti stopped the doctor before an injection to ask, "Are you sure you know what you have in the syringe?" However, after quite a long illness with quarantine and much anxiety, Ruth survived the scarlet fever, and the two women had learned to respect each other. As time went on, this respect grew into a long and lasting friendship.

Ruth had recovered fully. It was during the winter of 1921, and snow had fallen. All the kids – including Ruth – met on the highest hill in Zehlendorf to go sledding. (Zehlendorf still resembled a small town where all the kids knew each other.) To Ruth's surprise, there was a stranger sledding among them. He had curly black hair, and when asked his name, he said, "Bacigalupo." That strange and foreign-sounding name soon made the rounds. Somebody had the bright idea to shout "Bacigalupo" instead of the customary *"Bahn frei!"*, the warning the kids yelled, to clear the path before sledding down. Soon everybody screamed "Bacigalupo" before starting the descent, and they all got a kick out of it. (I cannot imagine that the Bacigalupo boy was very amused!)

Ruth found out that the stranger was called *'Bubi'* at home. She also learned that he was two years younger than she, the age of her sister Inge. Bubi and his mother had come from Italy for his grandfather's 70th-birthday celebration. On their way back, they visited Bubi's mother's close friend in Zehlendorf, who was none other than Dr. Alma Hempel.

Ruth never forgot the day she saw 'Bubi' for the first time. Much, much later, when she told me the story, she ended it by saying, "How could I have guessed then – that one day in the future – that boy's daughter would become my sister!" ... Life writes stories stranger than fiction.

Bubi's mother, Elfriede Bacigalupo, and Alma Hempel had known each other ever since they had studied medicine together. They had a special bond, because they had been the only two female interns in the hospital in Berlin. Their friendship had lasted, although they ended up living in different countries.

Elfriede Bacigalupo's father, Paul Antze, whose birthday they had been celebrating, was a homeopathic doctor in Berlin and then in Bremen. He and his wife retired later in Rapallo, Italy, where their daughter, my grandmother, lived. Dr. Antze was an avid golfer as well as a good chess player. When he lived in Rapallo, he swam daily in the Mediterranean Sea, in winter as well as in summer. Hedwig Antze, his wife, died in Rapallo in 1926, at the age of sixty-nine. Her family were Huguenots who had fled from France to escape religious persecution. The Huguegnots found a home in Berlin, after Frederick the Great invited them all to come to Germany. (At that time, it was said that every fifth Berliner was a Frenchman.) Paul Antze died in 1940 at the age of eighty-nine. Both he and his wife were buried in the 'non-catholic' part of Rapallo's cemetery, where later their daughter, my paternal grandmother, was buried as well.

The Antzes, my biological great-grandparents, had four children, two girls and two boys. Their eldest daughter, Clara Antze, married a very wealthy – and, it was said, equally eccentric – professor of *Sanskrit.* Clara Antze and her professor-husband lived in Switzerland, but traveled extensively. They owned a villa in Sestri Levante, the winter resort, east of Genoa and south of Rapallo. When still young, Elfriede Antze visited her older sister there during a holiday. She enjoyed it so much that she insisted on going back the following year, though no chaperone was available. With the excuse that she wanted to take care of her sister's children, while their parents were traveling, she went back alone.

A young man, Massimo Bacigalupo, had noticed the German *Fräulein* the year before. Now – seeing her with the children and thinking that she was the governess – he approached her courageously and introduced himself. He soon learned that she was the children's aunt. He began courting her and was so persistent that father Antze finally capitulated. Dr. Antze was not at all pleased that his daughter was abandoning the specialization of her medical education for a life in Italy.

Massimo Bacigalupo and Elfriede Antze were married in 1911. A year later, on June twelfth, their son, Giuseppe, later nicknamed 'Bubi', was born; twenty-one years later, he became my father.

During World War I, when the anti-German sentiment in Italy began, my grandmother decided to take her son and return to Germany, to continue her study of medicine. She left

Massimo & Elfrieda Bacigalupo traveling to her home, Bremen

her son with his grandparents in Bremen. She enrolled at the University of Rostock, the oldest university in northern Germany, where she specialized in pediatrics. She returned to Rapallo in 1918, after the war had ended.

My grandfather's parents had owned a pharmacy in Sestri Levante, and my grandfather, Massimo Bacigalupo, later owned a pharmacy in Rapallo. Elfriede, his wife, started her medical practice in the same town on the Italian Riviera. If it was difficult for a woman physician in Germany, it seemed nearly impossible in Italy. But my grandmother was determined. She said that being a doctor was her 'calling' not a 'profession.' With tenacity, she succeeded in what she set out to accomplish. She soon gained the reputation of being 'the good German doctor who is an excellent diagnostician.' Ten years after the birth of her son, Elfriede Bacigalupo gave birth to a girl she named Adreana. Elfriede met a German lady, with a daughter of Adreana's age. She invited her to come and take care of the children. *Frau Pfuhl* and her daughter, Waltraut, were to speak only German with Bubi and Adreana, so the native language of their mother would not be forgotten. Now, Bubi's sons and grandsons speak German as well.

Elfriede Bacigalupo kept in close contact with her friend, Alma Hempel. She was aware that her friend's marriage had failed after a very short time, and that now she lived alone in her townhouse in Zehlendorf. That was convenient in 1933, when Alma's old friend, Elfriede, needed a room for a young Italian woman with the name of Clara Orazi. Clara was pregnant, and Elfriede's son, Bubi, was the father. Alma Hempel agreed to take Clara for the few months until the baby was born. – The baby was I.

CLARA ORAZI

1940

The time was January of 1933, when Hitler declared himself *'Der Führer'* (the Leader), and it was not long thereafter that Dr. Hempel made the fateful telephone call to Mutti Uhlenbrock. She needed a room for a pregnant young Italian woman, with the name of Clara Orazi. Dr. Hempel explained that she was doing a friend a favor. Her friend's son was the father and she, Alma Hempel, had agreed to take Clara until the baby was born. She went on to say that she was in the process of redecorating the designated room, and that she needed someone to accommodate Clara 'for just a few days'. Mutti had room enough, so she agreed to help out.

When she first met Clara Orazi, Mutti was somewhat taken aback by her appearance. Clara had bleached blond hair, and wore more make-up than was customary in Germany. "But it took less than an hour for Clara to conquer everybody's heart,"

Mutti told me later. Clara only knew a few German words, but with her expressive gestures, everybody understood her. "She was vivacious, bright and charming," said Mutti, "She was like sunshine, affecting the whole family."

Since Mutti Uhlenbrock's daughters were close to Clara's age, Mutti felt much compassion for the young woman, pregnant and alone in a foreign country. She gave Clara all her motherly love and support, thinking 'what if one of my daughters were in that predicament?'

Ruth and Inge, twenty-three and twenty-one then, were not emotionally close to each other. But they both got very attached to Clara, and loved having someone else their own age in the family. Vati enjoyed the young, attractive woman as well, who brought so much laughter into his home. Clara also became a main attraction for Vati's eccentric travel acquaintances. There was an Arab who claimed to have a harem. That impressed Clara a lot. He offered, "If you come with me, you will be the favorite!"

With Clara around, life seemed happy, carefree and fun. Unfortunately, it was only an illusion, doomed to disappear very soon. Life was to change drastically for every one of them, and the future was ominous . . .

The political clouds hanging over Germany became ever more threatening. Before Hitler, people were hungry, without work and little hope for future improvement. The Versailles Treaty was so devastating, that even the most optimistic Germans saw no way of economic recovery. The reparations, ageed to by the victors of the First World War, were successful in keeping Germany powerless and economically depressed. The Weimar Republic – Germany's attempt of a multiple-party government – had failed. Out of the many parties, two emerged with considerable power. Poverty made the Communist Party, on the extreme left, an attractive choice for many; but for others, the National Socialists, on the far right, promised most hope out of their misery.

"A bunch of hoodlums, with an ex-corporal as their leader, who has been jailed," was Vati's opinion of the Nazis. Unfortunately, he and many others under-estimated the power of the Nazi Party, whose skillful propaganda spread like a religion and attracted more and more people. Goebbels, the propaganda Minister, knew the fine art of saying what most Germans were anxious to hear: "We shall give you work!" "You will have food!" "We shall give you back your self respect!" "Germany needs its colonies back!" "Since our national debt is prohibitive, we need to ignore it!" If enough people had read Hitler's book *Mein Kampf,* they would have been warned of what was to come. Many people owned it – because it was given out at weddings and all formal occasions – but only very few read it, and even fewer scrutinized it.

Even many of Germany's Jews were persuaded by Hitler's message. The Papal Nuncio in Germany – who had been named Secretary of State of the Vatican in 1930, and who became Pope Pius XII in 1939 – made a deal with the Nazis. He would influence the German Catholics to support the Nazis, in exchange for allowing the Catholic Church to continue as before. Without the help of the Catholic vote, Hitler would have never become chancellor. But even with the majority of the Catholic vote, there were enough levelheaded, mostly older German conservatives like Vati, that von Hindenburg was reelected in 1932.

Hitler was furious that *Hindenburg* had been re-elected president. Nevertheless, the Nazi Party had just enough seats in parliament, to allow Hitler to represent his party. Unfortunately, to nominate von Hindenburg again was an impractical alternative. He was eighty-five years old and twice out of retirement. Hindenburg himself must have realized that he was too old for the job. He named Hitler his successor because he thought Hitler could be manipulated – a political move that backfired.

"Hindenburg was senile and did not know what he was doing when he handed the leadership over to that Austrian,"

Vati Uhlenbrock moaned, and now he called the Nazis *"Verbrecher"* (criminals). It was too late! Nazism took over like a tidal wave. Soon anybody who said anything against Hitler was considered unpatriotic; was denounced, imprisoned and eliminated.

After a week's stay at the Uhlenbrocks, Clara had to move in with Dr.Hempel in Zehlendorf. There she was unhappy and lonely, because Dr. Hempel was away all day in her practice. Clara missed the Uhlenbrock family and especially Mutti's warmth and care. Every day she took the subway to travel the long stretch from Zehlendorf to the Kaiser Allee. Clara suffered from motion sickness that made the trip seem endless. But it was a whole lot better than being alone. Back and forth she went, until one day Dr. Hempel forgot that Clara was still in the house and locked her in. Clara, with the help of a German dictionary, worked hard to describe what could have happened if a fire had broken out. She picked the word *Feuersbrunst* instead of *Feuer.* (*Feuersbrunst* is something out of Dante's *Inferno*) The story about the *Feuersbrunst* became anecdotal in our house and was retold many times. After Clara described the possibility of those 'extreme circumstances' at the Hempel house, and her daily problem with motion sickness, Mutti was only too happy to invite her back.

Everyone was glad because Clara's cheerful personality was contagious. But Clara especially loved to be with Mutti. She followed her everywhere and said, with her cute accent, *"Ich bin Ihr Schatten."* (I am your shadow.)

Clara was very close to her own mother, who was living in Rome with her husband, an older daughter and a son. Clara kept re-assuring her mother that she was fine. "No need to worry about me, you most wonderful of all mothers," she wrote. Clara never once complained. She never allowed herself to admit how much she hoped to hear from the man she loved, whose baby she was carrying. But Mutti knew without being told, and she waited for the mailman as anxiously as Clara.

Mutti was told that Clara had been sent to her aunt in beautiful Rapallo, to rescue her from the pursuit of an admiring engineer. She also was to be diagnosed by Dr. Elfriede Bacigalupo because of a persistent cough. (The great fear at that time was tuberculosis.) The doctor, Bubi's mother, was convinced that there was nothing wrong with Clara's lungs. She was so sure of her diagnosis, that she had no objections to Bubi dating Clara.

Bubi and Clara enjoyed all the same pastimes, though none of them were very beneficial for Bubi's study of medicine. When the reality of Clara's pregnancy forced them to talk to Bubi's mother, it became clear that she would allow nothing and nobody to interfere with her son's education. Bubi was twenty years old, and his study of medicine – certainly not marriage – was his mother's top priority. Therefore, Clara was sent to Elfriede Bacigalupo's friend, Alma Hempel, in Zehlendorf. Clara and her mother agreed to the plan, in order to keep the news from Clara's father, who had just suffered a severe heart attack.

Mutti loved Clara like a daughter, and she was displeased with the way the Bacigalupos had handled the situation. Not knowing what else to do, Clara had planned to leave her baby in the care of the Catholic Nuns, until her father had sufficiently recovered to withstand the shock. At that time, Clara planned to bring her baby home to Rome.

Clara was generous to a fault. She gave Mutti beautiful gifts, like an alligator handbag (the one I unpacked and re-packed on my first train ride to Italy.) Mutti did not know how to discourage Clara from spending her parents' money. Clara went so far as to hire a limousine with a driver for Mutti. Needless to say, it was the last thing Mutti wanted or accepted.

Clara loved to eat. Her passion was the crisp German hard-rolls, delivered daily and hung outside the entrance door. She could eat one after another, spread with the good German *Markenbutter,* as if her stomach were bottomless. She had such a capacity to enjoy things that it made everyone share in her zest for life. Inge, Ruth and Clara became good friends, and spent every available moment together.

The months went by quickly. Mutti was at Clara's bedside on the nineteenth of June, when her baby was ready to be born. During labor, Mutti took every deep breath with Clara, held her hand in support and suffered through the pains, as if they were hers. Finally, when the baby was born, Mutti fainted from stress and exhaustion. Clara was fine and even happier and more cheerful than usual.

I must have looked somewhat oriental, because Clara called me, *"Mia cara Cinesina,"* meaning "My dear little Chinese." She said it so often, that Ruth finally shortened it to *Cisi,* a nickname so unusual that everybody wondered how it originated. It embarrassed me throughout my childhood.

After Clara had given birth, Mutti was so attached to both Clara and the baby that she did not want Clara to hand her child over to the nuns, as if she were an orphan. Mutti, not impulsive by nature, did what was most unusual for her. After getting Vati's consent, she said to Clara, "If you want to leave the baby with us, we will raise her as our own. But you must promise that you will never change your mind and take this child away from us!" Clara thought about her situation. By now, she knew she couldn't count on Bubi. Her father could not be told anything about the baby for the time being. She compared her circumstances with those of the well-established, cultured Uhlenbrocks. She herself had experienced the love and care of what she considered a well-to-do and solid family. She pondered what would be the best solution for the happiness of her baby. It did not occur to her that the Uhlenbrocks were old enough to be the baby's grandparents. Mutti was forty-eight and Vati Uhlenbrock was fifty-five.

Mutti told me later, "Never for a moment did I regret my decision to take you." But many times, Clara had told her other daughters that she regretted very much leaving me in

Germany. She told Catherine, when she was dying, "I have never stopped longing for your mother, my firstborn child."

Soon after I was born, when Clara was still in Berlin, Elfriede Bacigalupo came to see her grandchild. One day, before leaving on an errand, she announced, "I am going to bring all of you some chocolates!" Clara swiftly said, "But we only eat *Feodora!*" That happened to be the most expensive chocolate one could buy at the time. My modest Mutti almost fainted and never forgot it. From then on, whenever somebody promised something – no matter what it was – Mutti would say jokingly, "But we only eat *Feodora.*"

Bubi had written only one letter in all those months that Clara was in Berlin. She saved that letter. Bubi was so self-involved that he only talked about his own young and exciting life. There was not a word about Clara, neither the child nor their future together. After receiving that letter, Clara wrote her mother that she was not so sure that she still loved Bubi as much as before. She did not admit her disappointment, and explained that maybe after giving birth, a mother's love centers on her baby.

During this time, Bubi was on a tennis tourney. In the English newspapers, he was lauded as one of Italy's 'young, rising tennis stars.' On his way back, he stopped in Berlin to look at his daughter, and he made the observation: "A movie star she will not be!" Mutti never forgave him for those prophetic words. She consoled herself by calling him, *"Ein dummer Junge "* (just a silly boy.) The one she really blamed was his mother, for not insisting that he take responsibility for Clara and his child.

Clara died of breast cancer in December of 1979. She was seventy-one years old. My sisters Simonetta and Donatella were heartbroken. They had truly adored their mother as much as Clara had adored her mother.

BUBI

1950

It was 1950, and the first time I met my Italian father, Bubi. He was thirty-eight and I was seventeen. When I arrived in Rapallo, Italy, I was dazzled. Compared to the condition of post-war Berlin, the contrast was stark. Berlin was still a huge pile of rubble with little sign of recovery.

I'm trying to recall what Bubi told me when we were sailing on his boat. I remember he said that he had asked Clara to marry him – three years after I was born – but Clara had refused. Instead, she accepted a proposal to marry Bubi's friend and fellow student, Adreano Rimoldi.

Bubi also told me that in those wonderful early years, he spent his time playing tennis, sailing, playing cards and dancing with beautiful women. Whenever he counted down his passions he would add – with a playful grin on his face – "But not in that order!" He added, "While I gave my mother plenty of grief, I had a wonderful life!" All those activities were not very goal-oriented and left little time for studying. That lifestyle came to a screeching halt, when Bubi used his tuition money to buy himself an automobile. One bright and early morning, when he was quite hung over from the night before, he opened his eyes and saw his mother's face looming over him. It was time to become serious!

Frieda & Bubi Bacigalupo 1950

Among his university friends was Frieda Natali from Pennsylvania, USA, who was in Italy on a scholarship. Frieda studied with Bubi and changed her major to medicine because of him. She was exactly what his mother considered perfect for her son. But by that time, Frieda had waited quite a while for Bubi's proposal, and had decided to return to the United States. Her goodbye message was, "Should you decide to ask me to marry you, let me know and I'll come back!" 'Getting serious' for Bubi meant sending Frieda a cable to ask her to come back. Frieda returned to Italy and Bubi and Frieda lived happily married until her death from lung cancer in January of 1983.

There were quite a few years, when Frieda was not able to conceive, and Bubi contemplated – so he said – taking me away from the Uhlenbrocks. I later learned from Clara that she had insisted on giving me her surname, Orazi, and not Bacigalupo.

Massimo and Andrea 1951

She wanted to make it harder for him to claim me. Thank goodness, Clara's theory was never tested! Frieda gave birth to a son, Massimo, in 1947, and a second son, Andrea, in 1949.

Adreana, Bubi's younger sister, had two girls at about the same time and later a third daughter. It was ideal, because Bubi's boys, Massimo and Andrea, and Adreana's girls, Juliana and Roberta, were so close in age that they grew up together like siblings in beautiful Rapallo.

Bubi drove a motor scooter. I accompanied him sitting on the back seat of his Vespa. It was his favorite mode of transportation, whether he went to see his patients or went dancing.

Catherine with Andrea and his son Tomaso

Frieda arranged everything. It was she, who had insisted on my visit, so I would meet my father. It was she, who made sure I went on to Rome, to meet my mother, Clara. It was she, who invited Catherine to spend her high school summer vacations in Rapallo; a glorious experience for Catherine. She found a second home in Rapallo, and she was loved there like a daughter.

When I first met Frieda, I was very intimidated. She appeared to me like a general. But as time went on, I realized that she was a saint. Long after that first visit, she told me that she originally wanted me to come to Italy just because 'it was the right thing to do'. But, as a bonus, she found a friend in me. Those words I never forgot!

Bubi was very close to his mother. He respected and admired her. Therefore, it was especially painful for him that she, in later years, lost all memory to a point where she did not even recognize him. But when I visited in 1972, she astonished everyone when she called me by name, when I entered the room.

Unfortunately, my father had a travel-phobia; therefore he never saw where and how we lived in America. Because of Catherine's In-Flight-Service-Manager position with Trans

World Airlines, we were all privileged to fly for little or nothing. (I have the most wonderful memories of being pampered in First Class.) It enabled me to have a closer bond with my father than I had ever imagined possible. Steven and Kristine spent their honeymoon in Rapallo, a gift to them from Steven's grandfather. In his last years, he showed a great interest in Steven's life, and his only great-grandson, Jonathan.

Bubi and Frieda were extremely happy in their marriage, and Bubi had a very hard time after she died. He survived her by sixteen years. His heart gave out in May of 1999, when he was almost eighty-seven, the same age at which his mother had died. His father had lived to be over ninety.

1997

Two months before my father's death, Catherine called him with the happy news that she had given birth to a baby girl, whom she named Ginevra. He was overjoyed. For a long time, it had been his great wish for her to have a child. He died with the knowledge that this wish had come true.

The following is my father's good-bye letter, an insight into the script of his life:

GUISEPPE BACIGALUPO
A good-bye.

Now we are coming to the end. As I brought people and events back to memory, I relived the moments that were an important component of my life and I am sad to say good-bye to all for the second time. But now comes the evening, light and colors blend and the day envelops itself with melancholy that has a foreboding of the night that will come. It is the moment when one looks back into the past to bring forth the times that have made life worth living.

The first thought leads me to the women in my life, those wonderful creatures who, beginning with the first flirts of my youth, stayed with me throughout my life. They brought illusions, surprises and strong will, playfulness and wisdom but most of all great devotion and tenderness. So, first of all comes love, the great motor, basis of all human happenings.

Also I had the great advantage to live at this beautiful Riviera, among stone pines that seemed to grow out of the rocks and that bend down as deeply as if they wanted to become one with the sea and lend it a sea-green appearance. And there, stretched out on the boat, warmed by the sensuous sun, and enchanted by the waves that gently strike the boat, and lying next to a beloved body, that way one can achieve the illusion of happiness.

In addition comes the successful development of my profession, that started with little enthusiasm and not as a calling, but then, over the years, crystallized to a "Leitmovtif" that still today enriches my over eighty-five year old life. Because of this profession, I had the opportunity to connect with many people and realize what is really important in life.

Everything You Do and Have Done must Have Been Done out of Love.

On top of that there was a happy marriage which was never boring, instead ever kept lively, an incomparable partner, and stimulating sons, (friends as well), but most of all a sense of humor, the salt of life. Although it is the evening now, I still can say, when I look back: "It was a beautiful day. "

LAST NOT LEAST - AL

2002

Albert James Erickson – my husband for over fifty years – was born on October 1, 1928, in Denver, Colorado. He was the oldest of five children. A year after Al was born, his parents returned to Council Bluffs, Iowa. It is located on the east side of the Missouri River, across the bridge from Omaha, Nebraska. His father's family had lived in Council Bluffs for many years, and it was there that Al's father, Albert Tinley Erickson, had met his wife, Florence Larsen.

Al's father had a good job in Denver, working for the Sinclair Oil Co. He was locating property and establishing gasoline stations for the company in southern Colorado, Arizona and the Texas panhandle. To answer his mother's wish, Al's father left Denver to return to Council Bluffs. It was during the Great Depression, and Al's father had to take all kinds of jobs to feed his family. He delivered milk with a horse and buggy; worked in a chocolate factory (he never ate chocolate again, after he saw how unclean those factories really were) and eventually drove a gasoline-delivery truck, just to make ends meet. At that time, the young Erickson-family lived in a one-room house, just northeast of the city limits of Council Bluffs. Al's mother was a registered nurse. His father wanted his wife to stop working in the local hospital, partially out of jealousy and also so she would be with her child.

Father, Mother & Buddy 1929

They called Al, their first-born child, 'Buddy' because – so it was said – his responsible and supportive nature was apparent from early on. When he was just four, in December of 1932, he gathered wood and kept the fire going in their coalburning stove to help his mother. She was close to giving birth to her second child, Eldon. Most of the time, Al's father was away at work.

The age-gap of the boys, a little more than four years, and their very different personalities, made for many fights. Al was very serious and always aiming to please – especially his father – while Eldon was happy-go-lucky. Their father was a disciplinarian and very critical. He could always find something wrong with everything, and when he said nothing, it was a compliment. On the other hand, their mother was a very patient and caring mediator. She never complained. She had seen much harder times growing up on her parents' dairy farm. From childhood on, she had to do whatever work had to be done, including carrying heavy feedbags. In winter it snowed through a glass-less window right onto her bed.

I noticed very soon that all the Ericksons had two things in common; they were hard workers and they had a great love for animals.

From early on, Al was anxious to learn. His mother wanted to have him accepted in school at age four, just one month before his 5th birthday. That took persistence and only when the little 'Buddy' proved that he was able to handle whatever was expected of a first-grader, he was allowed to stay in the two-room schoolhouse.

Al & his dog 1934

After graduating from high school at age 16, he continued to live at home while studying at Creighton University in Omaha, a Jesuit school. He was there for two years, did well, and received a good and quite diverse education. But when he transferred to Iowa State University, he found himself ill-prepared for a major in Chemical Engineering.

Finally on his own (and not having to work for his father in his free time), he could read as much as he wanted. He had his nose constantly in books – but not necessarily chemistry books – and that exacerbated the struggle with his curriculum. Iowa State was a tough university. After the second quarter, Al was asked to take the third quarter off. The following year, when his grades had not markedly improved, he was advised to take off the rest of that school year. He found a job at the Omaha Testing Laboratories, where he worked for about a year and a half, trying to earn money for further studies. In July 1950, he learned – just a month before he was to be readmitted to Iowa State – that he was on the list to be drafted for the Korean 'Police Action'. He decided to enlist instead, so he could choose the branch of service he preferred. He joined the Corps of Engineers, and after three months of basic training in Fort Ord, California (near Carmel by the Sea), he was transferred to Ft. Belvoir, Virginia. There he was trained in topographic surveying.

Weekend pass from Fort Ord 1950

Armed with his newly acquired knowledge, he was assigned to a construction battalion stationed in Japan. It took sixteen days for the troop-transport ship from Seattle to Yokohama. They battled a typhoon for most of the way. Soon he was one of the very few who could still enjoy food – and there was plenty of it – because the demand for nourishment grew less and less as the sea became more and more violent.

He and six others were assigned to Camp Drake in Tokyo. There they spent two weeks working and waiting, while the Army was looking for their 453rd Engineer Construction Battalion. Finally they located his group in Beppu, Japan. Off by train the seven went to Beppu. Upon arrival, they were informed that their battalion was no longer there. That gave them the chance to spend two weeks in Beppu, while the Army once again looked for the 453rd Engineer Construction Battalion. Word came for the seven to catch a train to Sasebo, a port at the western coast of Japan. They were generously given five days for a train-ride distance of only four hours. They took every bit of their allotted time. On the way, they found a place to collect their first pay since leaving Seattle. They made it to Sasebo just in time to pick up their combat gear and get on the ship destined for Pusan, Korea. They arrived Easter Sunday morning 1951, greeted by a cold drizzling rain. They were given an equally cold and wet Easter breakfast, consisting of a congealed creamed-hamburger mixture on a cold hard piece of toast. They were very hungry, so they appreciated any food they could get.

Then they were loaded on a semi-trailer and transported 30 miles to the railroad station that was only a mine-filled block away from where they started. A bullet-riddled railroad car, with no glass in its windows, made them feel very uneasy. But it brought them north to Taegu, where Al and his six buddies got off. In the station they could rest on some cots, until the battalion truck picked them up. After another couple of days, they all moved north to Yong Dong Po with a convoy of heavy construction equipment. Their mission was to reconstruct a railroad-bridge between Yong Dong Po and Seoul. Al helped the surveying team, finally able to apply some of his training. Next, they surveyed for building a railroad-line from the port of Inchon (20 miles west of Seoul) to Kimpo Airbase in Seoul. Their job accomplished, they were all shipped to Koje-Do Island, located off the southern tip of Korea and southwest of Pusan. There, many of the North Korean and Chinese prisoners-of-war were kept.

Life became exciting, when the island commander agreed to meet with the senior Chinese officer in the POW compound. Very soon, word went out that the General had 'involuntarily joined' the prisoners and somehow had to be rescued. Another U.S. General was flown in and assigned the rescue job. He had the great idea to build a new compound and move the prisoners there, one by one. Everyone on the island was put to work to get the building-job done quickly. About a dozen tanks equipped with flame-throwers were lined up in front of the old compound. An hour was used to practice firing the flame-throwers, showing a lot of firepower! Next, the new General made a telephone call to the imprisoned General, telling him loud and clear that the troops were coming in and that nobody would make it out alive, unless they surrendered.

When the Chinese looked out the window to see and hear what was going on, they surrendered. Totally stripped, they were chased with a bayonet, one by one, to the new compound. When the old place – now empty – was searched, about 300 rifles were found. The only explanation for that was that when trusted POW's had been used to clean U.S. Army barracks, they had found enough rifle-parts to build a small arsenal for themselves.

**Doing the soils job
Korea 1952**

Soon, Al was in charge of the surveying team, and was also the chief soils technician. In the latter position, he designed and did the soils analysis for a small water supply dam on the island. After that job was completed, he was given the opportunity to run the NCO club. He was responsible for purchasing all the alcohol needed to stock the NCO-club, as well as the Officers'-club. Not a bad job that he held for his last six months in Korea!

After Al's eighteen-month Korean tour had ended, he was re-assigned to the Engineer School at Ft. Belvoir, Virginia. It was October of 1952, the same year and month that I had come from Germany.

Al and I met the following June. On August 15, 1953, Al was discharged from the Army and went back to Iowa. He returned to Virginia in September of the same year, intent on persuading me to marry him.

He succeeded. We married on July eighteenth, 1954. A month later, Al, Mutti and I drove to Iowa, so Al could continue his education. While waiting for me, he had gone to George Washington University at night. Those credits, as well as some from his Surveying and Soils courses, allowed him to graduate in 1956 with a degree in Civil Engineering. He had taken additional graduate-courses in Sanitary Engineering, his newly found interest.

In 1956, there was no lack of jobs for engineers, and he had many offers while still in school. He took a position with the Washington District of the Army Corps of Engineers, in their engineer training program that lasted for eighteen months. It involved moving from one branch to another, an opportunity to gather knowledge of the various branches of the Washington District of the Corps of Engineers, and who was running them.

After the training period, he chose the *River Basin Planning Branch* headed by Harry Schwarz, who turned out to be a mentor and a dear friend. Al's first project was the Potomac River Basin Study, at a time when America started realizing it, too, would have to do something about its water resources.

In 1967, the Washington District and the Baltimore District of the Corps of Engineers were merged and the main office was in Baltimore, MD. Al, at 39, now Chief of River Basin Planning, Baltimore District, did not want to move or commute to Baltimore, because it was located more than 50 miles from his home. During the merging process, Al was offered a job with the President's Council for Water Resources in Washington, DC, reviewing plans for water-resource development of the nation's rivers. In 1968, he became a GS-grade 15 when he joined the Federal Water Pollution Control Administration, in the Department of Interior. That subsequently became, in 1970, the new Environmental Protection Agency (EPA). He was a charter member.

In the spring of 1970, Al was working for EPA under Alan Hirsch, when he was told to go to a special meeting at the White House. The purpose was to find out what a NATO program called, *Committee on Challenges to Modern Society* (CCMS), was all about, and how it might concern EPA's water program. At the time, the U.S. director of CCMS was Patrick Moynihan.

When Al arrived at the white House, everyone was sitting around a large table discussing noise pollution, air pollution and the development of fuel-efficient cars. When Patrick Moynihan asked who was representing EPA's water program, Al said, "I am; but I am only here to gather information about the NATO-committee." Moynihan responded that the Canadian government was going to make a water project proposal, the following Monday in Brussels, and that he wanted a representative to be at that meeting. Al replied that he did not know who would be going, because he had to consult with his boss first. Moynihan replied, "I expect 'you' to be there, and to report to me at our next meeting here at the White House." He then added that if Al's boss had a problem with that, he was to call him. After the meeting ended, Al went back to his office to discuss the situation.

Alan Hirsch wondered aloud, whether he should go, or who else should be given the opportunity to represent EPA in Brussels. Al handed Hirsch Moynihan's business card, and told him that Patrick Moynihan said for him, Al, to be in Brussels on Monday morning. He was also to attend all regular meetings at the White House from then on. Should there be any question, Hirsch was to call the number on the business card. Alan Hirsch swallowed noticeably and said, "Then you better make arrangements to go." Little did anybody know that Al would spend the next 5 years working on this and other international projects. They were the most exciting and interesting years of Al's career –

Al left that Friday for Brussels to orient himself for Monday's NATO meeting. At ten o'clock on Monday morning, the Canadian representative made his presentation of a Water Pollution Control Project for International Rivers, flowing between two countries. As it turned out, the proposal had little substance, and the meeting ended after only one hour.

Official Passport Photo June 1970

Al was surprised that he had been flown overseas for such a poor Canadian presentation, and couldn't hide his feelings when he went back to the U.S. office at NATO. There the office director was worried about Moynihan's reaction and asked Al, whether he could put together a more appropriate proposal. He gave him paper and pencil and space at a desk. At three that day, Al had his ideas on paper and gave it to the director. A short time thereafter, the U.S. Ambassador to NATO came out of his office. He told Al to be ready to go with him to the Canadian Ambassador's home for dinner that night, and they would discuss the new proposal at that time. A gracious dinner ended up with a plan.

The Canadian Ambassador decided to use Al's well-received paper as the new Canadian proposal, the next day. It was agreed between the two Ambassadors and Al that nobody was to know from whom the proposal came. The next day, the new submission was accepted. Canada was to be the project leader and Belgium, France and the U.S. agreed to support it.

Every year, there was a get-together of the participating countries, which generally lasted a week. The four principal countries took turns, hosting the meeting in a pleasant setting in an international river area.

During this time, EPA created an Office of International Activities. Now, because of his international experience, Al was asked to represent the EPA at several meetings of the Organization for Economic Cooperation and Development (OECD) in Paris. He also traveled to Geneva to represent the U. S. at a few U.N. meetings concerning the environment. – In 1979, Al became a charter member of the United States Senior Executive Service.

When I think back over the many years of our marriage, I remember that Al was always working. There was the time, when he got up at three-thirty in the morning to measure the stress of steel bands on a water tower – proposed to be used as a radar scope – close to Ft. Belvoir. He was away for weeks at a time, for continuing education in Oklahoma and Texas. Every weekend was taken with Army Reserve duty, and two weeks a year with active duty. He was a Captain in the Army Reserve, when the Vietnam War was escalating. It became a real possibility that the Reserve units were going to be called up for active duty. It was not easy, but I insisted that he resign his commission. I have seen enough dead heroes. I hate war and everything connected with it!

Whatever work Al did, there was no task too small not to totally absorb him. He managed to squeeze in a lot of time working on our house. In fact, I think, there is not a corner in our home or yard, where Al's skill and sweat hasn't improved it. I don't know how we did it, but once in a great while we took a vacation.

When Al proposed to me – we were penniless and had not just two, but three mouths to feed – He said to me, "Never worry, I'll find work to feed us." He also said, "Whatever I'll end up doing, I'll work to make it to the top." I never even gave it a thought, and I did not know until years after Al's government service had ended that he had made his prediction come true. In 1984, at age 56, Al retired as a senior executive, level four.

Retirement was not for long. A friend talked him into getting a real estate license and joining him in selling and buying land and houses. But his interest was working with – and learning all about – computers. The first opportunity to test his knowledge was setting up a home-office for desktop publishing of a scientific journal. That experience came in handy when he later helped his friend, Jay Holmes, to publish *The Windmill,* the newsletter of the Mount Vernon Unitarian Church. It was the beginning of Al's real interest in our fellowship, where he became a truly dedicated volunteer.

Ironically, twenty years after Al refused to commute to Baltimore, he ended up driving there daily. Alan Moghissi, who previously had also worked for EPA, established the Office of Environmental Health and Safety at the University of Maryland at Baltimore. He talked Al into joining him there. Al ended up liking his work at the University so much that he commuted to Baltimore for ten years. The 100-mile daily round-trip was a good reason to retire for the second time, in October of 1999.

Now, more fully retired, in addition to his volunteering for Mount Vernon Unitarian Church, he takes care of anybody with computer problems who ask for his help. And whenever his now-grown children, or I, need him, he is always there for us – ready, willing and still able to help.

Mutti was right, "He has a shoulder to lean on!"

Printed in the United States
57477LVS00007B/16-39